Above THE LINE

A TWENTY YEAR CAREER INSIDE THE MOVIE BUSINESS

To Doug,
Thanks So Much
Enjoy iT!

LENNY MANZO

DOUBLE
SAW
PRESS
Boston, MA

To learn more about the author, visit: www.lennymanzo.com

Edited by Carlene Roche and An-Dinh Nguyen

All Cover Art by Lawrence Sampson

Photograph of Lenny Manzo by Josh Dreyfus

Interior Book Design by Daniel Middleton | Scribe Freelance

Set in Garamond Premier Pro

ISBN: 978-0-615-44272-3

Published in the United States of America

This book is dedicated to my friend and colleague Mary Feuer, who has helped me immeasurably throughout my career. I wish to express my humblest thanks for everything she has done for me. I love you Mary. Thank you.

Acknowledgments

I would like to thank the following people who have helped me along the path to publishing this book. In every artistic endeavor that I have created there have been family, friends and colleagues that have helped me see it through. I would like to thank Volker Nick Grün, Julie Pierce, David Caiati, Stephanie Schwartz, Michael Kalish, Carla Scheri, Ed Regal, Bill Miller, Stephanie Rosenfeld, Lawrence Sampson, Chris Streeter, Carlene Roche, An-Dinh Nguyen, Sarah Braucher, Lea Manzo, Nina Manzo, Kathleen Manzo, Lisa Manzo and last but not least, Lenny Manzo Sr.

When the writer is ready, the muse will come.

Above the Line: A budgetary term in the movie industry that refers to the director, actors, producers and screenwriters. Their salaries are the above-the-line costs. Every other item in the budget is below the line, including crew, locations, equipment, props, wardrobe, vehicles, special FX, extras, food and coffee.

Contents

SCENE 1

A Boy Grows in Brooklyn

I *once heard Ginger Rogers* say in an interview, "I always knew I was going to make it." For a woman who appeared in her first film at the ripe old age of 18, I can see how she never had a moment of doubt. Practically everyone who makes it says this with such conviction. Does any young aspiring artist hold another conviction? Even if you doubted yourself that's the way you tell it on *Letterman*. I'll tell you a little secret: the people who never made it in the movie business had those very same thoughts, until they gave up.

It's fine to set the bar as high as you like. The Hollywood dream is the new American dream. In years past, society was content to shoot for the white picket fence, the 2.3 children, and if we really had success we could build a gazebo in the backyard. Now that more people have their needs met they are free to shoot for the stars. We live in an age where people can dream and spend time pursuing that dream.

Where do I fit into this crazy Hollywood dream? Well, that is a loaded question, but since you asked ... there is an old joke that goes something like this: A guy walks into a bar and is hit by a nasty smell. "What's that *smell*?" he asks.

Some old-timer speaks up: "That's from me." The guy explains that he's traveling with the circus passing through town and that he's the elephant keeper. The elephant has bad digestion. Every morning, one of his tasks is to give Jumbo an enema. "I can never get out of the way in time," he says.

The other man is shocked. "You have to do this every day?"

The old-timer nods. "Sometimes twice."

"That's awful!" exclaims the man, horrified. "Why don't you find a better job?"

"WHAT!?! And give up *show business*?"

That's how it is for many of us in the movie business regardless of where we are on the food chain. Some are content to sweep the theater floor; others won't stop until they reach the top. I fall somewhere in the middle of those demographics. I look to earn my living and still try to advance. The reality of hitting the Spielberg level of success is slim. It could happen, but I can't think it will. For every Walter Mitty that comes to the movie world to follow his or her dream to make it and become a star, there are thousands who will never get a steady paycheck, let alone come close to grabbing the brass ring of success. Once one makes it inside the machine the belief is that the system works: "If it can happen to me it can happen to anyone." The dream is perpetuated for the masses and everyone thinks they can beat the odds.

In a way, I am one of those star seekers that I just semi-bashed. I am just more practical at it than most. I understand the mountain I'm climbing and though I strive for the peak I am also content to settle on a lower level where I can find food. If I find enough food along the way I might stop my upward mobility and settle.

There has been many a night I've gone to bed wishing I'd chosen a different racket. As country crooner Claire Lynch sings, "If wishes were horses I would ride, ride, ride." Bottom line, I'm not in a different line of work, I'm in show biz, and quite frankly I'm not skilled at anything else. At one point when I hit the skids, my father-in-law suggested I get tested by a career advising organization. He told me that it did a great deal for his son and it could help me. With their advice, he said, my brother-in-law modified his career and changed his life for the better.

Why not? I have an open mind, so I gave it a shot. The company was a posh organization with fancy digs in the Back Bay, the heart of Boston. They had an old brownstone building with a huge lobby and a lot of other unutilized space. The proctor gave me an overview and we were off to the races. I took all kinds of diverse tests: written, oral, aural, Rorschach. They poked and prodded for two days to see where my natural strengths lay. I met with my advisor at the end, waiting to hear how my talents would be better suited in the world. After hours of comprehensive testing I would find out the proper work that fit my personality.

He sat down and said, "Len, after looking over your tests and weighing out the results, I have to say, You Can't Give Up Show Biz!!! It's in your blood kid! It's why you live and breathe, it's what makes you tick and you can't shake it!" Actually the exact verbal transmission was, "You seem to be suited to the business that you are already in. I would advise you to continue on the path you have already chosen."

Sixteen hours and six hundred bucks later I was told I was already on the correct working path. I was hoping to get some inspirational idea and make a radical life change, which is something I support in anyone's life. However, after being clinically tested it was scientifically proven that I was already in the perfect job. Combined with the fact I couldn't do anything else, I stayed in show biz.

It does go a little deeper than that. At this time I'd like to give you a bit of the back-story. Let's use a cinema technique known as the flashback: everything goes out of focus and our faces become indiscernible. Now hear typical flashback music in your mind. Evoke the sensation of drifting through time. I would tell you to close your eyes at this point, but I think it might be hard for you to continue reading. For those of you who can close your eyes and still read, please do, so as to better benefit from the flashback experience.

Continue on in your flashback and find yourself back in Greenwich Village, circa 1967. "All the leaves are brown and the sky is gray," sings Mama Cass as we see hippies frolicking in Washington Square Park, playing music and dancing in the streets. The Brazilians are playing soccer near the south entrance and there are street performers juggling and telling bad jokes. The old men and the young hustlers play chess and other games of chance. There's music everywhere with guitars, African drums and hip 60's FM radio. The Steadicam (a mobile camera attached to the operator) leaves the park and the montage takes us down Bleecker Street, through Greenwich Village and to the Lower East Side. Continue down Orchard Street through the old Jewish market. It is Sunday and the street is closed off to traffic. Many people walk by the racks of garments in between the knish stands. The Steadicam weaves through the crowd, stands and stalls, and past the police barriers. The camera takes a hard left on Delancey Street and heads over the Williamsburg Bridge to Brooklyn, where the 60's have not hit as hard. It is more like the 50's: a few guys with long hair, a couple of people in paisley and the odd girl in bell-bottoms.

The camera goes through the blue-collar Polish neighborhood of Greenpoint, into the Italian section of Bushwick, where my parents grew up, and past Wyckoff Heights Hospital, where I did my first gig as a human. Continue a few blocks past the hospital to Grove Street. The camera hangs a left, works its way against the one-way street through the stickball game, past the little girls jumping rope, and finally lands on a two-story brick building for an establishing shot. Cut to the second floor, serpentine around the furniture through the railroad apartment to a 6' x 8' bedroom overlooking the street. There you will find a young boy glued to his 12" black-and-white Philco TV set, taking in the cutting-edge work of the day, which includes and is certainly not limited to, *Gilligan's Island, The Flintstones, F Troop* and *Bugs Bunny.*

I spent a great deal of my time as did most American "utes" (excuse my accent, I meant youths; see *My Cousin Vinny* for further dissertation on the Brooklyn accent) watching television. I watched my share of cartoons and sitcoms as a kid. Very early on, I began to watch the old movies. Back then TV wasn't flooded with all the "exciting" programming that we have today. On the contrary, the networks needed content, especially daytime and late night. There was an early morning movie, a late morning movie, a movie at 1 PM and three late afternoon movies. Often on the weekend I would stay up for *The Late Movie* at 11:30 PM, then *The Late Show* somewhere around 1:30 AM, and then if I could hold out I would stay up for *The Late Late Show* around three in the morning. That was the only time I saw *A Tree Grows in Brooklyn.*

The Late Show and *The Late Late Show* had the same logo, an animated picture of an apartment building with all the lights on. As the theme music kicked in, the lights in each window started to turn off. With only a third of the lights left on (because most of America was asleep) our feature presentation began. Later, when *The Late Late Show* came on, it would continue in the same manner, until all the lights, save one, were off. My father would always say, "That's our light Len!"

Movies inundated my life. My mother would encourage me to go to the theater on Saturday. Those were the last days of the double feature, except for Ape Day in the late 70's when the Ridgewood Theatre showed all five *Planet of the Apes* movies sequentially. I did the whole gambit that day, though I had seen them all. When I first saw the trailer for *Planet of the Apes*, I was 7 years old. It blew my mind. I had to see that movie. It was so wild, apes on horses herding humans into fishnets. That trailer pulled me into the theater. Another mind-blowing trailer that pulled me into the theater was for *Soylent Green*. This time it was bulldozers scooping up humans in order to quell a riot. I wonder if there was some correlation there.

My favorite movie as a child was *Angels with Dirty Faces*, starring James Cagney, Humphrey Bogart, Ann Sheridan and the Bowery Boys. It was released in 1938, a time when Bogie played second fiddle to Cagney. I met a young would-be screenwriter a few years ago, and she told me that she had never heard of James Cagney. I was taken aback. Never did I think that I could walk down the streets of America and meet someone who had never heard of Cagney. I asked my aspiring writer friend if she had ever heard of Humphrey Bogart. She replied, "Are you kidding me?" With iconoclastic films like *Casablanca*, *The Treasure of the Sierra Madre* and *The Maltese Falcon*, Bogie's legendary status clearly has surpassed Cagney's. However, in the day, nobody was bigger than Cagney. He was up there with any of them, Gable, Tracy, Garbo and the Duke. That was the crowd he ran with.

I need to say something about my childhood idol. I loved Cagney. I think it had something to do with me being from Brooklyn. He was also from New York and that came out in his tough guy persona. I related to his movies and felt a connection with him. The seeds for stardom were already planted in my head. I just didn't know it yet.

At an early age I embraced the idea of becoming a movie star. I loved the movies and the actors. I knew who they were and the movies they were in. By the time I was 16 I had seen most of the Hollywood classics. By the time I hit my junior year in high school I tried out for my first play. It was *Our Town* by Thornton Wilder, the classic American staple done in most high schools all over the country.

Like any naïve child I walked into the audition with delusions of grandeur, aspiring to get the lead role. I had a strong gift for memorization, a good sense of humor and a quick wit, which made me think I had some talent to be on a stage in front of people. Perhaps it was time to try acting.

There were only a couple of things wrong with my plan. First off, I wasn't as talented as I thought. I mean, I had some talent, but it was far from honed. Secondly, there were already students who had been doing it for two or three years. They were experienced at it. Even more important was the fact that they had built relationships with the drama teachers. At an early age I learned the most important lesson in the biz: it's not *what* you know, it's *who* you know.

I'm not telling you anything new. Show biz is about meetings, connections, referrals and, most important, uncles. The uncle in the biz cannot be underrated. Would doors have opened for Nicolas Cage without Uncle Francis Ford Coppola? Kate Hudson is great, but without Goldie Hawn leading the way, she'd just be another pretty face clawing her way in. Without Billy Ray to hold her hand, could Miley Cyrus have ever risen to such heights? Nepotism is the way of the world and it is more so in Hollywood.

Getting back to my own dreams, and looking back objectively, I wasn't ready. I hadn't developed any talent to act. What I had was a quick, spontaneous wit. I have always seen life from the humorous side. As a lad, my jokes would fly over the other kid's head. I was ahead of the curve when it came to sarcasm; I packed a dry delivery and a suspect tone, which often left me misunderstood as a child. It hasn't changed much as an adult. This information might be helpful while reading this book.

After the *Our Town* audition I had my first "don't call us, we'll call you" moment. I was not ready for the rejection. I didn't have an understanding of the stage and I lacked the guidance to get through it. I had the makings inside me, but I didn't have an iota of technique.

The thought of acting graced my brain one more time in high school. A year later there was a musical production that was having auditions. It was a 50's-style musical somewhere between *Grease* and *Happy Days*. I tossed and turned for a week. Singing on the stage sounded great. I only had one small problem: I couldn't sing a lick and I knew it.

I tried out for the choir at my Catholic grammar school from grades four through eight. Every year I would volunteer for the auditions. I have to say, I had no real interest in the choir. I just knew that this experience was getting me out of the classroom for at least an hour. I headed over to the church rectory with a few future tenors and some other deviant classmates also trying to scam some time away from the drudgery of parochial school in 1972. That is another story, for another book.

We arrived at the rectory and sat down in silence. The church had that natural effect on us. It was either that or the threat of violence that loomed over us. Oops, I'm starting to write that other book again. So we sat there and waited our turn. Eventually, the maestro called me over to the piano. He hit a key and I mimicked the note. He hit another key and I mimicked that one. After the third time he said, "All right Alfalfa, you can go back to class now."

The nuts and bolts of it was that at an early age I could not carry a note. Part of my life-changing career testing consisted of repetitive tonal responses. Though my advisor had said, "There's no business like show business," he did reinforce the fact that I did not have an ear for music. He did mention I could still continue to enjoy music as an audience member.

For more proof that I can't sing, ask anyone who has heard me do it. If bad singing were a crime they would have thrown away the key long ago. Compared to me, Lucy Ricardo is a diva. Even with the knowledge of my inability to harmonize I was still willing to give it a shot. So, I spoke to my mother and she said, "Audition, what have you got to lose?" Besides my dignity and self-respect, no, there was nothing to lose.

My good friend Carl also encouraged me to audition. So with their support, I rehearsed two songs, "Yesterday" by the Beatles and "Shake, Rattle and Roll," which was written by Jesse Stone and a big hit for Bill Haley and the Comets. After memorizing both songs I auditioned for my mother and Carl. It was unanimous that I drop "Yesterday." It probably would have been a great number to perform on *American Idol*. I would have been a shoe-in for a one-time appearance so Simon could have had his way with me. By default it was "Shake, Rattle and Roll."

The day of the audition arrived. I headed downstairs to the music room, where I saw my fellow classmates already waiting for the auditions to get underway. I looked in that room and I was scared to death. Up until that point no one had ever liked my singing. As I stared into that room, I knew no one in there would like it either. After 20 minutes of deliberation I left. I hopped on the bus home and was very happy with my decision not to embarrass myself. No doubt about it, it was the right choice. I am not a proponent of giving up, but there is a time to know when to walk away and know when to run. This was a time to run. No need to humiliate myself at 16. Humiliation is 10 times worse when you're a teenager. There was no way I would have made the chorus let alone landed a role.

So, at the cultivated age of 16, I gave it my best shot and decided to walk away from acting. I finished school and left home. I traveled a fair amount and found myself living in San Francisco in 1984. I was 23 years old. A lot happened to me in that time frame that shaped my character and moral fiber today. I'll tell you about it sometime over a cup of coffee or two.

Having matured I decided to take another crack at school. I enrolled at San Francisco State University. That was a great place to go to school, a nice campus with eucalyptus trees everywhere. The sweet smell of those trees would hit me two blocks away from campus. I had grown mentally, developed more confidence in myself and I wanted to explore my quick wit and extroverted urges, all G-rated of course.

Acting seemed natural to me. I enrolled in an improv class, which made the most sense, since my humor was spontaneous. I was a little awkward at first. It took me a few classes to get comfortable with the group. Once I did, my acting excelled. I did great work that semester, which led to extracurricular work. I auditioned for different things and I was cast in a small show. I finished the semester doing well in all my classes. I had embraced education in a way I had never known. School was finally something I could enjoy.

After the semester was over it was decision time. Should I stay in school, continue my studies and the process of becoming an actor, or should I travel? I really liked school, but the time factor concerned me. It was daunting to commit so many years to a degree. I still wanted to hit the road again. I wanted to go to Asia. I had hit one of the biggest crossroads of my life. It was tough, but I knew that my traveling was not finished. I still needed to go out into the world. I chose to put off my artistic needs for a different kind of education.

Since this is a story of my movie world you'll have to read about *The Travels with Lenny* at a later date. With a few years of adventures and a couple of near-death experiences under my belt, I landed in New York City in 1987. I found an apartment the size of a shoebox on the Lower East Side, and was happy to have it. If I was going to study acting and start the career I had always dreamed of, I needed more experience and more education. I took classes at the HB Studios, a serious acting school located in the West Village. HB had churned out the likes of Faye Dunaway, Jessica Lange and Billy Crystal. At least I was in good company.

These classes were a lot harder than improv; with improv, I could just react and go on instinct. I found delivering the canned lines took a bit more effort and skill. I didn't mind the challenge; I enjoyed the teachers and the process. Everyone here was more serious than in the California State School. It wasn't a mixture of actors and college kids; it was an environment with talented and dedicated artists expanding their craft. This was a step up, and I felt I was heading in the right direction.

This was my first experience surrounded by professional and would-be professional actors, and the first time I noticed that the level of insanity in actors was higher than in most people. Many great actors ride the razor's edge of genius and lunatic: Robin Williams, Jonathan Winters, Peter Sellers, Joan Crawford, the list goes on. It must be difficult on the brain when you are constantly acting like someone else, especially when you employ an acting style of complete character transformation. When Kathleen Turner did her one-woman show, I think she eventually believed she was Tallulah Bankhead.

This business naturally inflates the ego ... the more success, the more ego. The tabloids are flooded with stories of stars behaving crazy because many of them *are* crazy, and living amongst a small elite group of people who treat you like you're wonderful reinforces that you are "wonderful."

A thousand years ago the acting world consisted of one man per kingdom with a funny three-coned cap. Everyone would laugh and the king would dribble wine all over himself. That was show biz. In the 1800's, actors were still fairly low on society's scale. Then the silver screen happened, and that changed how we see actors. Our infatuation grew as the golden age of Hollywood ramped up the quality of movies they were making. Technology progressed and the stars jumped off the big screen. Even into the 1950's the average person thought acting was not a real career. It's fine for Gable and Lombard, but not for their child. "My son is going to college to be a doctor or a lawyer." But the next generation responded, "But Daddy, I don't want to sing in the choir," a reference to Al Jolson, whose father wanted him to go into the family rabbi business, or at least that's how the story goes.

As time passed, the ratio of working actors to nonworking actors became larger. Acting became a more acceptable way to earn a living. Fast-forward to today; hordes of people are trying to break into show biz. It's not just in front of the camera; there's an onslaught of people who also want to work behind it. You hear it all the time: "What I really want to do is direct." Everyone wants to make a movie. Part of that inspiration comes from all the bad movies that are made, and people get this idea in their heads that they can make a better movie. More often, they emulate the style of bad Hollywood movies.

We can see by the outburst and continued success of reality TV that people are dying to be in the limelight. Reality TV has given the illusion that there are more opportunities for the average viewer to help her budding show biz career blossom, that it is even more possible to get on a show and thus get, how do you say, "discovered." It has increased and validated the pipe dream for Josephine America and gives her hope as television brings her neighbors into the national spotlight.

Back at HB Studios in the West Village, way before I had grown old and wise, while I was taking acting classes and trying my hand at auditioning, I came to the quick conclusion that I did not have what it took to audition. I could not enter a sterile room in front of a bunch of strangers, get handed a script, and in that moment be able to deliver the goods. I never could hit a curveball and I couldn't do a cold read. I had to face the facts. If I was unwilling to audition, how could I ever hope to get any parts? How could I do it? I finally understood how far I would have to travel down this road before I could ever realize any success. I made the deliberate decision for the second time to break away from the art of acting, and I left the movie business before I ever really started.

Next, I examined the roots of my dream. Growing up in Brooklyn, I had few choices and even less interest in what was going on in my neighborhood. My childhood was spent watching TV and going to the movies. I'm not breaking out any violins here; I really didn't have much interest in that world. Movies became a major part of my life and I learned a lot of life's lessons from watching them. I can't say I got it all right. I know now that what worked for John Wayne doesn't necessarily work for me. I don't think trying to kiss your girl when she's blowing her top works anywhere except in the movies.

After deep psychological analysis of myself, some long looks at my motives and abilities, I understood the truth. I was not an actor at the core of my being. It wasn't me. To become a success, acting has to be almost as important as breathing. It has to be something that creates a void inside if unfulfilled. It should be something you would do for free if you couldn't get paid. It is that kind of love for the art that breeds great actors. Even though

I liked doing skits and improv, and respected the craft immensely, I faced the facts. I didn't want to act and I didn't want to take the steps necessary to make it a reality. I was glad that I had explored the art and left of my own volition. I made the right decision and walked away from acting forever— or so I thought. How about that for a cliffhanger?

I was now unfettered from my dream and I could continue the madcap life of a single man in the modern world. I continued traveling the globe to seek out new life and new civilizations. I lived in France, traveled around Europe and made my second trip to India. I was living my other dream: travel. I was happy with my choice and my freedom.

At this point I had lived and experienced life. I had laughed, cried, climbed a mountain and crossed a desert. I had been to about 50 countries and 47 states. Yes, I know you're the curious type; I missed Alaska, North Dakota and Alabama. I could have caught Alabama if I had only veered left! Who knew? Somehow all of that led me to Massachusetts. It certainly seems like I made a wrong turn somewhere! Why would someone choose to live here? This is a place for locals or people who aren't from the big bad city of New York. Hey, some of my best friends are New Englanders; I'm even related to some of them. I eventually adapted and in the course of time the good people of the Commonwealth accepted me.

So how did I wind up in this godforsaken—I mean, this beautiful landscape called New England, where the cultural fabric is woven through the tradition and the pride of the hardworking people who live here. Well, if you must know, it was a woman. Like any good movie, it's always a woman. Isn't a woman at the core of everything? We wouldn't really have a movie without the girl. Even if the movie is mostly men there is always the girl. One exception would be *12 Angry Men*, with Henry Fonda, a fantastic movie by the way, an old-fashioned film with one set and great, great acting. I'd bet they wouldn't have been so angry if there had been a lady around.

As the line goes, "That's no lady, that's my wife!" Yes, only a siren could have pulled me off the boat during my carefree youth. After running around the world I decided to settle down. Settling down was not without its growing pains. Before taking the plunge I was able to walk between the raindrops by avoiding a home. I moved around a lot, jumping from friends to family and from couches to campgrounds. I eliminated a lot of expenses, which negated the need to make much money. However, living in a steady place, I was hit with these things that I was unaccustomed to. They were known as bills. I had bills to pay and I needed work.

Roll Sound

It was 1990 and there I was, living in Marblehead, Massachusetts, trying to figure out my next move and doing some temp work just to make a buck. I found myself in the employ of a trophy manufacturer. I was in charge of putting their literature together. Translation: I stuffed envelopes. The first day on the job, the owner introduced himself to me and said, "Well, we make trophies here." That struck me in the funniest way and just as I was about to let loose with laughter, I noticed he was not smiling. He was dead serious, and I knew immediately he didn't have a sense of humor. After I stuffed enough envelopes to let bowling leagues across America know the new fashion in championship symbolism, I came to the fast conclusion that I was not suited for this line of work. I was in and out of meaningless jobs for about a year, and the jobs I did find were duller than daytime television. Without a sheepskin, what could I really expect?

I guess that's why the movie business was an easy fit. Once you are working on movies you can throw your degree in the closet, even if it is in filmmaking. The main ingredient the college experience offers to the movie professional is the connections made at school. If you didn't go to a prestigious film school or a big college like Harvard, where the alums take care of their own, you will still have to elbow your way into the room. A master's degree in film does not open up any doors by itself. Even though we live in a society that purports the pull-yourself-up-by-your-bootstraps mentality, it is a rare individual who pushes through by hard work alone. Usually there is someone helping with the bootstraps—more on nepotism later.

On a trip to New York I hooked up with my friend Rob, who was taking filmmaking classes. He was making a short film with a bunch of his fellow students and ascending directors. He asked me to be in his little movie. I told him I had given up acting, I had moved on, I had accepted my fate and I was living with that decision. I could look at the man in the mirror and say unequivocally that I was done. Kaput! Finito! Hasta la vista, baby! The fat lady has left the building. He said, "So what? All you have to do is hail a cab." Well, with that kind of encouragement, I figured I'd do it.

The sun was shining, but it was a blistering cold day. I stood there on 2nd Avenue just north of Houston Street freezing my something or other off. Even though it was a student project it was my first experience with the movie business. Basically it was a group of aspiring directors, each with an individual vision in this collaborative project. One woman in particular could not cooperate with the others; she was clearly the Stroheim of the group. I didn't know if she had any talent; what I did know was that she wouldn't listen to anyone else and as a direct result I was freezing. While they duked it out on the Lower East Side of Manhattan, Rob took me to a warm place. He knew my natural aversion to the cold. Heat, or lack thereof, is a recurring theme in this book.

I sat in holding (the area where actors and extras wait and wait) and eventually I did my "silent bit." When I started in the biz there was something in the SAG (Screen Actors Guild) contract known as a silent bit. It fell somewhere in the middle on the rate scale: less money than a speaking role, but more than an extra, and hailing a cab would have constituted a silent bit. That is, if this had been a SAG show. It wasn't SAG and I wasn't paid.

I had a good time, but I still had no interest in getting into the movie business. I just helped my friend that day and he kept me posted on his progress. After some classes and a few shoots he decided that he was going to work in the film business and become a soundman. He was already a musician and was highly familiar with electronics. He was on his way except for one thing: he needed cash. The soundman brings his own equipment with him to the show. He asked me if I would split the package with him, and we would split the revenue. I thought this was a great idea. I wanted to start something and I could see how serious Rob was about the endeavor, so I said "OK."

Because of my casual attitude toward work in general I was unaware that I was making one of my biggest life choices ever. It defined my life for the next 20 years. I didn't think about it in that light. It was a very cavalier decision on my part. I was actually looking to stumble into something. I often say, "I fell into this business by slipping on a banana peel." I had never considered film crew work before. The opportunity was there, so I grabbed it.

I was very excited by the new career move, and ready to dive in headfirst. I had only one problem: no money. I had some of the money, but not all of the money. I scrambled around and borrowed from friends and family to put my end together.

As we put the sound package together my friend suggested that I become the boom man. I had never even heard of the job, let alone thought of making a career out of it. He gave me the job description. "So, all I have to do is hold this pole," I retorted.

He said, "Yes and no. It is not an easy job." It didn't sound hard. I figured I would give it a try.

Everything in life always boils down to two ways of doing things and breaking into the movie business is no exception. The first is the best way, if it applies to you: you already have an uncle in the biz. As previously stated, show business is highly nepotistic. From the talent to the Teamsters, if you have a friend or relative who has treaded the path before you, he can easily open a door for you. This speeds up the process exponentially. However, it only applies to the few with royal blood. You might say it applied to me because my friend had already been in the business for six months. I knew someone already "in" that was willing to help bring me in. It wasn't like Lloyd Bridges and Jeff Bridges, but it sped up the learning curve a tad.

The other way is to get on the bottom rung of the ladder and start climbing up. Even though my friend was in the business, we were both essentially starting at the bottom. We didn't know anyone who could open up a door for us, not even a window. It was up to us to push our way inside and then upward. The movie business is highly competitive. Everyone wants to be in front of the camera or somewhere behind it. The sound department is as competitive as any other part of the industry. There were plenty of people already established and there was a line to get in.

As luck would have it, my first opportunity came quickly. My buddy signed us on to a two-day freebie in New York. He persuaded the producer to pay my driving expenses from Massachusetts. After gas and tolls I yielded twenty bucks. Many people start out volunteering on shoots until they get experience, building a resume which eventually leads to paid work. Slave labor is a common way to begin a film career.

So, there I was, on the set of my very first show. My friend and boss did not want me to let on that it was my virgin run. I pretended like I had done it before and tried not to appear "green." Essentially I kept my mouth shut and did what I was told, which is good advice for anyone. It does not help your situation to let anyone know it's your first barbecue or that you are still new to the job. If people around you sense that you don't know what you are doing, they will eat you alive. There is no compassion for the inexperienced. There is also no patience. If you do something wrong it will only be magnified by the fact that you were upfront with your co-workers. Then as time passes on the shoot you will be a magnet of criticism and the production fall guy. As I broke people in later on I would give out the same advice: "Mouth shut, eyes and ears open."

I broke in one gentleman and gave him the hide-your-inexperience rap and after four seconds on the set he divulged his new status in the business. He told me he could not hide who he was. He had to be himself. I guess everyone has to answer these moralistic questions for themselves. He had to follow his own treatise for living and ignored a lot of advice in the process. It's not rocket surgery, but the business works a certain way and if you want to march to the beat of a different drummer you might find yourself alone at the parade. When you hit the Mel Gibson level of success, tirades and idiotic comments are acceptable. I believe my former colleague is working at the Quickie Mart in Scranton.

Another problem with showing weakness, particularly in the sound department, is that you are already by default a pain in the neck to the production. The average soundman tends to be on the nerdy side, nitpicking at every horn, cough or footstep. Unfortunately, some do not know which battles to fight and more often than not they do not have the tact necessary to communicate their needs. I have found this to be more of a problem at lower levels of movie making. By the time a soundman makes it to the big show (big-budget Hollywood movies), he usually has sorted out his techno, geeky, over-the-top dysfunctions, or at least concealed them.

The sound department is unique because it is the only department not working on the picture, and the level of respect shown the department varies from show to show. This sets up the salmon-swimming-upstream syndrome. In low-budget land it is essential to capture all the dialogue on set. There isn't any money to go into post-production to do ADR (automated dialogue replacement). The big shows are going to do it anyway. They already have it budgeted. Bruce Willis told me on *Surrogates*, as I was booming the shot, "Don't worry about the sound, I'm going to have to loop it (ADR) anyway." Thanks Bruce! Does that mean I can pack up and go home now?

There are intelligent directors and cinematographers who understand the concept of good sound for a movie. However, many DP's (directors of photography) don't give a hoot about the sound. They are only concerned about the picture and how it looks. Sometimes they're even more concerned about the look of the picture than the movie itself. They get hung up in their lighting, use more time than allotted, cutting down the shooting time for other scenes or causing material to be dropped. This is probably more of a problem with independent features than the multimillion-dollar Hollywood shows. On the big-budget shows they can go into overtime or add days to get what they need. In the independent world a selfish DP hurts the movie.

The camera operator can mishandle the camera, the actor may flub a line, the assistant cameraman can mess up the focus, but God forbid you make a mistake with sound or dip your boom into the sacred frame. It's like you put a mustache on the Mona Lisa. I worked with a DP on *Monument Ave.*, who had classic holier-than-thou DP syndrome. On the very first take of the movie my boom operator had an accident. To his credit it was the only time anything like this ever happened and he was one of the best boom operators I have ever worked with. He was on a bench at a hockey rink and as he was backing up alongside the dolly he misjudged the distance of the bench. He came up physically unscathed, and saved the microphone, but the take was busted. When we were back in position the DP leaned over to my boom op and said, "You know, that was a good take." That was the first take of the entire production! Was that magic in a bottle we missed? I guess it was just Academy Award–winning stuff that we sound guys blew.

That's the landscape. There is no forgiveness for sound errors. If you want to be a soundman you better be good, because there is no patience for anything less than perfection. The actor can screw up until the cows come home. In fact everyone will have a nice chuckle about it. "Don't worry," the director would always say. "We'll just do it again. It's OK, no big deal, no worries mate, we have plenty of film, it's cool mon, no problemo, don't worry your pretty little head about it."

Meanwhile back at the ranch, which happens to be in Midtown Manhattan, I was thrilled yet clueless about my first day on a movie set. That day I had no idea I was crossing into a whole new chapter of my life. Actually, I would say that it was not just a chapter; it was more like a sequel. I would call it *Lenny Manzo Part II: The Movie Years*, Part I began at age 19, when I hit the road in my 1969 white Buick LeSabre. That car was suited for royalty. It fit nine comfortably. Well, it fit nine.

When I make Part I into a movie, the pitch will go something like this: "It's called *Lenny Manzo: The Missing Years*. It's Jack Kerouac's *On the Road* meets *Fast Times at Ridgemont High* with Sean Penn. You know, kid from Brooklyn hits the road, makes some money, loses some money, meets a girl, and gets his heart broken. It's a coming-of-age thing, I was thinking Edward Norton, but I think he's a bit old. What this part needs is some new blood. Anyway, the kid finds himself, resolves his demons and lives another day. This would also have been a great role for Pitt 20 years ago." This movie is in the first steps of development; I can only offer you a written trailer at this time.

Still at the Midtown Manhattan Ranch on that historic day somewhere in 1991, I showed up with my boss/friend in my Subaru full of sound gear, a few cases and a folding sound cart. Yes, thank providence, God or a fast-talking used car salesman for the hatchback. I just bought that car a few weeks before I had an inkling of my new career. A normal trunk would have been a handicap. The cart was about five feet folded firmly when flat; say that three times fast. That hatchback made my life so much easier. Was the power of fate already in motion? Is everything preordained? Should I have consulted with a local soothsayer? I was in the midst of big changes, though I didn't know it. Next time I'll pay more attention.

The piece was titled *Casting Call*, a short comedy, ironically about actors breaking into the movies. In the moment it was art imitating life, while life was imitating art. As the actors broke in on celluloid, my life mirrored the story. I was breaking into show biz in real life. Still, no way had I fathomed what a crazy world I had walked into. I had no idea what I was getting myself involved with, or how it would affect my life. It was only two years prior that I had retired before I started. Even though I wasn't in front of the camera, I was getting into show business. It didn't really penetrate my mind yet. It was a small shoot with an all-volunteer crew. It was more like a picnic than anything else.

The only thing I was capable of doing was the loading and the unloading of the gear. I had received a 15-minute tutorial the day before, but it was still confusing. I just hung out and waited for Rob to get it together. Everyone else was getting prepped as well. As we moved closer to the first shot I began to get strapped in with cables and headphones, much like a pilot. Dressed in full regalia, I was ready to go. I received a couple of last-minute pointers from my friend/sound mixer, and it was zero hour. We were ready to shoot.

This was a surreal moment. I've watched a zillion movies and had this love affair with the cinema my whole life. I was actually working on a movie, a 10-minute movie, but a movie. Then the magic moment came and the AD (assistant director) silenced the set then bellowed, "Roll Sound!" It felt like a dream or the time I was in a car accident and time seemed to slow down. I relished every second.

The mixer responded with "Speed." The tape passed over the record heads of the tape deck. The DP knew he could start the camera; the 2nd AC (assistant camera) called out the scene, "Scene 6, Take 1." The cameraman said "Mark it," the 2nd AC clapped the slate, everyone settled, the director called "Action" and from that instant I was in the movie business. That was a magic moment for me. I couldn't believe I was in the middle of a movie set. The rest of the weekend went off without a hitch. Everything went pretty smoothly. I thought to myself, "I can do this, this isn't so bad." I expressed that to Rob. He said, "Hold on there, it's good that you like it, but I think you are underestimating the difficulty of the job." I really did not understand what he was talking about. Since I had nothing else to compare it to, I thought I could do it.

This is how I was hoodwinked by the biz, set up like a bowling pin. When I look back it feels like a con job. Nothing premeditated. Just one naturally conjured up by the powers of the universe. My first job as a boom operator was so easy. I had actors who barely moved. Ninety percent of it could have been done with the microphone on a stand. It was all contained in two rooms. One of the easiest boom jobs I ever had. I can tell you one thing about booming: it is not easy. You have to dance around light and camera. You have to stay out of the way. You have to hold the microphone and pole over your head for an uncomfortably long time in awkward positions. I have not met a boom operator to date who does not have back troubles. This job is no *duck walk*!

One of the more subtle jobs of the boom operator is to act like Claude Rains. Not as Captain Renault from *Casablanca*, more like *The Invisible Man*. The boom op spends a great deal of time on the set, and must stay out of the way while achieving the goal of getting clear, pure, unadulterated sound. A good boom op goes unnoticed and gets the work done. It may not be the hardest job, but it is hard and it definitely is the most underrated.

While acting invisible on the set, it is most important to put the microphone into what we call the *sweet spot*, that place roughly 1 to 2 feet above the mouth on a 45 degree angle where the sound quality is the best. One of my favorite things to do was to walk backwards down the street and nail a *two shot walk and talk*. I could get the sweet spot every time! This shot usually uses a Steadicam and it is a dance to move with the camera and the actors. A good boom operator is Fred Astaire on wheels!

Are You Ready for Your Close-Up, Mr. Turturro?

My next job was on another below-low-budget movie. I was paid seventy-five bucks a day and that included a full sound package. Actually, I wasn't even getting paid; my equipment was, though. It was more valuable than I was, at least in perceived value. This was my first in a long line of bad movies. That is one of the problems with the industry. There are not enough good projects to go around. If you want to work regularly you come to the realization fairly quickly that content is not a consideration. If you want to get paid, you just don't concern yourself with it. Actors rarely have that luxury, never mind a crew person.

I did turn down one show because of content. It was one of those reality-style police shows where you bust in on some guy getting wasted on his couch with his girlfriend. I was asked to do sound for the arrest squad. I took the job right away, but as I thought about it, I had to cancel on this one. I didn't want to arrest anyone. I figured there was a chance that we could be arresting someone who was not guilty of anything. I didn't want that to be part of my day. To paraphrase Dr. McCoy from *Star Trek*, "I'm a soundman, not a gumshoe."

Major actors suffer from the same problem. There are many great actors, but not as many good projects. I often think of Michael Caine when this discussion comes up. He has worked nonstop throughout his career. He has been a part of many amazing award-winning films. In between all those gems there are some serious clunkers. It was important for him to keep working. If he waited for something good it may have taken years to get the right project. If he turned down too much he may have knocked himself out of the loop. George Raft turned down *The Maltese Falcon*. Some of my younger readers are going to say George who? Case in point, Raft was huge back in the day and on the scene before America knew who Humphrey Bogart was. Turning down the iconic *Falcon* hurt Raft's career and launched Bogie's. The bottom line is if you want to work regularly you'll have to take what you are offered. Meryl Streep, Tom Hanks and Julia Roberts can pick and choose, the rest of us take what we can get.

My first feature was my introduction to low-budget nightmare horror, and I don't mean horror as a film genre. It was a horror show due to the poor working conditions. Since I've been in this trade I've been in so many toxic environments, places I never would have walked into of my own volition and I soon learned that glamour had nothing to do with this business. We shot all night, we shot in the cold and we shot in the rain. Sometimes all the bad conditions would come together. There's nothing like making a dumb low-budget movie on a cold rainy night in February, in Queens. Now that's show biz.

The glamour is for the few and even then it is an illusion. Many actors are so bored on location that they go back to the hotel and watch television all night. Bruce Willis always talked about what he watched on TV the night before. Perhaps he was just keeping up with his peers or perhaps he was bored out of his mind at the hotel night after night. It doesn't matter, either way he's spending his evenings watching TV like everyone else in America. No judgment, just the facts, ma'am, just the facts.

What usually happens on a no-money extravaganza is that inexperience runs rampant through the production, and this movie was the poster child. The director was green and the producers were green. Hell, I was green, but I wasn't running the show. I've seen mistakes in this business made at the highest levels. Organizing a movie is no easy feat; in fact there are few who do it well. The big-budget producers are inclined to make more mistakes because there is more money to fix the problems. On an independent movie you have to find another way, since you don't have the money to fix the mess.

This show was always running late; the first day was 17 hours out of the gate. It was slim pickings for lunch and I brown-bagged it daily. Since I was so new to the industry I didn't realize I was being abused. Since everyone else was going along with it I didn't think much of it. I thought that was how it was.

I kicked around a bit in my first year, trying to get any work I could for the experience, also trying to do what I could to make a buck. My first year was a lean one. I did a bunch of college shorts that could throw me a c-note for my troubles. The film school kids would rotate the set positions or find a group who had diverse interests. However, it is a rare bird that goes to film school for sound. Everyone in college is either going to produce or direct. Since all the students dream of being the next Steven Spielberg or David O. Selznick, they find themselves over a barrel when it comes to getting a sound guy. I was able to squeeze out some coffee money from these shoots and continue to learn on the job.

Most film students are naïve when it comes to the commitment needed for this career. The reality of pounding pavement and hustling work has not yet entered their brains. It is partly the fault of the institution. The schools talk about film theory and get the kids hands-on experience, but in no way are they prepared for the harsh reality of climbing the Hollywood mountain. Many students upon graduating with a film degree never do a thing in the motion picture industry besides rent movies. The programs are flooded with kids who don't have a direction and think film would be cool. Sure it's cool, but you have to have a desire for it, you also have to have a fire for it. To make it into the crème de la crème and direct multimillion-dollar movies you have to have a burning drive that borders on obsession. Either that or be Kirk Douglas's son. That's a much easier route. Are you Kirk's son? That would help.

Later on, after I was an established sound mixer, I spoke at Boston University, Emerson College and other learning institutions on the subject of recording sound. As I yakked about the finer points of location sound recording, the students were bored out of their minds. I remember that vacant look from high school; I think I had it myself. I did the Vulcan mass mind meld and found out most of them were just thinking about getting out of there. They were thinking about their plans for the evening, a hamburger or the cute girl in the second row. She did catch my attention as well. They stared at the ceiling, doodled or just had that glazed, deer-in-the-headlights look. There were usually two or three who paid attention. Sometimes if the lecture ended early I would open it up to general questions about the movie business. Then they pricked up like rabbits popping out of their holes. Sound is dry; they wanted to hear about the set and all the juicy stuff that goes on there. Don't worry, I have those stories too.

At this early point in their lives the kids have high aspirations. The students can't concede the exalted director's seat; basically there are too many chiefs and no Indians, which created a small pocket of employment for me. I could at least wangle one to two hundred bucks a day depending on their desperation level. It is not uncommon for the college kids to hire professionals in certain positions, especially if the young stud had an overzealous project. Since film school is a training ground, it is expected that mistakes will be made. Still, the college flag was a red flag. Inexperience shines brightly and the production experience was not going to be fun. After doing the sound for a bunch of college shows the frustration level increased until I priced myself out of that pain.

After a year I found a job on *The Search for One-eye Jimmy*. I guess you could call it a job. I did the work, but I didn't get paid at the time. This is what is known as a deferred project: work now, get paid later—maybe. Since work wasn't flying in, my partner thought we should do this movie because it had a big cast: Samuel L. Jackson, Steve Buscemi, Jennifer Beals, Anne Meara and John Turturro. This causes me to pause ... inhale ... exhale ... and share my John Turturro story. John Turturro was booked on this show for two days. I surmised he was doing a favor for his brother Nick who was one of the leads. He arrived on set in full prima donna mode. Let's say he wasn't very cooperative from the start. Maybe he resented being on such a low-budget project, maybe the dog bit him, either way he was not easy to deal with.

A bit of back-story: My partner and I were completely broke. We were not making much money, especially on *One-Eye Jimmy*. This film may have been pushing our careers forward, but it wasn't doing anything about our more immediate needs, such as gas, food and lodging. We needed to buy some pouches for our wireless transmitters that the actors wore, which connected to their body mikes. After spending a combined twenty thousand on gear we were just tapped out. I was walking around New York City with four bucks in my pocket. My partner said his mother could sew some pouches for us. It was either that or fork over another fifty bucks each, which we did not have. So, we went with the sound plan of homespun wireless receiver pouches. The caveat and the point of this story, pun intended, is that we needed a safety pin to close the pouch.

As fate would have it, there was a shared destiny for that safety pin and John Turturro's backside. He let out a yell that would curl your hair, and went into a tirade that would put Joan Crawford to shame. This just fueled the fire that had been simmering all day, and it did not help his already disenchanted attitude. He was scheduled for two days but the production shot him out in one. Either he demanded it or the production was smart enough not to have his unwilling self back for another day.

Fast-forward a few years. I was lying on my mother's couch in Queens, flicking around the cable television and as a fait accompli I landed on *The Tonight Show*. Sitting in the chair was the aforementioned Mr. Turturro. The first thing out of his mouth was, "I was working on this low-budget movie ... " I knew it! I knew it! I knew he was going to talk about it. I felt it like mud on a pig. Then he went on to tell his side of the story, how he was a trooper, even while being literally stabbed in the back, and was able to finish the take. He said that there was something in his back and described the pain, but of course he finished the take and then pulled it out of his back. Dolly Parton was sitting just to his right with mouth agape and completely astonished. He said that he also gave us some money to buy some real pouches.

For one thing I never saw any money. I don't have much pride; I would have taken a few bucks even if it was an insult. I loved the bit about finishing the take. I had never thought about it before. A celebrity comes on a talk show and tells an anecdote. It had never dawned on me to wonder whether it was true or not. I just never questioned it. It was just a story. In fact it's all show biz, folks, it's all smoke and mirrors. You never know what's true or not. "Based" on a true story, based is the key word. They have to make it into something the public wants. Truth is not a necessity. Does it play in Peoria? Maybe he remembered it like that. Hey, maybe that's how it happened. I just remember the crew talking about what a jerk he was for the rest of the week.

The rest of the show was similar: long hours, bad food and many mistakes. For that matter the whole movie was a mistake. It was a heinous film; in some countries it might have been considered a crime. While we were shooting, it seemed funny to me, with a quirky offbeat feel and some amusing characters. Either something was lost between the production floor and the editing room or I was just way off base. I remember Sam Rockwell, who shows up at the end as *One-eye Jimmy*, giving a monologue that was cracking up the entire set. It did not translate to the screen. Plot and bad script aside, this was one movie that really did have a happy ending. Amazingly enough the producers *of One-eye Jimmy* ended up getting distribution and they paid the crew. I couldn't believe it. They paid us for our labor and the gear. Unbelievable! A miracle in the world of deferred freebies.

SCENE 4

Don't Shoot Me, I'm Only the Sound Mixer

Working in New York and living in Massachusetts was not working out very well. My life was in Massachusetts. The arrangement was making less sense to me. I pursued work in Boston and the surrounding area. I pounded a lot of pavement back then. Fortunately, I was able to do it over the phone.

It was good for me to cut my teeth in another city. I made all my big mistakes in New York, with crew people I would never work with again. In this business people are unforgiving when you screw up. By the time I began working in Boston I was an established soundman and I was able to create the perception that I knew what I was doing. Gradually I felt like I really did.

My second year was also lean, but not as thin as the first. I made 11K the first year. The hourly wage was probably about a buck an hour. Technically I only made a thousand, I had to put up ten grand just to get in the front door. That money put me inside; it was up to me find a chair and stay a while.

The second year moved along with its share of short films and miscellaneous jobs. I was really starting to enjoy my work at this point. The learning curve had flatlined. Even though I started in this business without an ounce of technical knowledge and even less technical interest, I had mastered the operation of my equipment and understood the fundamentals of good sound.

Before I mastered the operation of the gear I learned how to act like I knew how to use it. If you can't do, pretend. I pretended from day one, and I was glad when the faking came to an end. The business kind of tricked me into becoming a technician. I started as a boom operator in New York, but in Boston there were minimal opportunities for a freelance boom operator. If I wanted to work in Boston, I had to become a sound mixer. I had no desire to make that leap, but people were calling me to record sound. They had some idea that I could do it. A pattern began to develop. It was sink or swim and I kept throwing myself in the water. I learned how to swim and became a firm believer in that theory. There really is no choice; at some point you have to fly solo. One thing I learned how to do was keep my cool under pressure even when I was freaking out on the inside. On the outside I kept a stern professional demeanor.

Becoming a soundman meant learning how to operate the Nagra, the industry standard reel-to-reel recording deck. The poor Nagra, once the stalwart of movie recording for decades, has now moved into obscurity. It was a gorgeous piece of machinery and a joy to work with. This machine that was once valued at $13,000 is now sold as a doorstop at Kmart for $19.99. There's no crying in technology.

The first video shoot I ever worked on was in Boston. The camera guy owned the Beta camera. He was going over the camera with me and I had a confused look on my face. I knew that because as he was explaining it to me he said these words that tipped it off, "You have a confused look on your face." I brushed it off like I was distracted and applied my poker face henceforth. A green person on the set is like a nerd at a summer camp.

I got a big break toward the end of my second year. A film by the name of *Lost Eden* was filming in Boston with a lot of hubbub, bub. The director had received a grant for a cool million from the National Endowment for the Arts. I thought this was a great opportunity for me. The pay of course, was low. It was a flat rate of $275 a week. I did manage to get a decent amount for the gear, which brought me up to almost a grand a week. It was my highest paid job and a great chance to work on my first feature with a decent budget as a mixer.

The job was going well. I was getting great sound, and I was having a good time doing it. I was enjoying the August sunshine and the company of my fellow filmmakers. A wise man once told me, "When life looks like easy street, there is danger at your door."

Even though everything in the Lenny Manzo world was coming up roses, it was not the case for the production. The director was prone to changing her mind. Changing your mind is fine, but on a movie set it can be disastrous. A quick change in the schedule can add another hour or more to the day. A new scene meant a re-light and costume changes, as well as make-up and hair, which were huge because we were doing a 19th-century period piece. One of the few people not affected was me. I didn't have to make major adjustments. Actually, this only fueled the Lenny Manzo world. I would indulge in some extra downtime. I went outside to catch a breath of air, to shuck and jive with the crew, and have a cup of tea. Yes, that was in the days before I drank coffee, if you can imagine that. That story comes later.

This amount of downtime did not let up in the first week and continued on into the second week. By day eight we were two or three days behind. That was a bit much. Even though we were behind, the movie was coming out great and what we were getting was good. The production design was great, the cinematography was beautiful and we had a good script that was coming alive through great acting, but there was dissension in the ranks.

Some of the crew were sure we were not going to finish this film. They were actually outraged; they were viewing it as a piece of art that needed to be made. It was a woman's story set around Massachusetts textile mills in the 19th century with all the problems of mill life. The director was a woman. The DP, the production designer and the costume designer were all women. They were there because they believed in the movie. They felt that this film should be made. I was in favor of it being made as well. The difference was that since they were seasoned vets they were compromising their rates greatly. The key people on this show were artistically and emotionally attached to the film; they saw the money as a stipend. As for me, I was trying to make my way in the movie world. This film was a step up, I wasn't there doing the production a favor; this job was supposed to pay my bills. Pretty much like it is today and for everyone else who is earning a living in this crazy business.

There were grumblings and rumblings about being behind schedule. People complained, as they do on a movie set. Downtime is often filled with a lot of banter about what is wrong with the production. I still didn't think much of it. I figured it would work itself out somehow; it usually does. Either they figure out the problem or they cut scenes.

The lead actress, Cara Buono, had a hard out. She was going to work with Woody Harrelson in the western *Cowboy Way*. She was booked and that was a stone that could not be moved. After the first week of shooting it was fairly obvious we did not have the time to finish the film. In my small world it still amounted to six weeks of work, with the chance of more work doing the re-shoots. I had no issue with what was happening. I wanted to finish the movie like everyone else and would have preferred to do it right then. I needed that movie to be completed and distributed, so I could get some notoriety and build my resume on the success of the film.

This is how a mutiny on a ship happens. Sometimes there are legitimate reasons as in *Mutiny on the Bounty* with Clark Gable or Marlon Brando or even Mel Gibson. In every remake they were all justified in mutinying against the cruel Captain Bligh, but we didn't have a Captain Bligh. We had a director who kept changing her mind, something that I have run into many times since.

Well, the DP and many other department heads called a crew meeting without the production team, a strictly below-the-line affair. This was where my movie career went a little Felliniesque. It was not just a surreal moment; it was downright kooky. I had not been in the business long and did not have much to compare it to, but I knew this was an odd situation and not run of the mill. We started the meeting at lunch but it went into production time. The bone of contention amongst the heads of the creative departments was not only that we were not going to finish the film, but also that we were getting further behind every day, which would require re-shoots that they would not be able to come back to finish. Therefore again, the production would have to hire other crew to finish the work. And there-finally-fore, the current creative team's work would be bastardized. That left field thought led to righteous indignation, and the pervading perception was, "We can't have our work bastardized. How dare they do that to us?"

So, the only thing to do was to demand that the director step down and be replaced by the producer so we could carry on. That's the fact, Jack! I couldn't believe it! I was in complete jaw-drop mode. There were actually two things that I could not believe. One was the fact that these crew people were going to overthrow the production government by threatening to shut it down over artistic differences. The second was that I was going to lose my job, four more weeks of work and the feature credit that went with it. Needless to say I was not happy about the prospect.

On many a show I've seen the tug of war between the director and the DP. The DP would say to the AD, who acts as the set foreman, or social worker in such cases, "Why can't she do it the right way?"

The director would tell the AD, "Why can't she listen to me?" In general, I side with the director on this issue. It is not a coincidence that the word director is a very similar word to dictator. The only place in the world where I support fascism is on the movie set.

There has to be one person in charge of everything. If it were a democracy and open to debate movies would never get made, at least not on budget.

The movie is ultimately the director's vision and it lives and dies with her execution of it. If I was having trouble with a director, or for some alien reason I was so disgusted with how she was handling the project, and it was beyond anything I could stand being a part of, I would walk away on my own. I would not start an insurrection.

After some time of rocka-rocka at the crew hoedown, I decided to put in my two cents, perhaps for my own personal gain. Not perhaps, but yes, to save my job and the movement of my career. I said, "Maybe we should put it to her, that there is a problem and give her the opportunity to right the ship." I thought that it was a reasonable suggestion and a good compromise.

Everyone started yelling, "Stone him! Get him! Kill him! Lyyyyyyyyyyyyyyyynch him!" That may be a bit overstated. They didn't say exactly that. That was only the tone. They said, "Oh no! We can't do that! Are you kidding me! She'll only keep doing it! She's incapable of directing! It's all her fault, she does not know what she's doing," and on and on. I was shot down. It was like defending the monarchy in France during the revolution. How could I even suggest the thought of a compromise? The crew had developed a mob mentality.

The moment came and went and there was nothing I could do. I had to sit back and watch the movie crash and burn. It was very similar to the beginning of *The Outlaw Josey Wales*, as Clint Eastwood lies there almost dead, watching his house burn down with his wife and child inside. I realize that having a house burn down and your family murdered trumps losing a job, but I must point out that while Mr. Eastwood's experience was simulated, I was heading to the real-life unemployment line. As my plea fell on deaf ears, the crew agreed to walk off the project unless the director stepped down from her position.

The director's immediate response was, get this, "No." She did not want to step down from the project that probably took her years to put together. Go figure. The crew was steadfast. They were not going back to work unless the director stepped down. We were, how do you say, at an impasse. There was only one thing left to do: wrap the gear and go home. As the immortal Phil Rizzuto, former New York Yankee shortstop and broadcaster, would have said, "Holy Cow!" Never was that expression more apropos. I had to scrape my jaw off the floor. What was going on? Was this really happening?

I packed up everything in utter disbelief. I was moving slowly. I had nowhere to go. I was so stunned. Just as I was getting ready to leave, the producer came out to the set. He gathered the crew and told us that he would direct the movie in her stead and we could carry on. He called a department head meeting for the morning to make a plan.

I did breathe a big sigh of relief, but I didn't understand why he was calling this meeting. It seemed like a time waster to me; we already lost a half-day of shooting during the mutiny. We were way behind, bringing us to this crazy crossroad and now we were going another day without shooting. I surmised the production people, especially the director, needed some time to figure out some options. Regardless, there was a department head meeting in the morning. I was dying to know what we were going to talk about.

So there we were on the Group W Bench waiting to see what the heck was going to happen. At the meeting—or shall I say, in this corner, with a combined weight of 325 pounds, the producer and director, and in the opposite corner, wearing blue trunks of righteous indignation, the director of photography and other department heads. The bell rang and the director was the first to strike: "I will be watching from a monitor in the next room. You can't expect me to just walk off the project. I am not walking off the project."

That left hook out of the director's mouth was the straw that broke the DP's back. She told the director, "You have shot yourself in the foot and won't go to the hospital! I'm out of here!" She turned and walked out the door faster than you can whistle "Dixie." The gaffer and the key grip were of the same conviction: "If she goes, we go." They left right behind her. Within 12 seconds we lost three departments.

This created quite a stir in the room. For the movie version of *Above the Line*, there is a cacophonous sound of people in a confused panic. There are dazed looks on the people's faces. The camera is focused in a wide shot on the producer with his hands up as he tries to grasp the commotion of the room and quell the temporary chaos. Cut back to the doorway where the

DP is standing: She is gathering her stuff, and then she walks out followed by the gaffer and the key grip. The camera pans through the pandemonium of the crowd and lands back on the producer trying to calm everyone down, unsuccessfully. The camera continues to pan left to the director, who is seated alone, but unshaken externally. Hard cut to our hero in the corner, which is me by the way, maybe played by Johnny Depp; I think it would be a perfect role for him. We hear my brain rumbling in a voice over: "Oh my God, what is going on here? I have only one card to play in this absurd game." I stand up with confidence and conviction. Camera dollies back as I walk across the long room in slow motion; the background audio is becoming muddled. We see other crew members frantically gesticulating again and no recognizable sound. I am walking with determination and intent. I head straight for the director, I stop in front of her and the camera zooms in for a close-up. I tell her in no uncertain terms, "When you shoot this movie I am ready to do sound." She thanks me, and we play some knock-off *Star Wars* music here; I don't want any copyright issues. Fade out, end of scene.

I was not part of this Bolshevik movement to overthrow the director. Don't get me wrong, I am for due process and everyone having a say. There is just no place for it on the film set. The movie set is a fascist state by necessity. There is one person with the creative vision and everyone else is there to support that vision. To quote Tony Randall as Felix Unger in *The Odd Couple*, "The director is in charge, without it, there is anarchy." It is so true, and *Lost Eden* was the perfect example. The crew took over the ship, and instead of saving it, crashed it on the beach.

Let's try to look at this thing from both sides. Over the years I have examined this debacle many times. My final assessment is that even though the DP had a valid point, that the movie would not finish on time and maybe the DP couldn't come back for the re-shoots or would not want to, the bastardization of her work was a little too farfetched an accusation for this cowboy. The task of the alleged future bastardizing crew would have been to match what was shot. They would have received notes from the former crew people and brought back the same costumes and props to create the same look of the movie. The bastardization argument was absurd and pretentious.

Movies do re-shoots all the time. This was not outrageous behavior; it was standard textbook filmmaking. If you don't get it done, you come back and finish another time. There must have been other issues that I was not aware of. I can only believe that the rift between director and DP was large enough to end the show. I have been in worse situations where the conditions were poor, the unpaid overtime was out of control, and the movie was much worse in quality.

The DP is actually the only person who really has the power to spearhead a strike. The DP is the director's right hand. It is the job of the DP to support the director. I believe there were unknown elements that transpired between the DP and the director that led the DP to lead the rebellion. It was not just artistic integrity. Artistic integrity would have been to finish the film, or at least try to finish it. Finishing funds could have been raised, especially for the quality project that everyone seemed to think it was.

So, what happened to our hero? Again, that's me. The movie shut down for a week, while the production regrouped to find more crew. I of course, stayed with the project. Just as we were about to get going again we shut down for the last time. I never received an explanation for the final wrap. Perhaps the funding was pulled, perhaps something else. Either way, *Lost Eden* was officially lost and it sank like *Cleopatra* at the box office.

There was an upside. Since I stayed with the project, I wound up getting paid through practically the whole show. Most likely because I supported the director and the production. I know everyone did not get paid. I put it on my resume; I just didn't talk it up. When asked to explain it I describe it as a 19th-century period piece that I did the sound for, nothing more. It was legit, but there would not be any notoriety for this film. I had to get back into the water and find another job. It wasn't the boon for my resume that I anticipated, but I did get paid. I also walked away with a story I've been telling for years and now have a chance to share with you. All debacles in life make great stories and great movies.

SCENE 5

My El Mariachi

Halfway through my second year I was immersed in the low-budget movie scene in New York and Boston. The independent movie scene was growing. *El Mariachi* was just released and claimed it had made been made for just $7,000. Of course that doesn't count the seven figures that Paramount dumped into it for theatrical distribution. *El Mariachi* was one of the first rags-to-riches indies of the 90's. It put director Robert Rodriguez on the map; more important, it opened a floodgate of want-to-be filmmakers who thought they too could make a movie for under ten grand.

As Mr. Rodriguez parlayed 7K into a Hollywood career, it sparked many light bulbs in many heads. Inspired by the guerrilla filmmaker, there was an explosion of kids with cameras. Everyone wanted to film the next *El Mariachi* and be the next Robert Rodriguez. Such aspiration has its trickle-down effects. For every emerging Quentin Tarantino making the next indie hit, there is the need for a Lenny Manzo to do sound. Alas, I made my living off such dream seekers. But mine is not to cast judgment, mine is to show up at 6 AM with a microphone to record dialogue.

When the call came to do *Meter Madness*, the producer said, "You know, it's kind of an *El Mariachi* thing." I didn't know if that was supposed to entice me or warn me. They had some money and I still needed experience, so without knowing it I signed onto one of the worst low-budget movie experiences of my career. The tragedy of this movie is that I could have changed my entire experience had I been a tad savvier.

The deal with this show was that we towed a yellow taxi from a cube truck around Midtown Manhattan for two weeks. Normally, in any tow rig, the sound guy gets into the cab with the driver. In the early stages of my career I had never been in a situation with a tow rig. As the head of the department, and the only one in the department, I had to figure out what I was going to do. I set up my rig in the back of the cube truck. Big mistake. Instead of being cozy in the cab of the truck with the air-conditioning, I sat on an apple box (a wooden box roughly 20" x 12" x 8" used for various purposes on every film set which also makes a practical night table) in the back of this smog-filled cube truck for over 90% of my working day. It was the most toxic environment I have worked in to date. It does compete with the sewage plant on *The Box*. Oh, I almost forgot about the dilapidated underground set below the power company in Providence, on *Underdog*. That was like going into a coal mine every day. There were odors down that hole I have not smelled since.

No, this movie was not fun. We worked 15 hours a day and there was barely anything to eat on this show; in that way it was very similar to *El Mariachi*. I also made the mistake of agreeing to work 10 days straight without a day off. Even the Big Guy rested on the seventh day.

On this show I became fed up with the flat rate. I was also fed up with filmmakers who were clueless about managing their day. Let me tell you one thing about movie making: it takes time! It is a long, tedious process, and then things go wrong and it takes longer. Maybe this producer knew how to manage her day. After all, she crammed into two weeks what should have taken three, and saved herself some cash due to my naïveté. There are some directors such as Clint Eastwood and Woody Allen who are famous for short days. Their days are usually about 10 hours. That's how brainwashed we are in this business; we think a 10-hour day is short.

On union shows there is no such thing as a flat rate. After eight hours you go into time and a half, and at some point depending on the contract double time kicks in. I hadn't reached the union level yet, and the only work I could scrounge was on the flat rate clueless production. I did however, start to take matters into my own hands. One thing all these low-budget pipe dreams had in common was the first shot in the morning. It would usually take three to four hours for many of them to get the first shot off. I would just come in two hours later. It never made a difference and they never waited on me. It made my life easier and allowed me to avoid sleep deprivation.

As a producer or director you are so vested in your project that loss of sleep means nothing. Getting the project done is the only thing that matters. You can sleep when the project is over. As a crew person you move on to the next show and the next sleep-deprived situation.

Sometimes there are legitimate reasons why a show goes longer than 12 hours. Perhaps the location is only available for that day, or the production has to shoot out the actor. It's not easy to manage this circus. The production staff has to jump through many hoops to keep the show flowing.

Sometimes unforeseen events occur. There are many logistics that have to come together in a series and come together quickly. Sometimes things just happen. This is what I have dubbed "The Broken Window Axiom." Part of good management is to plan for the unforeseen. At the end of the shoot a good producer will have some add-on days in the budget and will have made arrangements to be available in case the shoot goes over. She has to figure that the movie will go over the allowed schedule. If she doesn't have a stash left in her bag of tricks she will find herself in a lot of trouble.

In any movie situation you do what you have to do to "get the day" (to shoot everything scheduled). If 17 hours gets you what 12 couldn't, then the shop stays open all night, and you finish the day's work. It will cost more money to come back another time to finish. So make sure you get the day. Get the day already. The downside to this pace is the decrease in productivity. Things start taking longer. People are less attentive, nuances slip through the cracks, problems snowball and dominoes fall. It also creates an unsafe environment, especially handling heavy equipment or driving vehicles.

The producer can sometimes be overbearing and go too far. He has a lot of power to gum up the works big time. I've seen some producers hover over the director like a nagging mother-in-law (pick your own ethnicity; I'm not touching that with a 20-foot boom pole. Don't you just love audio humor?). It all depends on the balance of power; he who has the power has the power to muck it up.

Then you have the actors. This is where water can really be thrown in the gas tank. Sometimes the actor becomes a big monkey wrench because of outrageous demands and not being a team player. It could take forever for the actor to be satisfied with his or her make-up, especially a disgruntled one. As good as some actors are, they don't always get the big picture, pun kind of intended but not really, but it is a pun and it works and I used it and I kept it, so I guess I would say at this point, it is intended. The actors need to go through some process to work through their art form. They sometimes don't understand that the director usually has a better idea of what the role needs and how it should be played. It is up to the director to coddle the actor, scare the actor or whatever works to get the performance he needs. Sometimes there is no getting through to the big know-it-all actor who can't take direction anymore. Al Pacino in *Heat*, I rest my case.

The director can throw a show out of whack as well. He sets the entire tone of the movie. Any of the above-the-line crowd can hold up a shoot. In our jargon-filled industry we just couldn't call it management and labor. It isn't that black and white anyway. The producers, the writers, the actors and the director are all above the line. Everyone else is below the line—a term that is not exactly complimentary for the bottom-feeders, but neither is bottom-feeders.

I like the idea of a strong director with a strong vision. However, it is not unwise to seek counsel from the great team that has been assembled to help you. This is the problem for the less, shall we say, "gifted" directors. They have the fascist-director thing down, but not the talent of the great ones. This is known as mediocrity. The way you fit into this category is by not being aware that you have shortcomings. If you are aware of your weaknesses, you are not mediocre, you are still progressing because you understand where you are. If you know you haven't reached the epic proportions of Cecil B. DeMille or Ridley Scott, then you are still on your way. To know what you don't know is the beginning of knowing.

My second year was coming to an end and I logged a lot of miles going back and forth from Boston to New York. I didn't mind in the beginning, but the commute was getting to me, and Mom's couch was getting uncomfortable. The proximity of her apartment to the Long Island Railroad was also disconcerting. For some reason I was having trouble sleeping through the passing trains.

It is true that I am a native New Yorker, and all that stuff about taking the boy out of the city and not being able to take the city out of the boy is all true. I am a New Yorker at heart and no matter how many years I live in the country, I will always be a city kid. However, this city kid left the city for a reason. He wanted a different pace of daily living. He wanted to smell the flowers, so he didn't want to go back. I will now go back to talking in the first person.

It was at this point I decided that I was going to do my own thing, be my own man, and focus on my career in Massachusetts. I talked it over with my partner and he bought me out. I took that money and reinvested it into my own package and went even further into debt.

SCENE 6

The Poseidon Adventure

In my third year of the biz I was enjoying myself at work. I was getting comfortable in my craft and even though work wasn't pouring in I was feeling a forward progression. I learned quickly that the New England winters are a very barren time for the movie industry. I got wind of an independent feature shooting in Upstate New York called *Upstate Story*, a working title later changed to *Heavy*. The sound mixer job was between me and another more experienced sound mixer; for some reason they chose the person with more experience. It was a movie with some name actors (Liv Tyler, Shelley Winters, Deborah Harry, Evan Dando). Even though I didn't get the job, I was in the conversation. I saw this as progress.

Just before *Heavy* was about to shoot principal photography, I was called to operate the boom. I checked my schedule and I was available. The mixer told me the rate and I checked my schedule again. Unfortunately, I was still available. I had nothing else going on so I signed on for the first week.

It began in a civilized manner; we did the standard 12-hour day. I thought, "This is OK, the money isn't good but the movie is good." They weren't killing me, so I signed on for another week. It was a setup. As soon as I committed myself, the wheels fell off the ship and it got ugly. On a union show if they do this to you there is compensation. Even if you are suffering, the paycheck eases the burden. On the low-budget flat rate indie, there is nothing to ease the pain of free overtime. In retrospect, it was crazy to be abused like that. That's how it is for new people in the industry. They need the experience so they get dumped on. That job paid $50 a day. On some days it worked out to $3.14 an hour.

Heavy was director James Mangold's first film. He has since gone on to make *Walk the Line* and *Knight and Day*. Jimmy, if you are reading this I'd like to call in that favor now, and see what you can do about hooking me up somewhere. We do go way back and when you think about it, you really owe me. Would you work for me for fifty bucks a day? Look, I'm not holding any grudges; just drop me a line and we'll talk.

It was on *Heavy* that I worked with the Hollywood heavy, Shelley Winters. If you said, "Who is Shelley Winters?" you should watch *Swimming with Sharks*. Guy (Frank Whaley) is holding court with his wannabe cronies, the four of them all dressed in suits, and he tells a great story about how his boss Buddy Ackerman (Kevin Spacey) interviews Shelley Winters. Buddy tells Shelley he wants her to come in for an audition. Upon entering Buddy's office Shelley puts an Oscar on the table. He doesn't know what to think about that, and continues talking about her, the role and the audition. She pops another Oscar on the table. Same story, he continues to speak about the audition and she puts the third Oscar on the table and tells him, "Some people think I can act!" All of Guy's cronies chuckle at the industry story, but then ask, "Who is Shelley Winters again?"

Shelley was big in the day and does have three Oscars to her name. She made no bones about telling us that more than once. She was lying in a hospital bed for a number of scenes including her death scene. As I was waving my boom pole over her bed checking it against the light, so as not to throw shadows over her face, Shelley told me, "Don't worry about it honey, they'll never see it. I won three Oscars." I gave her a chuckle and then she continued her rant.

She ranted from the time she arrived on set until she left. Sometimes it was jokes, sometimes it was insults. Either way, Miss Winters was "on" all the time. She was a product of the business. I don't know the back-story, but at that point she was gone, she was Hollywood Toast. One day she came on the set, insulted everyone in her tracks, reached her spot next to the director, sighed heavily and apologized profusely. There was no joy left in her work. It was on this set that I realized how great an actress she was. She transformed her nasty bitter self into a nice, sweet old lady. It was clear that the Hollywood life had taken its toll. In that same hospital bed a few hours later she was doing the death scene with Pruitt Taylor Vince who played her son in the movie. After the take she insulted him and inferred he was stealing her scene. This was some real old-school Hollywood nonsense, which I had read about, but never witnessed. She was definitely a throwback to the Hollywood of yesteryear.

When she insulted Pruitt he didn't take it well, or suck it up. He told her off, walked off the set and threw a chair for good measure. That hospital ward was as quiet as a church. The pin drop would have rocked the silence of that room. I honestly thought the movie was over. I thought, "How is this guy going to come back here, and work with this woman?" Well, that's just what happened. I don't know how it happened or who talked to whom, but after some time to regroup they were back at it as if nothing had happened.

There were some good things about *Heavy*. That was the first good movie I ever worked on. It was a good script with good acting. Working on it was another story. The drag about this one was that I was stuck in the middle of nowhere. It was a gorgeous area in the U.S. golden triangle of New York, New Jersey and Pennsylvania. I was stuck either on the set or at the motel. The food on all of these low-budget fiascoes was across-the-board bad. The problem with *Heavy* was that there was no other option. On other shows, if I had a problem with the food, I just bought something from a store. Here, there was no store. There was nothing to eat except the daily gruel served by the gulag. They took bad food to another level.

SCENE 7

Sausage and Cinema

I *have been complaining about* the food from the start. It's time to take a moment and talk about the food. Here's the deal. It is customary in the movie biz for the production to serve lunch. You work for six hours and then eat. Lunch is catered and ready. You walk over to the buffet, or take a short shuttle in a 15-passenger van, eat for a half hour, then go right back to work. When on location the production supplies all the meals including an evening meal, or they give you a per diem to get your own food. It is part of the business and you expect this as part of the deal.

Since I was making such short money I saw the meals as a big part of the compensation package. I felt entitled to be fed since everyone else was fed. I also have my own built-in food issue. I'm a vegetarian. I don't eat any beef, pork, chicken or seafood. I do eat dairy. Being a vegetarian is run-of-the-mill now. Many people today have food issues. Back in the early 90's there was little awareness of vegetarianism and even less understanding of it. I ate a lot of bagels and pizza in those years. I was on a shoot where the producers liked me a lot, and went out of their way to accommodate my food needs. I was thankful beyond belief, but they still couldn't pull it off. Half the time I ended up with a condiment sandwich. Even with good intentions it was difficult to satisfy my dietary requisite. I decided to fend for myself and not mention it anymore. Most people didn't care, and at times they found me annoying. All they saw was some sound guy whining about his lunch. So I let that go. It was better not to give people reasons to not hire me.

When I worked the big show, the food was so much better. The caterers on these movies work only on movies. They have a truck with stoves, ovens and everything else that goes in a kitchen. And out of this little 25-foot truck they cook for a hundred to three hundred people. They can handle anything. They do two meals a day, breakfast and lunch. You can order anything for breakfast, eggs, waffles, burritos, smoothies, sandwiches, French toast, rye toast ... if they have the ingredients on the truck they will make it for you.

We have one other element of food on the set, known as craft service. The single most uttered phrase in the movie industry is not "Action" or "Cut," it is, "Where's craft service?" The craft service department supplies their fellow craft people with snacks and beverages throughout day. When I first started in the biz, craft service provided a few bagels, muffins, chips, salsa and candy, maybe some fruit. It was no big deal. Now it has become very big. There are hot soups, sandwiches, cakes, crackers, cheese plates, falafels, calzones, crudités, parfaits, fondues, other French words, vitamin water, mineral water, energy drinks, caffeine drinks, ice cream, more cake, pies, chocolates, chocolate strawberries, fruits, nuts and on and on. On big movies there is a nonstop stream of grub, and not just at the craft service table. The craft people walk around the set as if they are working a cocktail party, serving shrimp or English muffin pizzas, and when the sushi hits the set, the crew swarm the craft person like locusts.

On the big show they eliminated the food problem. There is plenty of food and variety; there is always something to eat. They pay you well and feed you well. For that you perform your daily tasks and keep your mouth shut. I don't mean that in a bad way. Once inside the machine, one can make a pretty good living. It's all specialized work and the production companies demand a high level of skill from all the crew. I feel like a hired gun on these big projects when I'm doing some kind of lower totem pole job, but when I was in charge of the audio department for a film, I felt like a major contributor. Later, when I was doing assistant work, I felt very disconnected from the movie. More on my fall from grace later.

Even though I was well compensated financially for my efforts and I received some perks to sweeten the pot, the job experience wasn't all gravy. The biggest problem on many movie sets is the hours. When you jump onto a project, you know it's going to be 12 hours a day. That is the standard and we all accept it. A 60-hour workweek is tough, but when it gets over 70 hours life has less meaning. Friday night's shift, which has been dubbed "Fraturday," works its way into the early hours of Saturday morning, so the weekend is shot before it starts. As a veteran video playback guy put it to me on *Mall Cop*, "We wear golden handcuffs." We are fettered to a high-paying, time-consuming occupation.

It was worse years ago when the production scheduled six-day weeks. The six-day workweek has gone by the wayside for the most part. The producers finally figured it out.

"Why are we working six days a week, Sid?"

"I don't know, Harry, why are we working six days a week?"

"I think it's to save money."

"I think you're onto something, Harry. Do we really save enough money?"

"When you think about it, it's not really a big savings at all."

"So, I guess we don't need to work Saturdays, do we, Harry?"

"I think you're onto something, Sid."

"You are so right, Harry. Screw working Saturdays."

We only go to a sixth day when we are behind schedule or there is some issue that must be scheduled around, such as a location only being available on Saturday. The above-the-line folks try to make it as convenient as possible for themselves. When Adam Sandler shot down the block from my home in Essex, I heard he had a basketball court and a pool right on location. This business is not just about the money; it is also about the amenities.

Everyone is resigned to working the 12 hours. It is the 14-hour day and beyond that is the killer. It is not so bad if you are on location. If you're not home, the only other thing to do is go out with your co-workers. You may as well hang out with them on the set and make money. The problem for the locals is they would like to experience some home life after work. People would like to go home, see their spouses and children. The children, what about the children!?! (That last line should be said in a high, shrill, desperate, excited, pathetic, overly caring voice. Try it again, this time with feeling.)

The quandary is also the crew person's expectations. It is agreed that the 12-hour day on a movie set is a standard day. Even though 12 is the standard everyone aims for, the norm is to go over that. I see many people crack on cue when the production goes over 12 hours. It is naïve to have any expectations when working on a movie.

There are two things you never want to see get made, one is a movie, the other is sausage. For a dissertation on sausage you'll have to find another source. As for movie making, the process at times seems overwhelmingly stupid. "Hurry up and wait" is the oxymoron that plagues the industry. The production spends hours getting something ready, and then all of a sudden the panic button goes off. They freak out about losing the light (the sun going down) or for no explicable reason they scramble to set up something then abruptly stop and do it another way.

As a soundman I have a front row seat for all the nonsense that comes with the movie ticket. Many of the seemingly absurd decisions again have to do with actor availability. You wonder why we are doing the living room scene when we haven't finished the work in the kitchen. It is a time waster to stop shooting in one room, do something else then go back to that room. That's because the actor we were shooting in the kitchen has to leave so we have to come back to that scene later when he is available.

On *The Town* with Ben Affleck, we had to come in at four in the morning. I can tell you something about starting your day at 4 AM. It's worse than finishing your day at 4 AM. I have never heard a set so quiet in my life. Not counting the Shelley Winters/Pruitt Taylor Vince chair-throwing episode. At that hour people are not talking and they are in a bad mood. I had to get up at three in the morning to make the Charlestown call. At least there was no traffic.

The reason for the baker's call time was because Jeremy Renner had an event later that day; he was receiving an award and they wanted to accommodate him. No one asked about my schedule. We were all very, very, very happy for Jeremy. I'm sure he would have done the same thing if the situation were reversed. If he was forced to come in at 4 AM or lose his job, he would have come in. That's just the kind of guy he is. He is devoted to his craft, which is why he avoids eye contact with the crew. He is so into his character that if he indulged in any kind of pleasantry with a co-worker it would burst the artistic bubble and he would lose the magic.

SCENE 8

Viva Las Vegas

Before I started working on movies I went to the movies a lot. I love the movies. Who doesn't? You must like the movies too; otherwise this book would have no interest to you, unless you're my mother or my Aunt Eleanor. They would be reading my book regardless, but of course, they like movies too. It is universal, we all like the movies. I once spent time with a holy man in the Himalayas of India; he loved the movies.

In my first few years of filmmaking I frequented the theater even more. After all, I was in the business and so movies meant something else to me, I had an even stronger connection with them. Audience participation changes with success in the business. Once I started working regularly I had less time to go to the theater. Then once I started my family that sealed the deal. I rarely went out to the theater. I only watched movies at home.

When I lived in Manhattan and before I ever set foot on a movie set, I would pass by shoots in the city. I would stand around and watch for about 10 minutes. The experience was a hair above watching paint dry. To the untrained eye there was nothing going on except a bunch of people standing around drinking coffee, eating snacks and yakking their heads off. After a few minutes of watching a film crew socialize, I would move on.

Years later, I found myself the one behind the red felt rope, as onlookers stopped and watched in fascination at the movie set. I was in the middle of this new coffee clutch, and I really liked it. Sometimes it would take hours to light a scene. I would enjoy the nice day talking about movies and sports or making jokes about the production.

"Can you believe how long this thing is taking? What the hell are they doing in there? These people are so clueless. What is taking them so long? Oooo the cheese platter is at the craft table." I would analyze in amazement, but I didn't care. This lifestyle suited me. I liked my job and I enjoyed the perks. I didn't mind being there all day. I also knew that when the movie was over I would have plenty of time off.

When I was a young man, just making my way into the world and forced to support myself, I would take various jobs. I found myself waiting on tables or washing dishes. I would come to work with a good attitude, make jokes, listen to music in the kitchen and make the most of my work environment. I spent a large chunk of time at work, and I wanted to enjoy myself there. This is where my work ethic differs from most; it is important for me to enjoy my time at work. If work was a part of my life, I wanted to get the most out of it. As I washed dishes I would sing and enjoy the music, if I had a few hours to kill on a set I would chat or read a book. Sometimes I would amuse myself with a game of cards or dice. On *Ratchet* I often played dice with the genny op (generator operator), another set person with a lot of time on his hands. While the boys set up the lights I would go into country club mode.

Later, when I worked on the big show I found other crew people resentful of my indulgence in downtime. If there was nothing to do, there was nothing to do; I wouldn't create unnecessary work to occupy myself from myself. I would make the best of the situation as I always had done. It was after work at the bar and three cocktails later that people were able to share their true feelings. Sometimes on set they would give me a verbal jab that reeked of indignation. The irony is that if you could take a magic wand and have us exchange positions so that their downtime would be increased, they would refuse that deal. It is something that cannot be learned overnight. It is part of a greater lifestyle choice. There are some people who have to be doing something all the time or they go nuts. Perhaps the thought of using their brain is too much for them. One must always remember there are two kinds of people in the world: those who like downtime and those who don't.

At an early age I developed the fine art of hanging out. Underrated by many and achieved by few. It was the mastery of such technique that helped me through the day on a film set. Those who had not acquired such skills were less fortunate during the massive breakdowns that naturally occurred on a movie set. I believe one of Siddhartha's three qualities was hanging. He could think, fast and hang. However, my intent is not to ponder too deeply into philosophy. It is to charm and entertain. Thank you so much for coming.

The downtime between projects was also great. I loved being able to do other things with my time. I enjoyed the business-imposed hiatuses. A traditional job would have me working every day all year, with the exception of 10 holidays and two weeks' vacation. I preferred the erratic schedule.

One of the disadvantages of the freelance life is the commitment to always be ready to work when the phone rings. I have blown so many personal commitments due to work. Usually, the more my personal event meant to me, the better the job offer. I was in the business for seven years before I refused a job for a personal commitment. That is the commitment; you have to be available for the work if you want to succeed. If you get a call you have to go. I would be having a glass of red wine sitting by the fire when the phone would ring at 9:45 PM: "Can I speak to Lenny Manzo?"

"This is he, who this be?" Remember, I was drinking wine.

"Oh hi, this is Kate from *Last Minute Productions*, it seems like we need a sound guy for tomorrow, are you available? Oh great, call time is 5:30 AM. Thank you so much." There goes my evening. I would never turn down work in order to enjoy myself socially. It is not done. As a freelance technician you must say yes, first and foremost because that is how you have set yourself up to make a living. Secondly, if they wind up hiring the other guy, who is just as good, maybe not as charming, but still an excellent craftsman, there's a good chance he could get the next job with that company. Work breeds work. Every time you work with a new bunch of people you open yourself up to more leads in the future. No one ever turns down work because they don't feel like working. It would be one thing if you had the two-week Hawaiian vacation planned, but not for minor plans like a weekend on the Cape, a friend's birthday party, or even a wedding. I took a job early in my career and blew off a friend's wedding. The job was so big I had to do it. In retrospect, it was the right decision; I can't even remember whose wedding I blew off.

The next film tale requires another flashback. This one takes us back to 1973. Steve Miller Band was on the radio and gasoline was cheap. We find our humble hero still in Brooklyn and he's grown up a little. His tongue was slicker and his streetwise was savvier. He was developing his survival skills at the time. Pardon me, but do you mind if I switch back to the first person? I don't want to disconnect myself too much from young Lenny Manzo.

Third person is good for the flashback Chinese master/Grasshopper–type scene. You know, when young Kwai Chang Caine is learning the secrets of the world and how to snatch pebbles and such things.

I used to hang out on the corner of Palmetto Street and Onderdonk Avenue in Ridgewood, New York. Ridgewood was in Queens, which abutted Bushwick, in Brooklyn, the place of my birth. It was on that corner I spent many a day and night playing poker. I have always had a good head for games. I've played all kinds of board games ever since I was a kid and cards were no different. I won constantly. Many of the other kids were just learning, I had a seven-year head start, and most of them were under the impression that poker was just luck. Now that is funny.

The elevated M train was about a hundred feet away. And on this very corner, a historical event happened in 1970. They filmed a portion of the famous chase scene from *The French Connection*. Gene Hackman was chasing the train in his car and not 50 feet from where I spent a great portion of my youth; his car crashed into a fence. The writing was on the wall dear reader; the die was cast long before I ever set foot on a movie set.

Yes, when I was just a young lad hanging out on the corner, as the other kids watched all the girls go by, I was honing my skills as a gambler. It just enveloped me. Was it the excitement of the wager? Was it the gamesmanship? Was it the competition? No, it was the money. I liked winning the money. You might think that is the obvious answer. Well it is not. Many gamblers get caught up in the game and excitement. I liked the games, but I liked winning. As I grew older I viewed my gambling more or less as a part-time job. I usually knew what I was getting into, and won. Sure, I lost sometimes, but that came with the territory.

I began my poker career at the early age of 6. My family used to have a penny ante game on Saturday nights. I would stand next to my mother with my eyes just above the tabletop to see all the action. Of course they wouldn't let me play. I was just a kid. I was dying to get in that game. Contrary to the famous Kenny Rogers song, she let me count the money. I like that song "The Gambler," but there is some bad advice in it. You do count your money at the table. That's how you keep track of your progress. The gentlemanly thing to do is to not be seen counting your money at the table. And you thought you were only going to get movie insights here.

My first wagers came from pitching pennies in the street in fourth grade. Every morning before school we would get there with our pennies and nickels. In those days I didn't keep track of my results, but as I recall I held my own, except when the big kids just took the money. My school encouraged gambling. The school would set up a yearly bazaar with dice and cards. The games were so rigged that it made Vegas seem like a good deal, but it was all for the Lord. When you lay your money down in the church basement it is of course for a good cause. The church only condones gambling inside church walls.

By sixth grade I was the class bookie. I would book bets for the racetrack and offered only 2 to 1 odds. How could I lose? This was one of my first entrepreneurial ventures. I was quite proud of myself, especially the 2 to 1 odds part. I went home and told my parents what I had been doing. Much to my surprise they were not happy with my money-making scheme and ordered me to shut down the betting window. "But why? Don't you get it? I can't lose; I'm only giving 2 to 1!" That logic meant nothing to them.

I stopped the bookmaking, but continued to gamble. My first gambling mentor was my late Uncle Charlie. He was an intelligent man who was raised on the wrong side of the tracks. I liked him a lot. He married my Aunt Gail who had introduced me to many of the basic card games. It was Aunt Gail who taught me how to play poker when I was 6; it was Uncle Charlie who taught me how to gamble. Uncle Charlie was kind of like James Cagney, a tough guy from the Bronx. He was a heavy gambler himself; sports, cards, dice, it didn't matter to him, he loved it and that's what attracted me to him. He was also an artist and a writer who couldn't apply himself properly. We did discuss other subjects like Greek mythology; I'm not totally crass.

One day I told him that I lost two bucks on the Jets game. He asked, "Why did you bet on the Jets?" I told him, because that was my team, I liked the Jets. Then Uncle Charlie gave me a piece of advice that has stuck with me my whole life. He told me, "Never bet with your heart. Bet if you can win, not if you like the team. If you bet with emotion you decrease your chance of winning." That logic spoke to me and for the most part I stayed away from the home games unless I thought I could win with them.

What dear reader? What has all this have to do with the movie business? All right, all right, keep your shirt on. This philosophy stayed with me and I carried it into the movie world until my dreams became reality. I was working on *Squeeze*, and every Saturday night, no matter what time we wrapped, we played poker after work. By the second week into the shoot the post-work poker party led to on-set gambling. I had a little side shelf on my sound cart, where a pair of regulation Vegas dice would sit, welcoming all comers. The gaming festered by the snail's pace at which we were shooting. Day in, day out, we would shoot, joke and gamble; ah the life of burgeoning filmmakers, so young, so naïve. I was living the dream. I was working on a movie, getting good sound, having a great time, gambling with everyone and winning.

One bright sunny day on a back street of Boston, the production came to a grinding halt. Left to my own devices I started my usual craps game. The bigwigs were off conversing somewhere on some point of cinema, and left the entire crew with nothing to do. Idle hands are the devil's workshop. Everyone began to mosey on over to the lower east side of the set, where there was quite a colorful craps game going on. Half the fun of a dice game is being able to call out kooky phrases, like, "Daddy needs a new boom pole," or just the traditional, "Come to papa!" When film jargon meets gambling lingo you are in slang heaven.

The game was getting louder and I was fueling the fire. Finally the dice came to me and I hit four passes in a row. I celebrated by digging into my losing crew members with cheap phrases such as, "Better luck next time" and "You must be lucky at love, monsieur." I rambled on how I couldn't be stopped, which brought out some friendly venom from my colleagues. They started a wall of negative energy trying to bring down my mojo. I was yelling back at them, and I coerced the make-up guy to sing "Viva Las Vegas." I covered all the bets and called in the winning number 11, using the Vegas chant, "Yo lev, talk to me eleven, give me eleven, one time, just one time." The make-up man continued to sing and a dozen or so crew members started chanting, "No, no, no, no, no, no," over and over again.

The game grew progressively louder, a scene that easily rivaled the basement craps scene in *A Bronx Tale*. With my knees on the ground I covered all the bets while shaking the dice high above my head. I called out above all the sound, "This is it. YO LEV! GIVE ME NUMBER ELEVEN!" I rolled the dice; the camera zooms in on the upturned 6 and 5. The crowd was silenced; they turned and walked away in unison. I raked in the pot.

Without a doubt the sweetest dice moment of my life and a story I've been telling for years. Despite the low pay we all had a great time on this movie.

There was a point when the gambling became a problem. People could not discern the proper time for such things. It started to get out of hand. There was a moment when it was in the way of my work. It wasn't serious, but it was in the way. Sad as it was, I was forced to close the floating craps game during working hours. Once my craft was being threatened I saw it differently. I learned that lesson fast enough. I was happy for a while to be a part of that debauchery, but I realized it could not continue and have not gambled on the set since. Want to bet?

The Big Show

The industry's nomenclature is huge. There is a name for everything. That is the sure way of sniffing out a green set person. Vernacular that is standard fare on a movie set is like Greek to anyone else, unless you live in Greece. Then I can't use that analogy. If you are Greek please substitute another foreign language here that is equally difficult so that you can grasp the analogy.

We call the last shot the martini. An extension cord is a stinger. The honey wagon is a traveling office with men's and ladies' rooms. There are also various pieces of equipment that only exist on a film set: you have polecat, onkybonk, cheeseborough, baby, junior, baby double header, baby triple header, hanger, joker, bucket, single, double, silk, solid, snakebite, slider, siamese, scrim, snoot, squib, saco, no Vanzetti, trapeze and French flag, not to be confused with French hours.

French hours is a ridiculous concept that occurs on a union show. Someone from the production staff gets the bright idea to ask the crew if they will consider French hours if the production goes late into lunch. If agreed upon the crew will wave meal penalties for several hours. If they do not go over a certain point, there will be no penalty; if they go past a certain point, all the penalties will be retroactive. The caveat to French hours is that the crew must agree unilaterally, so it is defeated as soon as the question is asked.

Most names and terms have evolved from somewhere and everything is abbreviated. We use the trucker's CB code for the bathroom: "I'm going 10-100." But that wasn't short enough. It has now turned into "I'm 10-1," which technically means receiving a poor signal, but not on a movie set. The second-to-last shot is called the Abby Singer, after an AD who always called the martini when there was still another shot to do. I have been a proponent of naming the third-to-last shot the Abe Vigoda; I heard it once long ago and I believe it is finally catching on. On the set of *Surrogates* there was a heated debate on whether or not Abe Vigoda was alive. We immediately called on the Internet gods to settle the dispute. Not only was he still alive, he was still working and is still working today as he is pushing 90. That's show biz, like the "Hotel California": once you're in you never leave.

There were a couple of big movies coming to the Boston area. One was *Celtic Pride*, the other was *The Crucible*. I had not worked on a big movie for more than a day. I thought it would be helpful to see how audio was handled on the big show. I went after *The Crucible* because it was closer to my house in Marblehead. I spoke to the mixer and was hired. I signed on as the cable man. This is the third position in the department. The bulk of this job is to run cable, move gear, operate the second boom mike and do what the boss tells you, with a major emphasis on the latter. Even though film is a collaborative effort, that collaboration ends with the keys. It is a rare key who looks downstream for an opinion.

In all departments there is the key who is in charge, then the second, you guessed it, is second in charge, followed by the thirds. No matter how many others there are in the department they are all called thirds. You could have 10, even 20 thirds, but no fourths. In the AD department the thirds are called second seconds. The reason for that is an overwhelming need to create as much slang as possible. Lingo is huge in this racket. A rose is still a rose and would smell as sweet; a third is a third and smell does not come into play, not in a good way, at least. The AD department is managerial; that is possibly why they came up with the higher falutin' name.

The film set is run similarly to a military operation, with the director sitting at the top of the pyramid. We could also use the mafia analogy, where you have the Don, then the Cappos, the lieutenants and again the soldiers. Since they base their operation on military style it is actually superfluous to mention it. I just like to say Don and Cappo.

Just below the director are the DP and the production designer, then the keys, seconds and the thirds. The production assistants are at the bottom, unless you count the extras, that really is the bottom. Sound is like its own branch of the military; it's sort of like the CIA, but in a good way. The production office is like the Pentagon. They perform all their tasks away from the set and sometimes I don't meet the office personnel until the wrap party.

The system works well when the head honchos have their act together. If there is dissension in the upper echelon, it will be felt in the trench. On the big show chaos equals cash: the less organization, the bigger the paycheck. There are various penalties written into the contract to deter the production from taking advantage of the crew. For example, lunch is due six hours after call; if it is late there is a meal penalty. This continues every half hour until lunch is called. The issue is not the food, it is the break. If a production were not held accountable, the meal break would be abused. This abuse I did not mind. Since there was always something to snack on I would rather go without the break and be compensated. Apple is designing a new iPhone app specifically for the meal penalty. Every time another penalty is incurred, a cash register sound rings. It's called "Ka-Ching."

On the last day of *Pink Panther Deux*, they just flat out asked us to waive the penalty because they wanted to finish early. They gave the crew the option of breaking for lunch on time or no break and no penalty in the hopes of getting out early. This actually created a bit of hoopla on the set. Many of my naïve colleagues were in favor of getting out early. They thought waiving the penalty would be fine and thought the staunch union crowd should have been somewhat lenient in a unique circumstance. My business manager would have been proud of my stand that day as I stuck to the party line. I pointed out that it was illegal to renegotiate the contract and that we were forced as union members to honor that as such.

I want you to know I'm not strictly a by-the-book kind of guy, but as a worker you want to hold onto any of the benefits the studios have agreed to. We went back and forth on this issue and it was squashed. So, what did the production do? I know you're dying to find out. They skipped lunch and paid the penalties. The production had already planned on working through lunch; they just made a fleeting attempt to save some coin. They waived the early-day carrot in front of a worn-out crew and several bit. Some might see this as good business tactics; others might see this as sleazy. I'll let you, my devoted reader, make your own judgment.

Back on Hog Island, a beautiful island off the North Shore of Massachusetts, 20th Century Fox was prepping to shoot *The Crucible*. The pristine untouched nature made it a perfect place to recreate Massachusetts in the 1600's. The sets were brilliant and the landscape was lush. It would have been a paradisiacal place to come to every day and build sets—you know, the great outdoors. The only imperfection in this scenario was the colony of greenheads that lived in them there parts. This is one bad-ass bug that makes a mosquito bite feel like a kiss. These guys bite and bite hard. They come out for several weeks during the summer in big numbers and they are nasty. There was no break from the greenheads. The set builders were out there every day under constant attack. Aaaaaaaaaah, the love of film.

It was necessary to jump through a few hoops just to get to work. I had a half-hour drive to the parking lot, and then a short walk to the ferry. Upon arriving on the island, shuttle vans were waiting to take the crew to the base camp, where all the trucks were. It was a bit confusing the first day, but eventually we found the set.

The first shot was a wide establishing shot looking down the hill to the center of the old town. Everyone was dressed in traditional Puritan garb. There were all types of livestock milling about: pigs, goats, chickens, dogs, horses and antelope (no antelope, I just wanted to see if you were paying attention). This was the biggest set I had been on to date and it blew me away. The magnitude of it overwhelmed me. They constructed an entire colonial period town to resemble Salem, Massachusetts. I could tell that it was just another day at the office for everyone, and so that's how I conducted myself. I wasn't going to act like a country boy on his first day to the big city. I was impressed, but kept it to myself. My mother didn't raise any stupid children; I played it cool, real cool, cool, cool as a cucumber, I mean ... all right, you got the idea.

After my first awestruck experience, we made the shot and had to move down the hill. We had two carts, a stand and sandbags to hold the stand, which held our wireless antenna. We brought everything down for the next shot. We made the next shot and then we hiked back up the hill with all the gack (equipment). We shot there and went back down for the next shot and on and on for the rest of the week and the rest of the shoot. This was a factor I hadn't even figured on. Up until then my job had not really been a physical one. My sound cart was heavy, but I never had this amount of running around.

The mixer on this movie had three times the sound package I had, which is standard at this level. It was something I was not aware of or prepared for. It made for a very physical job.

On top of the new physical components of the job, I didn't hit it off with my New York colleagues. We had our ups and downs. That was when I learned that no matter what went wrong, it was my fault. I wasn't totally clean. I made mistakes, but I was also blamed for the ones I didn't make. This job was long and hard. The boss was thin on patience and felt I was inexperienced. He could have been right. I had never been a third on a big show for more than a day. At the end of the first week we had words and I threatened to quit. I did quit for about an hour. I told him on Friday to get someone else for Monday. He was over a barrel so he convinced me to stay. It felt good to speak my mind. The option of quitting was easy for me at the time. Boston was busy, as it always was in the fall; I knew that I could get on the phone immediately and find work, so I had nothing to lose.

Monday wasn't pleasant. The only communication was work related. It was not comfortable. So when lunchtime came, I didn't eat with my audio counterparts. In the beginning of a show everyone sits with his or her fellow department members, as we had also been doing, especially because we had never worked together. I had to work with them; I decided I didn't have to eat with them.

The silence between the mixer and me went on through the next day. This time at lunch the boom operator came up to me while I was in the lunch line and told me where they were sitting. I said, "OK." I perceived this as some sort of olive branch. They were sitting with the camera department. I sat down and again nothing was spoken. I ate my lunch and didn't say a word. By the end of that day the mixer broke the wall of silence and cracked a joke. I'm not the type to hold a grudge—well, not for too long—and I wanted the situation to get better. I responded and the relationship improved.

I gave this job everything I had. Either I wasn't up for it or the mixer was overreacting. It probably was a little bit of both. I had less of a problem with the boom operator. However, she would pick the oddest times to berate me. It was usually when she misunderstood the situation. Once the mixer went home sick, that put her in charge and I became the boom operator. She asked me where I would do the next shot. I said to the right of camera on a ladder. Well, she had me experiment with every other spot I could fit into until she put me back in my original spot. She was satisfied with the way she found the place for me to stand. I bit my tongue.

I did learn a few things, though. I learned that the mixer wasn't doing things much differently from me. He had a few gadgets in his bag of tricks that I hadn't seen before, but I figured those out in the first week. The learning experience I was hoping for didn't happen. He was also one of the few sound mixers that didn't want to talk. Most sound guys will talk to you about audio until they are blue in the face, probably because everyone else in the world is uninterested. He was not of that ilk.

I lost nine pounds on *The Crucible* and that was while eating three heavy meals, snacks and chocolate cake every day. I did feel pretty fit, which was a sidebar of the hell job. When the movie came out I hated it. I could not view the film objectively. Every scene reminded me of the ordeal I went through. I sat in the theater and thought, "That was when the boom op yelled at me for not carrying the gear fast enough." "I remember that day, it rained all day." "That was the day I had a 101 fever and was delirious." When I saw it in the theater I felt physically ill for the entire 2 hours and 4 minutes. It was almost hypnotic. The disgust and pain I had with that job came pouring back.

Eventually, I was able to separate my personal experience from the movie. Ten years later I found myself in a hotel with a remote control in my hand. I clicked around until *The Crucible* popped up. I watched the whole thing and it was great. It was very well crafted with stunning camera moves, gorgeous cinematography, top-notch acting and great sound. It was the same movie; the only thing that had changed was my perspective.

SCENE 10

It Is Better to Rule in Hell than to Serve in Heaven

I *didn't mind being an assistant*, I just don't like working for somebody else. Way before I ever stepped foot on a movie I had trouble with authority. I could never handle abuse of power in the workplace and I was quite indignant about it. As a sound mixer I do have to answer to the producer and the director. However, I am usually treated with respect and my opinion is sought after in matters pertaining to sound. It is not the same when one works on the lower rungs of the ladder. Many times when someone is in charge they feel they have the right to be inhuman. They believe they are entitled to yell or have a tantrum; after all, they are in charge, which naturally makes them better, and permits them to have rude behavior. I went back to the independent movies to continue working my way up the crooked show biz ladder as a sound mixer, rather than Hop Sing for someone on a big movie.

After *The Crucible* I expanded my audio package and invested in more microphones and other gear. I was inspired to beef up my sound package, but I had another idea. I felt I could pay for the additional gear by renting it out to other up-and-coming sound guys. This is where you start to find out more about the real me. As you are now aware, I had no real audio aspiration before embarking on my movie set journey.

I have a slight entrepreneurial bend. I like sales and usually try to figure out a way to make an extra buck somewhere. As the sound mixer I would buy the tape and batteries and resell them to the production. It was commonly done when I first started. The big companies sort of frown on that nowadays. They prefer doing business with a third party. They prefer giving that money to someone who is not already working for them even if it costs them more.

It was helpful to make the extra cash. My natural abilities were geared more toward sales and making deals. It was only natural for me to expand and try to make a little bit on the side. It was a natural progression. I was officially in the rental business. It had a lot of upside. The equipment went out and I stayed home. This was a concept that resonated with me.

Year 5 started off with a bang. I actually jumped on a movie that was shooting a week before Christmas, the week after and the first week in January. They are the three deadest weeks on the movie production calendar. To this day it was the only job I ever worked between Christmas and New Year's. I closed out 1995 with a nice cherry and hit the ground running in the New Year. The other great thing about this little low-budget baby: it was shooting right in my own backyard. Most locations were five minutes from my house. Wow! It was also the first and last time that ever happened. I went home for lunch every day; I felt like a Frenchman.

This little independent movie was a fun one for me. I came in, did my job, had a good time and went home. Many things happened on this show, but the funniest and most absurd story is the one I will share. The AD was in a bit over his head. He was a young man who hadn't much experience. The AD position has a lot of responsibility. The production rests on this position as the world rests on the shoulders of Atlas. This is the person that keeps all the logistics in his head for the entire movie. He keeps it moving and on schedule.

It was the second blizzard of the show, or just another New England winter day. The snow had subsided, but there was a mountain of it on the ground. It was cold and cloudy. We were doing a shot of a car coming up a hill. They were having momentum issues with the vehicle starting and stopping on the ice. The AD and the DP were discussing it and had completely opposing viewpoints. Both men were getting upset and after much discussion the final dialogue broke down like this.

"It won't work," said the AD.

"It will work," said the DP.

"It won't work."

"It will work."

"It won't work."

"It will work."

"It won't work."

"It will work. It will work!"

At that moment our poor AD just snapped like a dry twig. He started doing pirouettes in a berserk manner mimicking our European-born DP and screaming to the high heavens, "It vill verk! It vill! It vill verk!" I was standing next to the make-up man, who was just bent over in uncontainable laughter. He was in complete knee-slapping mode. It was so over the top, I would have laughed if I wasn't so awestruck. The kid cracked like a raw egg on a breakfast grill. I didn't know if my fellow craftsmen had exchanged words before, or if the movie was too much for the young man, but either way something triggered him, and the scene was not pretty. The DP was quite angry and threatened to quit in that moment, but like with all other movies with incidents that seem to go too far and appear to have done irreparable damage, we continued, and nobody quit. The movies have a strange way of bringing out the drama in all of us.

SCENE 11

Pucker Up and Pour Me a Cup

"*And then Johnny Fontane* comes along with his olive oil voice and guinea charm." Every day on my next show I heard the lead actor do his Jack Waltz from *The Godfather*: " ... and she was the best piece of ass I ever had! And I've had 'em all over the world!" I lived with this sideshow for four weeks. I did enjoy it the first sixteen times I heard it. Hey it's a great line, but don't beat it to death. Some actors are on all the time. They can't stop; it is the "Look at Me Show," all day long. Of course many of them can't help themselves. Most of them don't want any kind of exchange; it is not about connecting, it's about showing off. They just spout all day and everyone smiles, chuckles or guffaws depending on how much ass they think they have to kiss.

There is a thing about ass kissing in this business as opposed to other walks of life. Anywhere else, it is frowned upon to kiss ass. Not in show biz. The more ass you kiss, the more people will respect you. They really respect you when you are kissing ass so much and the people whose ass you're in a love lock with don't even know it. I worked with an AD on a project and the star had the AD rolling in the aisle. He'd finish his little laughing spectacle wiping a tear from the corner of his eye. He was so good at ass kissing that the ass kissee only felt it on a subconscious level. In turn, the ass kissee thinks this guy is doing great work: "This guy is all right, I think I'd like to keep him around, he should be on my next project," a tried-and-true method of getting to the top.

Now hold on you ass-kissing novices out there; you can't start thinking that you can just kiss any ass that comes by and thus pucker your way to the top. No, this is not what I'm talking about. This is a skill that needs to be honed. To be good at it, you need to kiss ass in a way so that the ass kissee does not even know it. If the ass kissee knows you are kissing his ass you can still have good results because people do like to have ass kissers around, but it is slower for upward mobility. You need to kiss ass in a way that really blows the smoke so far up the ass that it filters into the brain, mixes with the ego, and makes them think you are a competent professional who is good to have on the job. This knowledge comes in handy, as it is easier to recognize others who are kissing ass all the way to the top. Ultimately, you can't really trust an ass kisser. The ass kisser can also be the back stabber. A back stabber is usually an ass kisser, but an ass kisser is not necessarily a back stabber.

What's up at the top besides the money and the glory? Well, the glory is an illusion. Are bubbles bursting all over America? There is no glory! I repeat, there is no glory! Yes, there is a jackpot waiting for anyone at the end of the Hollywood Rainbow. If you make it, there are gobs of cake to have and to eat.

There can be glory for the true artist, the person who is acting or making movies regardless of financial success or status in the world. If someone has the need to create and is able to achieve that artistic connection, that is the glory, which has nothing to do with red carpets. If the goal is the red carpet then you've missed it. You wouldn't be alone; there are many glory seekers living for their moment in the sun. For the movie business to have a real significance in your life the art must be the glory. If the desire is for the destination rather than the road then it will just be a job. The art must be at the heart. You like that? "Art at the heart"—there's a t-shirt in the making. Let's green-light that, Harry! If acting does not resonate to the core of your being, I would imagine there are a number of things you could do that would be easier than the competitive entertainment business. That can be said of any job you are not fully immersed in. However, I'm not here to preach, only to pontificate. Motives should be questioned before embarking on a journey that easily has a 90% failure rate.

Outside of the Daily Jack Waltz spectacle, this little movie in the North End of Boston was another fun experience, and it changed my life forever! Fade out aaaaaaannnnnd cut!

What was this grand life-changing experience, this transformation that occurred, this metamorphosis that had taken place? What was this monumental moment from which there was no return? Well, dear reader, I walked through the door of the Caffé Vittoria and ordered a latte, then another, then another and another and on and on. At 34 I joined the ranks of the Hollywood caffeinated. Coffee and I didn't always hit it off. The coffee at the Caffé Vittoria was brilliant. Sitting in the café in the middle of the day, drinking said coffee was more brilliant. Doing it more than once a day, most brilliant! By the end of the shoot I was drinking four lattes a day, four lattes a day and everyone on the bench got up and started yelling, "Four lattes a day!" And we had a good time sitting on the bench, drinking lattes, talking about the movies, talking about our movie and having a great time on the Group W Bench. There's that Group W Bench again. I couldn't leave you hanging too long. It is from Arlo Guthrie's "Alice's Restaurant," the 1967 classic still played all over the country on Thanksgiving Day. A must listen.

The Caffé Vittoria turned me into the coffee drinker I am today, a man who cannot imagine his life without coffee. A man whose coffee reputation precedes him wherever he goes, a man who loves a good cup of coffee and loves few things more. This love affair began innocently and to be honest it wasn't a pure love at first. I hope you are sitting down. I would imagine you are sitting down because you are reading. Unless you are on a crowded subway and my book is so riveting you can't put it down. All right, here it is, my big confession, in print for the entire world to see, and I'm ashamed to say it, but yes, I used sugar. Yes, it's true. I just felt with the tell-all book I needed to put my cards on the table and make a clean break. Let's get all the skeletons out of the closet. Now you know everything.

The sweetness in the bitter drink seemed natural and right. Then one day I weaned myself from sugar. Coffee never tasted better. I implore any coffee drinker worth their salt to give up sugar for one month and develop the taste for coffee in its natural way. After this experiment you will be converted, and you will reach a level of enjoyment unknown to sugar consumers everywhere. I came into that show as a *tea*totaler; I left a full-fledged coffee drinker.

I have been drinking coffee for the last 15 years. It has become an integral part of my life. I love coffee, as I expect most people who drink it also love it. As with anything in life, it always breaks down into two categories, two kinds of coffee drinkers: the ones who love it and the ones who really love it. You can guess which category I fall into.

It really adds to the creative process. There are many artists who have leaned heavily on the dark brew. Frank Zappa drank it black and by the bale. Honoré de Balzac would stay up all night drinking strong hot coffee, creating characters and laying down great prose from his inkwell. It worked for Balzac and Zappa, it works for me. Notice the commonality: we all have a Z in our names.

I haven't looked back. I drink coffee to this day. On the set people know me as this coffee connoisseur, or if you prefer, coffee nut. It's all perspective, but suffice it to say, coffee and I go hand in hand. The early years of my coffee addiction—I mean, coffee drinking, I had four or five double lattes a day. I admit that was excessive. I am much more composed in modern times and only drink two cups a day now, unless I go into production; then all bets are off.

Show business runs hard on coffee. There are a few *tea*totalers, but they are in the minority. In the middle of the day a Starbucks run is often a highlight. It is not always possible to find the good espresso. The remote locations make it impossible unless you're producing, then it simply amounts to figuring out who is best suited for the task of fetching. As a producer I would often go alone for coffee to get away from the show for a moment. I would sit down for a few minutes to relax and collect myself from the constant on-the-go energy. Producing is a lot of work, unless you are producing on the big shows, then you are sitting in your big chair, calling the studio several times a day. You know it's your chair because your name is on it. There's usually a cup holder and a pouch for your magazines. The ottoman is optional.

There is a big difference between producing a Hollywood movie and an independent movie. Independent producers have to work. On a big movie they hire everyone else to do the work. Many of them are glorified babysitters. They sit behind the monitor in the clichéd director's chair, eating nuts and berries, reading the paper and reporting back to the studio: "Hi Sid, everything is fine here. Uh, yeah, we did go over a little, but we got the day … I know it was 17 hours, Sid, but Antonio is doing some really incredible work here. His artistry is masterful and the actors are really responding in a way I've never seen before … we never did get the crane shot, it only cost us 9K, but it was good we had it, it gave Antonio confidence just knowing it was there … we did have problems with the hotel scene, we shot the first day and it was fine but it snowed the next. I asked Antonio if we should come back another day since it will be hard to match 3 feet of snow at the pool, he thought we could fix it in post."

SCENE 12

Another Phish Story

As *the enlightened philosopher* Lao Tzu once said, the first part of a job starts with a phone call. Perhaps I am paraphrasing, but I received a call for a location job in Upstate New York. It seemed the band Phish was putting on a big spectacle in Plattsburgh. It was not just a concert; it was an arts and music festival. Seventy thousand people would eventually show up to hear six sets of music and enjoy the artistic expression of the band on and off the stage plus three nights of camping and whatnot, heavy on the whatnot.

They offered me a good rate, meals and accommodations, and it was a full week of work; I was psyched. The concert was on a weekend in mid-August. I arrived the previous Monday to start work. The name of the event was the Clifford Ball, named after an obscure airman, which had something to do with the band's quirky sense of humor. I had heard of Phish before but I had not heard one note of their music. I was highly intrigued because of the 70,000 Phish pilgrims coming in from all over the country.

During the event they used multiple cameras; I was on the main team with the director, a publicist and a DP. The first night we had a production meeting, I was there by circumstance, not because I had anything to say at this meeting. As you have already noticed I do have a lot to say, they were just not interested.

We were on location having dinner while the director, publicist and DP discussed the shoot. I sat there in silence as they talked about the creative portion of the documentary. It was at that moment I discovered that this brain trust had no idea what they were going to do. With one week before the event it appeared that this was their first meeting. They seemed to have quite the creative freedom as they bandied about ideas and concepts. After scratching their heads long and hard they came up with the idea of weaving the town of Plattsburgh, New York in with the concert and the band. They wanted to combine the economic collapse of Plattsburgh, due to the army base closing, with the upcoming music and arts festival. I didn't understand the correlation or why they chose it; I think there was something artsy behind it. It's not that I don't like artsy. I like artsy when it is appropriate, or if it is a decent idea, or if it is actually artsy. This idea sounded ridiculous to me.

Be that as it may, I had my reasons for being there. I was going to make a buck and have a good time in the process. On our first day, the filmmakers set up in the middle of the street, photographing the back streets of Plattsburgh. It seemed rather precarious to me with cars going both ways and since the shot was MOS I figured I would extend myself by walking up the road to make the traffic aware of our presence.

An MOS shot is sans sound. The legend of MOS is that German director Lothar Mendes, on the 1931 set of *Ladies Man* starring William Powell and Carole Lombard, would say in his thick German accent, "Mit out sound, mit out sound," because a) he could not pronounce the word "with" or because b) "mit" means "with" in German, hence without sound, or because c) the American crew heard it that way. There is no real proof, but I have always embraced the folklore of the crazy director screaming, "Mit out sound, mit out sound!" It is just so romantic.

Back in Upstate New York, I was doing my best to keep my fellow filmmakers from getting killed, until the three of them screamed at me in unison, "Get out of the way, we want the cars, watch out!" They continued screaming and gesticulating as I walked off the street. Note to self: Do not be proactive with help. A simple "Can you move please, you're in the way" in a normal tone of voice would have accomplished the same result. I probably shouldn't have assumed they wanted help with the traffic, but they set right up on a double yellow line on a busy street. Was that guerrilla filmmaking or just plain stupidity? For the remainder of the show I did my job quietly, and I withheld my two cents. I made sure not to cross the line by doing production work. The screaming, however, persisted. The DP was constantly micromanaging me and telling me how to record the sound, and I was getting quite frustrated with her telling me how to do my job.

Because it was a video job, the DP and I were tethered together like Siamese twins by a snake cable, which sent audio to the camera and sent back a headphone feed. It is unlike film, where the sound is recorded separately. I usually stay very far away from the camera team on a movie set. Is this possibly my smooth segue into camera people? I have had my share of problems with camera people. The DP is in the driver's seat and crossing the DP would not be wise; it's a balancing act from the beginning. The DP can make a soundman's life miserable. By withholding information or lighting him out of the scene, he has the potential to be the soundman's worst enemy on set. With that knowledge in hand, it is up to the sound mixer to get a read on the DP as soon as possible. Very often they come dressed in sheep's clothing; they act very nice until they feel you are getting in their way. DP's are sometimes overzealous and it is their way or the highway. That mentality trickles downstream to the rest of the camera department, and worst-case scenario, you have a department filled with pretentious, self-important, chichi technicians. Every other department has to kowtow to the DP, first because everyone is subordinate to him, and second because he is in charge of hiring. Even if he doesn't have direct authority over your department, he will make "recommendations."

On *Evening*, we would wait an extra half hour every night for the camera guys to finish their work before we could load our stuff on. This drove my boss nuts as he fostered crazy ideas of going home at the end of his workday. There was no cooperation or consideration. They do what they want, when they want. In the world of film crew, camera is King. They are the camera department (sound trumpets here).

For many years camera and sound departments have shared a truck known as the camera truck. Make no mistake, it is not the camera/sound truck, it is the camera truck and there's little question about it. In recent years, the truck situation has changed. The camera people have what they wanted all along, and that is a camera truck all to themselves. Since being banished from the camera truck, sound now shares a truck with the video playback guy. Now all are happy clams in their own respective trucks.

How does the expression go? Some of my best friends are camera people, and they are great to work with, but some of them have blown so much smoke up their own lenses it affects their egos. Self-inflated ego is not restricted to actors and directors; it is contagious and you'll find it in any department on any given show.

We now return to Plattsburgh, where the week has progressed, and the camera lady is still breathing venom all over me. This arrangement was causing me to fester inside. I thought she should be concerned about her own work, as she and the other two bigwigs were making some kooky art documentary, as opposed to covering the arts and music festival.

Friday came and it was going to be our first opportunity to shoot the band. The first shots would be of the band members on their tour bus driving in through the gates of the Clifford Ball. The bus was sweet; it was made to tour and quite comfortable. It was a cool scene; we did some interviews on the bus. Trey Anastasio, the lead guitar player and vocalist, did most of the talking, while Mike Gordon, the bass player, noodled on the banjo.

The bus was great and I would have liked to have stayed on there all day, but before I knew it, we arrived at the concert site. We followed the band backstage and eventually onstage where they performed the sound check. The sound check was hot as they jammed for about an hour. I was already sensing the magic from these guys and I was looking forward to the concert.

Saturday came and the big three decided they would pick two young women from the crowd and follow them for the weekend to see Phish through their eyes. They chose two nice young girls who barely knew a thing about Phish. This was a mistake for several reasons. These young women were isolated from the scene. Phish has a huge underground following that goes from show to show all over the country. My esteemed colleagues would have been better off finding a couple of young kids that were heavily into Phish and show the band's connection to the audience. Being immersed in the scene, we could have also spoken to their friends and filmed quite a cross-section of fans. The most ironic thing was that there was a production assistant on our crew who was a big Phish head. She had offered to hook the production in with people she knew who were on tour following the band around to various shows. Of course they ignored the offer. I thought they should have at least used her as a resource; they asked her nothing and spent the weekend chatting with two young girls who may have not seen Phish since.

We were putzing around the parking lot and I could hear the opening licks from the band. I was festering even more; I really wanted to see this show, and find out why 70,000 people trucked up to Plattsburgh to see them. I realized that the girls had no idea what time it was, or when the show was starting. I hedged things a bit and whispered to one of the girls when my team wasn't looking, "Hey, the concert should be starting up right around now."

She immediately informed her friend and they said, "We have to go."

We followed them and stayed with them for the rest of the first set. My new friend, the camera lady, aka the Viper, told me to put microphones on the girls so we could hear what they were saying, since my boom mike was out of reach for the shots. I was fed up with her derogatory tone, and so I told her that I couldn't put the microphones on them because we had just met them. I explained to her that if we lost the girls in the crowd I would lose very expensive equipment. It actually wasn't just a line; we had just met them. But cooperation goes both ways; since she seemed to have something against me, I wasn't going to help her.

Later, when we were backstage, I spoke to the head producer. He told me not to worry about the liability. I should wire the girls and if anything happened, he would be responsible. My mind was at ease and the producer was a nice guy, so I was happy to do anything for him. We didn't shoot much after that. I enjoyed part of the second set and all of the third set that first night. It was a great night of music and I had a great time hanging out backstage.

On Sunday morning, the second and final day of the event, a colleague told me that he overheard the Viper lady badmouthing me to the producer and saying, "Maybe we should fire him," "him" meaning me. In the words of the immortal Popeye, "That's all I can stands, because I can't stands no more." I reached inside my shirt and pulled out a can of generically marked spinach. I squeezed it until the lid popped open and the spinach jumped out of the can and into my mouth. It traveled through my entire body while expanding all of my muscles as a sea shanty played in the background. My animated fantasy came to an end. Unfortunately, I couldn't clobber the DP, and unlike Popeye, there was nothing I could do, except blow steam out of my ears

We were cruising around the parking lot with our two young ladies when the DP decided to take a break. The Viper lady put the camera on the back end of an open pickup truck. I pulled my gear together, headed over to the truck, took the audio mixer off my shoulders and placed it next to the camera. Unbeknownst to me, someone had placed a half-empty bottle of beer on the open pickup gate, and I inadvertently bumped into the beer.

Only a few drops splashed out, but they landed on the camera lens. "Oh ... my ... God! What am I going to do now?" The right thing would have been to inform the DP immediately that there was beer on her camera lens. I have a lot of respect for the craft, and I do take my professionalism very seriously. I did the only thing any secure person in the industry would do. I opted not to tell her and let her figure it out on her own. She would have lit into me like the Fourth of July. Though she wasn't a very pleasant woman, she wasn't stupid. It did not take her long with her astute cinematic eye to figure out that there was beer on her lens. She freaked out while I was whistling the "I'm Minding My Own Business and I Don't Know What Is Going On" song, very similar to whistling "Dixie."

Later in the afternoon I was making some adjustments with my equipment when the camerawoman again felt it necessary to kibitz about the audio. I snapped, "Would you please just let me do the sound, thank you!" I hit the wall with that final straw. Once I had heard that she badmouthed me to my boss and tried to get me fired, I did not feel the necessity any longer to hold back. She was flabbergasted, much like one of those high-society dames in a Marx Brothers movie: "Well, I never!"

We wrapped at a fairly reasonable hour, and again I was allowed to enjoy the concert. During this time I was becoming friends with Carla the Phish head and film crew production assistant, who was very nice and very cool. We went out into the crowd to join her friends to take in the last set. I had a great time as Phish smoked that set, not to be confused with smoked fish. I know that was a bad one, but I just had to. After the concert was over, I had crossed over from employee to fan, and have seen Phish many times since.

Even though I was chained to the biggest pain-in-the-butt cameraperson I have ever worked with, I still enjoyed the week's work. The rest of the crew, the situation and the atmosphere were great. It was fun to see the inner workings of the rock and roll world, watch them put the festival together and crescendo with the Phish concert. It was not only a good job, it was a great experience. Working in the movie business does let you see things out of the ordinary.

Oh, I almost forgot. When this documentary was all said and done, the angle on the army base closing never made it into the movie. The two teenage girls that we spent three days following never saw any screen time.

They did use our shot of the cop stopping the tour bus on the side of the road, and the only interview that made it into the final cut was the mayor of Plattsburgh talking about the festival and the boost for the town. All that creative mumbo jumbo was hacked out. Just saying ...

SCENE 13

Lenny Manzo, Come on Down!

The fall of '96 was rolling in and I was having my biggest year to date. Because the year had been so heavily frontloaded, by August I had already passed 1995 at my own personal box office. I was getting a fair share of commercial work. After spending years on features, a commercial felt like a paid vacation. Everything moves slower on a commercial. There is no sense of urgency. A commercial is only 30 seconds and sometimes you do more than one spot in a day, but on a movie you are shooting upwards of five minutes of screen time in a day. The commercial world is much lighter work at a slower pace.

Another reason a commercial feels like a day on the golf course is due to the convention of creative types from the agency huddled around the monitor deciding whether the housewife should take one or two bites of cereal. They would discuss each nuance to death until they all agreed. After they hashed it out, they would tell the director what to do. Here the director was more of a glorified middleman. Creative power varied from shoot to shoot, but for the most part he'd get the info and relay that to the thespians. The actor and director could go through whatever artistic process they needed, as long as the actor took two bites of cereal.

My first commercial was a McDonald's ad. This time I was called at ten in the morning. They needed me there by one. They had just added a line on the spot and needed a sound guy stat. I was very excited because it was one of the biggest commercial outfits in Boston. I was also very excited because the commercials paid well: less work for more money, a true axiom of the biz.

I arrived and immediately put my rig together. After about a half hour I was set up and ready. I was taking a deep breath of relaxation when the AD said, "We're ready for sound, are you ready, Len?" Like any other movie making superhero I responded in the affirmative, "Yes, I am ready." I wheeled my cart closer to the set, rigged the mike and went to work. We did that scene several times over 20 minutes. After the last take the AD called out, "Cut ... sound is wrapped."

I continued in my superhero sound mode: "My work is done here now. But whenever there is a cry for sound, I will be there. Wherever a location is void of a recording device, I will bring it. And most of all, whenever a production screws up at the last minute, I will fly in to save the day." I rolled into my driveway well before the evening rush hour. Now that's a good day at the office.

The commercials were fun and easy. I would have loved to have done more of them. I eventually had several regular clients, but it was not enough to sustain me. I would always have to take a movie over day work. I could never get enough commercials. When I arrived on the scene in the early 90's, it was already sewn up. Twenty years later it is still basically the same crowd: Steve, Louie and Jean. There's a lot to be said for getting there first, staking a claim and holding onto it. Hey, you know I love you guys, especially you, Jean.

Ninety-six was just cruising along. Since I had already surpassed my previous year's earnings I was quite relaxed. The town was so busy that I had a little flexibility with the job selection. I noticed I was turning down lower-end work, which meant I was making more money. Everything was jelling, so when *Next Stop Wonderland* was about to start shooting in Boston, I didn't even think about trying to get on this movie. I had already worked on several features and between commercials and corporate videos I was holding my own.

Let me give you a quick word about corporate videos. I'd rather hang out at an old folks' home on a Saturday night than do another corporate video. Boring took on a new meaning. As I gained more experience I set up my gear with my back facing the work in case I fell asleep. I wasn't trying to fall sleep, I just couldn't help it. Listening to some corporate big wheel analyze the success of the dental floss market in Northern New England in the third fiscal quarter after the last ad campaign where the packaging changed from blue to light blue put me to sleep faster than any over-the-counter sedative. Like I said before, I don't take a job based on content.

I was fine with the way the wind was blowing. Since the year had been such a financial success already, I could also rest on my laurels. I had worked so hard the last five years, scraping and hustling, I was in a position to coast.

I didn't turn down work; that would be a cardinal sin in the world of the freelancer. I just let the phone ring and didn't fret none. In the movie version, I will be sitting poolside, martini in one hand and a big fat cigar in my mouth.

Then the wind shifted and Jeeves brought me the telephone. "What is it, Jeeves?"

"It's *Next Stop Wonderland*, sir, it appears they are in need of your services. It seems the former mixer has taken a powder, and has left them for a better position on a better movie. Shall I tell them that you are too big for your britches, or will you take the call?" Jeeves was always bitter about not getting that job over at the Wayne mansion.

Naturally, I took the call, and of course I took the job. This film was shooting for about six weeks and it was a train I could ride all the way to Thanksgiving. It was a fine way to close out the year. On *Wonderland*, I had the pleasure of working with Hope Davis. She was just getting notoriety for her work so she was an excellent casting call. That is the rub on independent movies. They can't afford a big star, but if they have their eyes peeled they can find one on the rise, and by the time their movie comes out, the star has hit the heights. It is not always easy to identify the diamond in the rough. Hope's rising popularity was a great negotiation point when it came time to sell the film. She gave a very solid performance. She is a great actress.

I need to say a word or two about the word "actress." In this overly conscious politically correct world we live in, there is sometimes a backlash. We are so paranoid about saying the wrong thing. I refer to the de-gendering of the word actress. So, being respectful of the PC society we are in, I ask you to allow me to have some indulgence when I use the word actress. I know some of you PC'ers may take umbrage, but I like the word and find it beautiful. Isn't that what an actress is: beautiful? When I started my career the word was still in vogue. Now the women are lumped in with the men. I love the word actress; it is charming, radiant and has more power. It's a better word than actor. Actor becomes generic and the male and female lose their identity due to the merging of the vernacular. "Ooo! *The Merging of the Vernacular*, let's put that one into development Harry."

I also like the word "waitress." It doesn't sound condescending to me; I believe that is why people have walked away from it. The current alternative, which is "server," sounds much worse and lower on society's scale: "Good evening, I'm Kay Francine, I'll be your server tonight." Do you really prefer that? Does Kay Francine even like saying that?

I used to wait tables back in the day, and I hated those restaurants that had the policy of introducing yourself. Let us now use the the-world-has-two-kinds-of-people-that-come-into-a-restaurant metaphor. There are the people at a restaurant who hear your name and it leaves their heads on contact—they are the majority. Then there are the other people who latch onto your name like a stray dog. "Lenny, could we have some more bread? Lenny, could we have some water? Lenny, this is overcooked. Lenny, why do you have that butcher's knife in your hand?"

Did anyone ask the collective wait staff of the U.S. what they would like to be called? I accept the word server because that is a mountain I am unwilling to climb. As for the word actress, I will stand my ground on the basis of art and beauty to the bitter end. It has more panache and eloquence; it has charm and grace. It even has more of a show biz quality. To me it's a term of respect for the female artist. When I think of Claudette Colbert and Rita Hayworth, I think actress. It is the same today for Meryl Streep and Scarlett Johansson.

I enjoyed working with Hope a great deal. She was upbeat, nice and always professional. I have not enjoyed working with any actress or actor as much as her. I make this point about Hope first because it is true, second because it is also rare. Actors have a tendency to—do I dare say it—be full of themselves. There, I said it, I said it and I'm glad. I said it because it's true. You can work alongside an actor for 10 weeks and on the last day of work they will walk by you like any other pedestrian on 5th Avenue. They don't see you. They don't want to see you. Many actors avoid eye contact with the crew. I used to work for Arthur Frommer, the travel author and businessman. I worked in the mailroom and when he passed me in the hall he would say good morning or good afternoon. If he had more time, there would be a "How are you?" thrown in there. This is just simple human courtesy that people have with each other in the same workplace. We are, after all, on the same project, but some actors just see the crew as an extension of the equipment. They look down their snobby ski-sloped noses and see a crew person as a chain gang member rather than a craftsman.

Today's actors are today's aristocracy. They parade around like the stars they are perceived to be. We love them, enjoy them and want to be them. They give us hope for our own dreams. Due to reality TV, ordinary people believe they have more of a chance to bust through and be discovered. By the way, no one is "discovered" anymore. The last person to be discovered was Lana Turner, at the drugstore. The story goes, she skipped out of high school one day and headed down to Sunset Boulevard to a drugstore or café. She sat down at the counter and ordered a Coke. Somebody thought she was hot, and the rest is history.

Reality TV has made it possible for everyone to dream about their 15 minutes of fame. Without studying the craft, they try to hit the show biz lottery by getting on some crazy show. They hope to get enough exposure and parlay that into a career, after they sing a song, woo a woman or eat some bugs.

The other big contributor to the show biz lotto is the Internet. YouTube, Vimeo and the agglomeration of other movie sites out there are giving hope to the untalented. There is no rhyme or reason as to what is going to go viral. I am in awe of what my daughters show me on YouTube that has 10 million views. It reinforces the idea that anyone has a chance. That can't be argued against, but neither can the fact that most people don't.

America is filled with budding stars and more talent than ever before, but there isn't enough room for everybody, especially at the top where everyone wants to be. The ones who are up there already are trying to kick the new people off, but they keep coming back like a bad zombie movie.

There was a buzz on *Wonderland* about a great deferred deal. If the movie hit it big so would we. At that point I put little stock into a deferred deal. Even though *The Search for One-eye Jimmy* paid off, there were at least ten other low-budget promises of success that never amounted to—as the expression goes—one thin dime. I felt it was naïve of the crew to be excited about the production's promise of riches.

The deferred contract always brought out the cynic in me. Many low-budget movies offer future bounty as enticement to lure you into the project. Many indie shows will dangle this carrot in front of you in lieu of pay. They think it is a valid offer because they are confident that they are going to sell their low-budget flawed indie. They believe they have the next

El Mariachi that will grace our screens. "If the *Blair Witch* people could do it, why can't we?" That is often the cry of ignorance on the low-budget sets.

I scoffed at the deferred money. Ha! I laughed in its face. I was satisfied with my on-the-spot paycheck. So I never gave it a second thought. Most of the stuff I worked on did not see any success, so I didn't have any expectations. I was content to be working, and to end my year with a six-week job.

It did turn out that *Next Stop Wonderland* was in fact the gift that kept on giving. We didn't finish on schedule and they added a few days. The following summer they had reshoots, but at real rates instead of low-budget rates. To my surprise, *Next Stop Wonderland* sold at Sundance for six million. A great coup for the producer; he did an excellent job negotiating that deal. That sale guaranteed the deferred money. The check finally came six months after they sold the movie. I still couldn't believe it.

The fateful day arrived; the scene was similar to the FedEx truck deliveryman at the end of *Bowfinger*. I heard the truck coming down the street and some type of bell went off inside me. Without reason I was pulled by some energy force to my front porch, much like the tractor beam on board the U.S.S. Enterprise. It was early in the morning and there was a thick mist, very similar to the "Dragon's Breath" in *Excalibur*. The noise was getting stronger, but I couldn't see the truck. Then there were two beacons of light shining up the driveway. The headlight beams illuminated the fog much like a Michael Curtiz movie from the 40's. Is that referential enough, or am I overdoing it? The camera ramped its speed and everything was in slow motion. I walked toward the truck as it continued to drive up the gravel path. As the truck drew near, the FedEx logo racked into focus. I saw the driver's silver tooth glisten as a piece of sun pierced through the cloud and reflected off it, not unlike in the Orbit gum commercial. I stopped walking and let the truck drive up to me. He came to a screeching halt; I think he needed a brake job.

He wasn't dressed in normal FedEx attire. He had on a ten-gallon hat, a leather vest, leather boots and leather chaps. Aside from the silver tooth, he was a dead ringer for John Wayne. He pulled back the sliding door and stared me straight in the eye. "Howdy, Pilgrim! You be Lenny Manzo?" He spit out some of the tobacco he was chewing and missed my dog's head by two inches. I looked at him, I looked at the spit, I looked at him, I looked at my dog, and I looked back at him. I stared him straight in the eye and said, "I am ... Lenny Manzo." We stared at each other for what seemed to be an eternity. With both of us standing our ground he broke the silence and said, "Sign here."

I held the 1-ounce envelope in my hand. Normally, I would tear into a letter that had good news in it. This time I walked back into my house to savor the moment. I grabbed my coffee and sat on the couch, took a sip and leaned back staring at the envelope. I finally opened my mail, and took the check out of the envelope without looking at the amount. I covered it with a piece of paper and I pulled back the paper to reveal the amount in reverse order. I squeezed it out like a poker hand. I slowly revealed each number starting with the pennies: so far 37 cents. I took another sip of coffee and was ready to get down to business; it was like being on *The Price Is Right*, except I already knew I was a winner. Yes, it was Bob Barker and not Drew Carey. It had to be; it was 1997.

So fantasy Bob said, "We have a five, Mr. Manzo has won five dollars so far. Shall we look at the next number, audience?" In true *"Price Is Right"* fashion, the audience responded in unison.

"Yes!!!"

Bob continued, "Let's see the second number ... it is an eight, Lenny Manzo now has eighty-five dollars!" The crowd applauded and I smiled a little. "Let us now look at the third number ... it is a nine, number nine for Mr. Manzo, Mr. Manzo now has nine hundred eighty-five dollars and thirty-seven cents, that is almost a thousand dollars!" The crowd really started to cheer and I was getting very excited to see the next number. I had figured out in my head that it could be a 6 or 7. If I was lucky it would be an 8 or a 9. So Fantasy Bob came over to me and asked me, "How do you feel, Len?"

I replied, "Pretty good, Bob. I'll be feeling much better when I see the fourth number."

"Well, what are we waiting for?" said Bob. "Audience, are you ready for the next number?"

To which the audience gave a resounding reply: "Yes, Bob!!!"

"OK, folks, let's see the next number!" There was a drumroll of course, and the number slowly came off the giant check to reveeeeeeeeeeeeeeeeeal ... a four. "Ladies and Gentlemen, Lenny has won four thousand nine hundred eighty-five dollars and thirty-seven cents!!! Let's hear it for Mr. Lenny Manzo!!!"

I smiled a contented smile. I thought I was going to get more from the movie, but this was found money and I was happy to have five grand. I thanked Bob Barker for his part in the good news and began to walk off the stage. After a few seconds, I heard Bob call me. "Len, where are you going?"

"What do you mean, where am I going? I have my check now and I'm heading directly to the bank. Where should I be going?"

"Lenny, hold on to your hat, sit back down and get ready for this. Audience, should we tell him?"

In a thunderous response: "Yes, Bob, let's tell him!"

"Lenny Manzo, you lucky fellow you, you are not going to believe this. You have another number on that check, and if you will excuse the pun, check it out!"

It turned out that Bob was right, there was indeed another number on that check: that little old lonely number one was sitting itself right in front of the four, for a grand total of $14,985.37. In the immortal words of Phil Rizzuto, "Holy Cow!"

I could not contain myself. I jumped out of my seat and like John Turturro I let out a yell that would curl your hair, or straighten it if your hair was already curly. I was out of my mind with joy. I put on some celebratory music and danced all over the living room like Tom Cruise in *Risky Business*, but without the Bob Seger song. After a lot of hootin' and hollerin' the adrenaline let up a bit. I jumped in my car and sang all the way to the bank, laughed too.

It was a big year all around. My second child was coming and I was buying my first house. We planned to close sometime in November. We couldn't wait because we were living in a one-bedroom apartment with my first daughter, whose crib was in the living room. Our second child was due mid-December. There was a crack in the schedule where we had a couple of days off and that was when I planned to close and move. Doing anything during a feature is tough enough but moving is really insane. My wife could not help due to the condition her condition was in. A few of my friends agreed to help. On the first day off we closed without a hitch. I was a proud owner of a three-bedroom Cape with an outbuilding that I call the barn.

The next morning me amigos came over to load up the cube truck. Between the house and my storage bin it took us well into the evening. I set up the bed and the crib, and went to sleep exhausted. I awoke at 5:30 AM and I went to work with a haze around my head, which remained for the rest of the show. I never recovered from the move. I was so burnt out I was like the walking dead. There wasn't enough coffee on the planet to keep me awake. The normal movie schedule was tough enough, but the added dimension of the move was too much to handle. I was somehow on autopilot. I made it through the rest of the show in a fog.

SCENE 13A

A Pick-Up

"*All's well that ends well*," said Shakespeare, and I agree. I finished the movie, my baby was born, and I still live in that house today happily ever after. At least if the movie ended here it would be happily ever after. Since life goes on, as we all know, no matter how good one has it, there is no real happily ever after. There are bills, problems and struggles. I ended my best year in the movie business and my life was changing, my family was growing, and that meant my responsibilities had increased at home.

Children: this is the rub. Having kids and working full-time in this business creates a stressful way of life. The industry is flooded with traveling freelancers who are barely home year in and year out. Most of these people are usually divorced. That is true of the workers and especially true of the stars. It is a rare couple in Hollywood that can hold it together. For people who seek to live an alternative lifestyle it amazes me how fast they are ready to tie the knot.

This business worked well for me up until I had kids. The demands at home took a priority and the fun frolicking film life became more of a pain than a pleasure. When I was not married, but still not single, I enjoyed the travel. Being on location is the best way to make a movie. I could throw myself into it 100% and not have to deal with anything else. When a production takes you on the road, pays for your housing, feeds you and gives you other perks, it becomes something else. It becomes a lifestyle. It can be viewed as summer camp, prison or somewhere in between depending on your attitude. You work all day and then hang out with the same people at night and on the weekend. There is almost no separation between work and play. So if you're into your work, which most people are, then it is a great experience. It is even better if you're young and single.

I have several friends in this business who have embraced the travel and have gone all over the world in their respective crafts. I was just starting to get that work when my first child arrived. I decided I didn't want to be away from the family. It was a big crossroads for me, and it changed the direction of my career. I don't regret that decision. It was the only one I could make. It is such a big question. How will you manage your family and career together? It is difficult to make it work, especially if you are still climbing the ladder and are obligated to take anything, which makes it hard on the home life. If you are successful then you are working all the time, which again makes it hard on the home life.

Either way it is a razor's edge, and very few manage it successfully. The best course of action, if you want to be in the movie biz and you must procreate, is to wait until you establish yourself. If you have not reached your desired goals you will be forced to compromise somewhere. If family becomes your life you will be forced to settle shy of your career vision. If you are a career-driven, brass ring grabbing, ladder climbing, tunnel vision career person, you will end up alone like Michael Corleone at the end of *Godfather II*. I still can't believe he actually killed Fredo!

If you work crew, put in the time and learn the craft, you will eventually be able to earn a living. The only thing that will hold you back is your personality, walk personality, talk personality, smile personality, charm personality, love personality ... I think you get the idea. There is a huge social factor that comes along with making it. To climb the ladder you have to be able to get along with people. It sounds easy enough, but it is not so easy for some. Everyone is wired differently and some people cannot fit into this paradigm. There are lines that should not be stepped over. Unfortunately for some, they don't know where these lines are located. They don't even know these lines exist. These people live at the bottom of the hire list and get called as a last resort. Of course they don't get why they are not getting called and if you explained it to them they wouldn't understand it anyway. They couldn't fix it if they wanted to.

There are some people who manage to get past their nasty selves and find themselves working fairly regularly. They are working because they are very good and usually the nasty people who are good find themselves heading a department, where they usually just wreak havoc downstream. You can't wreak havoc upstream or else you'll be asked to exit stage left. You can in fact wreak havoc anywhere if you are the star. You are the money; you are why people are coming to the theater. The execs in Hollywood couldn't care less what the field producer or director or anyone else on the set has to put up with in order to put a film in the can. When some actors get this power they lose touch with humanity and go off the deep end, similar to world leaders when they have total control over their countries. Power corrupts and then the star has no idea of himself. He thinks he is correct and everyone yeses him so he'll never know what type of beast he has turned into.

We had an interesting experience here in Boston as we watched Kevin James walk through the prima donna door. His first movie in Massachusetts was *Paul Blart: Mall Cop*. He came, did his job and that was it, no fuss no muss. One hundred eighty mil at the box office changes a man. Anyone who generates that kind of money on a $30 million movie moves into a different status. The demands get bigger. Why not? He's the reason for big money coming into the studio. So, on *Zookeeper*, the 35 feet from his trailer to the stage door had to be lined with heaters. Hey, it's cold in Massachusetts in October. On another cold evening, after several days of work by the riggers putting a dozen or so tractor trailers together to support a huge blue screen, the big moment came to shoot the scene and the cameras were ready for our boy, he got out on set and again he was too cold. OK, that was 40K nobody would miss. Let's just cut down on the pizza to make up for it

It is not uncommon in the history of Hollywood to jump through hoops to accommodate the star. It's even worse if it happens away from the set and laws are broken. It has been going on since the golden age of the studio system. In the old days, the studios were able to hide such antics from the press. Today, everything is on Page Six of the *New York Post* and other entertainment rags and shows. It is all part of the package and everyone is waiting for the next Lindsay Lohan train wreck. You would think such negative behavior would alter the continued success of Miss Lohan, but instead it is part of the whole show, on and off the screen; there is no separation. The public eats it up, which proves the old adage: There is no such thing as bad publicity.

Fortunately or unfortunately, I hadn't such problems. I was content with my portion of happiness that the universe was offering me. The baby arrived and so did the New Year. I was fully immersed in the Boston movie scene. It had taken four years to lay a stake down and develop my claim for work. In that time, I'd seen others jump on the movie train whose careers took off from the day they jumped on board. I had also seen others struggle for years before getting any recognition. As an actor or director you can go your whole life and never get anywhere. You can't count the number of would-be stars there are in the world. There are so many people who have the same dream of becoming a duke or a princess in the glamour-filled world of cinema.

Manzo's Waterloo

Everything was now clicking on all cylinders. I had a good reputation and I was getting enough work. My entrepreneurial eye started to wander again. I decided it was time to grow the LEN-INC Corporation. I was already hawking my sound gear around town. I saw a niche I could dig into. Every movie uses walkie-talkies for inter-departmental communication. It was common for the soundman to bring walkies to the show. So when the next movie rolled into town, I picked up some walkie-talkies.

I caught a break in February. There was a half-million-dollar feature called *Enough Already* coming to town. It was great to get right back on the horse early in the year. I had the added dimension of the walkies in my sound package, growth and prosperity were abundant and I was at the top of my game. "Top of the world, Ma," à la James Cagney in *White Heat*. If you didn't get that reference you must absolutely run to your Netflix account and put it in your queue.

I worked the five weeks right after the groundhog saw his shadow. We certainly had our share of nasty weather, and there were a few times I couldn't find any shelter, but overall it went well. No complaints about getting work out of season.

As *Enough Already* was ending there were rumors of a seven-million-dollar movie in the air. I worked with one of the producers several times, so I was in. I was the sound mixer on *Monument Ave.*, my biggest job to date and the biggest job by any local sound mixer. I had boldly gone where no sound mixer had gone before.

There was only one good thing about getting this job: that was getting the job. After that, this job went downhill quickly. The first thing that went south was my staff, or lack thereof. They wanted me to work shorthanded. In retrospect, I really needed a cable person for this job. This job was a thrash and on a thrash you need help. I had always been able to make do and I'd never had a paid third before, so I didn't know how to negotiate for more help. On one hand, I was excited just to have the opportunity to work on such a big show. On the other hand, I should not have accepted this and unbeknownst to me, the stage was already set for disaster.

Then I met the director, which did not feel right from the beginning. The director never gave me the time of day; he barely spoke to me and never listened to my suggestions. He ignored me and was rude. The DP was of the same ilk. I never felt like I was on board on this show. There was no sense of collaborative effort at all.

I had a rough first day and before I knew it my job was in jeopardy. I thought they were overreacting. They also were asking me to mix the movie differently from how I had done it on other movies. I was trying to cooperate but it wasn't working out.

There were a couple of above-the-line people who were friendly toward me. Around the ninth day of production they started to avoid me. I sensed something in the air. When the mafia takes you out they act like your best friend up until the moment they put a bullet in the back of your head. With film people, they all move away from you like you're a leper. Producers are bad poker players in that respect; they tip their hands in that way. I knew something was coming, and finally one day the ax fell. At the end of the second week I received the proverbial pink slip in true movie fashion. It was a grand Hollywood ending at 6 AM, standing in the rain at the end of a long all-nighter. I looked like Rick in *Casablanca* at the Paris train station after Ingrid Bergman stood him up. Losing Ingrid Bergman would give me more to cry about, but this was my Waterloo and I was depressed. It was the longest ride home I ever had. I had been going along so well and in my head this was a major setback. I was also on the hook for all the new gear that I had purchased for this job.

To add insult to injury, they asked me to come in on Monday because my replacement couldn't start until Tuesday. Naturally, I thought these people had a lot of nerve asking me to come in and help them out for Monday. The only reason they fired me a day earlier was because the new boom operator was a friend of mine. He told the production that if they didn't tell me, he would. I had two choices: stand on pride and tell them to go screw, or come in one more day and make about five hundred bucks. I knew they would just hire another local guy for the day and manage, so I swallowed the last bit of pride I had and went in Monday morning for the most depressing day at work I ever had. The director was the nicest he had ever been to me, a true prick. He actually has passed away since then. Is it wrong to badmouth a dead guy? If he were alive I'd feel the same way. Does one's status rise in passing? It worked for Nixon. Perhaps it doesn't sound it, but I buried my animosity a long time ago, no pun intended.

At the time, I felt like I had failed and not lived up to the requirements of the job. In retrospect, I'm not sure that really was the whole truth. I heard that the reason I was hired was because the mixer they wanted was not available until the third week of the shoot. I spoke with many of my colleagues about it after the fact and they believe I was set up from the beginning. I have no real proof, but I don't think it was farfetched when I look back at the whole rotten experience. The editor was on my back every day. He had some valid criticism. He also seemed to have invalid things to say. It made me unsure, which showed weakness, and then things got worse. In the end it doesn't really matter. I lost my job and lost an opportunity to keep moving up. I didn't know where it would take me, but not being able to finish the movie was not going to do a thing for my resume.

The devastation of this experience made me depressed for several weeks. Despite the big blow, I still had to continue to work. In this feast-or-famine business, things can change on a dime. I was out of work and the town was slow. The work dried up like a Kansas dust bowl in summertime.

Up until this point there was constant upward momentum. I had some ups and downs but there was always forward progress. I felt my career had broken down. Besides losing the job, I was on the hook for all this new equipment that I had just purchased. I was going to use my kit fee (equipment rental) from *Monument Ave.* to pay for the gear. I had this extra debt, the brand new big fat mortgage, and the even newer little Manzo in the house. This was cause for alarm.

The depression over the movie lingered as the demands of fatherhood increased. The business no longer worked as smoothly for me. Babies were waking up at all hours,

I wasn't sleeping and there were more responsibilities at home. I was handicapped because I didn't want to take any more out-of-town work. I received a few offers that summer that I had to refuse; I didn't want to miss my daughters' first steps or any other milestone, even a minor one, of my children's growth. If you leave a 7-month-old baby for six weeks you come back to a different kid. I didn't want to miss that so I missed the work. It put the reins on my career, but I made my choice as we all do, and I chose to stay close to home.

The fun disappeared and making movies became more like work. It hadn't felt like work before. It hadn't felt like work even in the hardest moments. Even in the wettest, coldest, nastiest moments that really sucked. I just thought, "Oh, this sucks." That particular situation sucked, but it still didn't feel like work.

My depression increased as I boarded a film called *Getting Personal*. The producer had me over a barrel and was squeezing me on the dough. He had someone with less experience waiting in the wings to take the job at a lower rate, but he wanted to give me the first chance. So, I went from a seven-million-dollar movie to a seven-hundred-thousand-dollar movie. Again, this did not help my depression. My energy shifted and people were getting the feeling I didn't want to be on the shoot. I still did my job and recorded the best sound that I could, but I was not my happy-go-lucky self.

As time passed I regained my dignity, at least in my own head. Losing that job never affected me getting other work. I made too much of it at the time. Later, I met many people who had similar stories of being fired from a shoot; at the time, it just seemed like it only happened to me. By the way, there were six others fired off *Monument Ave.* It was not a smooth experience for several people. And we all lived to tell about it.

SCENE 15

Manzo Bounces Back

As *the summer went on I* adjusted my attitude again. I realized that I couldn't carry on in the same way. Even though I wasn't happy about my career, I decided to keep it to myself. I know an unhappy camper finds his way to the ranks of the unemployed easier. I needed to work more than ever. So, I strapped on the poker face again. Life moves on and the calendar takes care of everything. I had survived the worst and was still making a living.

The fall arrived on schedule, and as it usually does here in New England, it brought in work. My walkie business started to take off in ways that I hadn't conceived of. At first I just brought the walkies to whatever movie I was working on. I figured out that I didn't need to work on the show to rent them the walkies. I unearthed a whole new revenue stream renting walkies to the commercial world.

Since there were other companies that were already renting walkies to productions, I had to do something that would make them switch over. It wasn't too hard since the competition had old gear and was overpriced. I had better equipment; all my walkies were brand new. And the major card played that sealed the deal was that I delivered them the day before. I lived 45 minutes outside of Boston. I might as well have been in Vermont, so I took that hurdle right out of the game. Between the walkies and the sound gear, I had developed a new business.

So, time passed, I rented equipment, recorded sound and paid the mortgage. The movie world was losing its appeal. I was pushing 40 and what was cool a few years earlier became more of a pain. I moved away from the movies as much as possible. I embraced day work and hopped between commercials and corporate videos. This work was easy enough, but there was never enough to go around. The rental business was no longer extra cash, it was a necessity.

I was not enjoying my work. I was bored and it was no longer satisfying me. I wasn't thinking about quitting. What would I do? There are not many places you can go with feature film experience except to another feature film. It was a bit frustrating. At the time, Boston had a low ceiling for sound mixers. I could pick up a job on a small show under a mil, but the big shows always brought the mixer in from L.A. or New York. Since I declined travel jobs I was stuck with what the Boston market had to give. There wasn't much room for me to grow. For better or worse, I was still in show biz.

I managed through the winter, eventually the snow cover left, the flowers bloomed and before I knew it, summer was upon me. I was moving along and making ends meet when another indie was getting off the ground called *The Gentleman from Boston*, later re-titled *Beacon Hill*, a bomb by any other name would blow up just as loud. I heard through the grapevine that they offered the job to somebody else in town. Well, that settles that. The power of fate, in Italian it's *la forza del destino* and in German it's *die macht des schicksals*. In any language, I was off the hook.

While *The Gent*, as it was affectionately referred to, was in pre-production and getting close to the start date, the soundman received another offer, a better one I'm sure. That made me the only game in town. So I did what any self-respecting professional would do in this situation: I held out for more money. Not much more, but I wanted more because they called me second. Had I been the first call I would have agreed to the rate. It was out of principle. Isn't that what people say? It's not the money, it's the principle. NFL football players say it's respect. They want to be shown the proper respect. Respect or principle, I made them give me more money.

It was summer and I was booked, but I was not happy. I was feeling daunted by the work, I wasn't interested in it and it was putting me in a bad mood. I shared my plight with a friend. I told her about my lack of interest, why I didn't want to do the movie, why I was in a bad mood and blah, blah, blah. She confirmed with me that I was going to do it anyway. She said I had two choices at this point. It does seem to boil down to two choices in this dualistic world of ours. Either I could do the movie and be in a bad mood, or do the movie and be in a good mood. That was the bottom line. That was the truth; I was going to have this experience regardless, so what the heck. It was weird, I was so wound up about doing this movie and these simple words from the right person at the right time made me see it in a different way. That small shift in thought taught me a lot.

I donned my happy-hat and the attitude shift came immediately. I began to embrace the movie from that point on. Not only did I embrace it, but it turned out to be great. We had a good crew and we had a lot of fun. We signed on to a 12-hour daily wage guarantee, but we usually only worked 10 hours. There were a couple of nights when I was able to stop at the bar for a beer. That never could have happened before. I would always have to get in my car right after wrap because the turnaround to the next day was so short. Not on this show. This movie became a daily party. It was fun and easy.

I had changed my perspective about my work. I got my second career wind. There was no turning back now. I knew I was here to stay. I would just make the most of my career options. And the options were coming in. Coinciding with my better attitude were better jobs. I was getting a lot of commercials, and I found my way onto the best short film I ever worked on, a great film called *Dog Days*, a post-apocalyptic-era drama. Another great crew with one of the best DP's I ever worked with, Evans Brown.

Len, Why Is Your Face That Color?

So I was sitting at home minding my own business; what else would I be doing at home? And the phone rang. I asked my wife, "Who is it?"

To which she replied, "It's opportunity, dear."

"Hmph, that's odd," I thought, "opportunity doesn't call, opportunity knocks." This intrigued me. I picked up the phone and it was indeed opportunity. It turned out to be the biggest film ever to hit New England and it was shooting right down the street in Gloucester. As luck would have it, they needed a second unit sound mixer. And as more luck would have it, I was available. It was *The Perfect Storm* and the perfect job. This would be a nice feather in the chapeau. I had never worked on a movie this large before and the location was the icing on the cake. Did I tell you it was down the street from my house? As freelance filmmakers we get terribly excited about a job near home, especially because living on the North Shore of Massachusetts, it rarely happens.

I had never worked on second unit before, but I knew one thing about it: it was easy. Usually there are no principal stars on set. We do establishing shots, stunts and special effects. Dialogue is practically nonexistent. Here is the typical irony of the biz: this was my biggest job, most money, highest credential and least amount of work.

Even though the job was on second unit, it was still the big show, a $90 million movie. On my first day I showed up early. I wanted to be ready in case they threw a curveball at me. This job auspiciously kicked off as one of the AD's told me that the schedule had changed, the crew was already out on a fishing boat and that I should just hang out in holding until they returned. In other words, "Len, take the morning off." Don't mind if I do.

Holding was a big warehouse where the extras were hanging out; it was also the same place breakfast and lunch were served. I wound up sitting in holding all morning. It was rather educational witnessing the four caterers working nonstop, transforming breakfast into lunch. It was like watching it on a time-lapse camera. These guys never stopped, the breakfast buffet was cleared away and the lunchtime smorgasbord was set up. The food on this show was top shelf. They had beef, chicken, fish and a vegetarian option daily. I can't remember which was bigger, the salad bar or the dessert bar. That particular day they added the pasta bar. There was no expense spared; food was not an issue on this show.

Later, when I worked on more big shows and observed the caterers again, I realized that it was the toughest job on the set. For one thing, they don't stop; you walk over to their station any time of the day and they are working. They usually start their day somewhere around three in the morning in order to have breakfast ready at six. If lunch is postponed for a few hours they stick around, which means they get out later. They are not guaranteed proper turnaround time, and often they don't get enough sleep. After they pack it in for the day, they have to do the shopping, and then they bring the dishes back to the hotel where they are washed. They somehow squeeze in their personal lives, like showering and brushing their teeth. I said personal, not social; a social life would be impossible. The amazing thing is that the caterers always manage to stay upbeat and keep a sunny disposition. I tip my hat and raise my glass and thank them for all the food they have provided.

Finally, my crew docked and came in for lunch, which is when I received my first instructions for the day: I was wrapped. They were going back on the boat in the afternoon and I wasn't needed. I never unloaded my gear. What a stroke of luck for me. Sure, the obvious good fortune was I went home early; the really good news was that I didn't have to go on a boat. I had recorded sound on boats twice for two different movies with the same result. I found myself laid out at some point with my face turned green. Boats are not my bag. On *Next Stop Wonderland* I lay on the deck until they called "Roll sound," stood up for the take, hit the record switch, hung on somehow until "Cut" was called, then it was right back on the deck. Do we have time for another fish tale here? I think we do because I have a page quota, so I better give you a nice little story that will interest you and fulfill my literary needs.

I was 17 when I went shark fishing for the first and last time. I was fine on the way out to sea, enjoying the ride and the oceanic air. It wasn't until we cut the engine that everything changed. It didn't help that I was the first one to jump into the shark seat and was trying to wrestle a shark into the boat. I thought, "What do I have against this poor shark? I got no quarrel with him." I let go of the rod, unfettered myself from the seat and lay out on the deck the rest of the day.

On *Ratchet* I had to sit in a motorboat on the high sea for hours. Like my shark experience, we just drifted, and shot our actors on the other boat. The AD tried to move me for some reason, but she gave up quickly; there are some advantages to having a green face. By the time I was on *The Gentleman from Boston* I had learned my lesson. I sent my boom operator out to sea to record the sound. He loved being on a boat and I was an official landlubber. I am willing to do a lot for the sake of film, but boats are off the list henceforth and forever. Now I just have that put into my contract—as if.

On *The Perfect Storm* I had been saved from the boat, and had gone home early. Everything was coming up Manzo again. The second day they put me to work, but it was simple stuff and most of it was MOS. You now know the legend of MOS, but in the modern world it means "Manzo Off Set."

There was some sound on this show and I recorded it when it happened, but most of the time I sat around drinking coffee and enjoying the summer weather. One night I waited for my call time until about 10 PM. I called the office and they said the day was pushed and the crew had the day off. They still had to pay me for the late cancellation, and as we say on set, "Ka-Ching!"

At some point one of the AD's pulled me aside and told me that I was only there because the producers and director were bored in dailies. They just wanted to have some sound for comfort and amusement. Basically she was saying that my work wasn't necessary and not to worry about anything. If I couldn't get the sound or if it wasn't up to proper standards it didn't matter. To quote Harry Chapin, "Another man might have been angry, another man might have been hurt ... I stashed the bill in my shirt."

That statement would have offended many a soundman worth his salt. I was worth my salt; I just had no pride about it. If you remember, I swallowed the last of my pride on *Monument Ave.* Remember there are no atheists in foxholes. Don't scratch your head too hard, it doesn't go there. I needed to close the chapter with some type of metaphor, but a juicy pride quip eluded me. My skin is thick enough to handle some off-the-cuff, below-the-belt L.A. AD remark about my superfluous presence. I've often watched money be thrown to the wind on these big-budget extravaganzas; it was nice to see some of it being blown my way.

SCENE 17

Crossing the Line

In 1999 the second phase of my career began. I wouldn't call it a sequel, more like an intermission. That's not right either: it was more like a new season of episodic television. That is most accurate; I like the TV analogy. I just don't like TV—stay tuned.

Even though I came back from my catastrophic demise on *Monument Ave.*, the truth of the matter is that I was never really a technician at heart. Technology never resonated with me; I learned it because I had to. After eight years, I thought about making a change. Not to worry, I wasn't leaving show biz.

I tried my hand at AD work on a couple of small projects that went OK, but I wasn't particularly moved by the experience. A good AD is like the maître d' at a fancy restaurant: he knows what is happening on the set at all times. He makes sure that it runs fluidly; if a problem arises, he handles it or delegates it. The AD is a very valuable cog in the movie wheel, if he is listened to. He keeps an eye on the script and keeps the show on schedule. He makes sure the day's work gets done and creates options when the production hits a roadblock. This position is the heart of the movie set and without it the production would come to a halt like an engine running out of oil.

Starting in a new department meant starting at the bottom. I jumped on a couple of shorts and was hooked in with some very inexperienced people who didn't value my contribution. They were always jumping away from the plan and making stuff up as they went along, which is not how I like to work. I am from the Hitchcock school of filmmaking. I don't believe in catching lightning in a bottle; you put the lightning in the bottle during pre-production, then you'll have it. Chasing new ideas in the moment and deviating from the plan will have you lose out somewhere else.

The AD experience left a bad taste in my mouth. I quickly decided that this was not my path and I didn't want to find myself working that close to the idiot trust when I had no real power. I didn't have any credentials as an

AD or any real experience so I would have had to kick around at the bottom and work with the newbies to get experience, which seemed more like babysitting than being a part of the process.

I started to think that I should have been producing at this point. I had been watching on the sidelines for years as people screwed up their shoots left and right. Why shouldn't I embrace the delusion of grandeur? It was clear most others were groping in the dark. So I figured that I should start doing a little groping too, G-rated of course.

They say, "When the producer is ready, the job will come." If they don't say it, then I just coined a phrase. I was ready to make the shift and coincidently enough another friend of mine named Rob was starting a production company and wanted me to be involved. His vision was to make all types of media and eventually make movies. He often felt over a barrel when renting gear so he bought his own equipment for his shows and also to make a buck on it in between. He bought the cameras, I bought the lights, and we went to work. The stars were initially aligned and business was overflowing.

Before I knew it, I was producing my first commercial and it was on location in New York City. A commercial was the best way to start my producing career. It is all the same stuff as a movie, only condensed; you need actors, stuff, insurance, more stuff, locations and other stuff. Basically, it's all the same stuff.

I was on the other side of the fence. I was above the line. I made it to the top of the food chain and I did it without even knowing I was going there. I saw an opportunity so I grabbed it. My personality was much more suited to producing than sound. I like the deal making, the communication with the departments, the managerial faction, putting the pieces together, and most of all, I really liked having input into the creative portion of the project. As a soundman I was not consulted about any of my cinematic knowledge, but as a producer my opinion mattered.

I'm not going to sit here and tell you that my first production went perfectly. We had some glitches and problems. The biggest problem we had was getting the truck into New York City. My driver was taking the truck down in the middle of the night to avoid traffic and that plan worked well right up until he hit the Triborough Bridge. The key word here is Tri, at least the key prefix. He sailed through Massachusetts and Connecticut right into the Bronx. He made it to the bridge and somehow missed the big green sign for Manhattan and found himself on Northern Boulevard in Queens. That's when my phone rang. He said it wasn't marked. My panicked driver was freaking out. He was lost and exhausted. I kind of let it gloss over me at the time, because I had to roll with my objective in the moment, which was to safely land the truck. That sign is about 30 feet wide.

The worst part of it was that he was in the only part of Queens that I did not have a complete handle on. If I were there I could have figured it out, but if I were there I would not have driven into Queens. We talked on and off throughout the evening which was cutting into my rest for our first shoot day. I was the last man standing so I had to make sure it all worked out. He did find his way to the city, but did not find his way to the parking lot where I had a deal arranged. As mentioned earlier, this situation falls under the broken window expense, money spent on many times unnecessary, avoidable or unavoidable problems. There are so many logistics being compressed in such a short time period that some things don't always happen as planned, and in this case it was an extra ninety bucks for a botched parking job.

The trick about producing is that you have different circumstances to work around every time. The labyrinth of production is infinite, and the skill that is needed is to keep a calm head and coolly figure out your approach. You never know what can go awry. Once I auditioned an actress who was sweeter than a peach pie on a Sunday afternoon. As the shoot progressed she started to become more demanding to the point of being unreasonable. At that point she had my back against the wall. It was too late to replace her. She was already screen committed; I barely had enough money to get the movie done. I couldn't stop production, fire the lead and hire someone else. There would have been so much film to trash and the amount of time it would have taken us to re-shoot with a new actress would have blown the budget. I bit my lip, swallowed my pride and held my tongue. I admit that this is a lot for the mouth to do when you're not saying anything, but there was no choice. I was forced to juggle the schedule. Pride is your biggest enemy; the important thing is to not take it to that level. This business calls for a lot of sucking it up, not to be confused with sucking up, aka ass kissing, which I have already gone into in depth.

If you sit on your own high horse then you will lose the battle and the war. You do have recourse; you never have to work with that person again. There is a credo that I now live by: "If someone ever screws me in this business, I will never work with that person again, unless I absolutely have to."

You would be surprised how many people have uttered the words, "I'll never work with that guy again." A situation comes up, a deal is struck and somehow that jerk you can't stand is in the middle of it all. You throw on the fake smile and get back to work.

Producing held a fascination for me. I knew on my first gig that I was more suited for this role than the way I came up through ranks as a soundman. It was a natural fit. I liked everything about it. I liked to make the arrangements and cut all the deals. I especially liked cutting the deals with the crew people. Since I had been a crew person so long it was the easiest part of the job. I knew what they wanted and I spoke their language. Crew people are easy to understand; they are working for a living and want to be treated with respect. I have found the respect portion is what is valued most. Sure the money is important, but after the monetary agreement has been made, there is no more talk of that, and the only thing left is the job, the conditions and the respect. I have found that when the crew is taken care of, they feel it and they will go the extra mile for you. It really just comes down to minimal human decency. Who doesn't want respect? It is all Rodney Dangerfield ever wanted.

I needed to be the one making the deal. I have found a big problem with communication in this area. I have seen many disagreements happen over misunderstandings caused by poor expression of the human language. I know how to make it clear and make sure all the P's and Q's are dotted and crossed.

I also liked being part of the creative process. When I recorded sound no one above the line wanted my opinion on anything besides the audio. I would not volunteer it anyway. I was cured of that on one of my first jobs. It was a college job and the actress asked a simple question, which I knew the answer to. Just like anywhere else in life when a question needed answering and I had the answer, I would, well, answer it. After that the sound mixer communicated to me through my headphones and very nicely told me that I was a lowly boom operator and that I should not talk to the actress. Let the director handle it. "Okie doke," live and learn. It made sense. I certainly wouldn't do that on a big set if Russell Crowe had asked a generic question in my direction. I would speak back to him if he asked me directly, and only directly. As a boom operator I kept my mouth shut.

Sometimes actors would say something to me on set, it would turn into a conversation and then they'd get this look in their eye: "Oh, My, God! I'm talking to this guy now, how did that happen?" Birds of a feather, they didn't know me or want to. I did notice how differently people treated me when I put on my producer's shoes. I was actually blown away by how much nicer the actors were to me than when I was a sound guy. They were sooooooooo nice and friendly. It was eye opening.

By spring of 2000, I was fat mad crazy busy, and also in the most stressful part of my career. Being busy was great, but I was working seven days a week, from sun up to sun down and beyond. I ran a rental shop with gear for every department. I still freelanced as a sound guy. My walkie business was booming, and now I was starting to produce commercials and music videos. At least when I just worked on a movie I had a day off. Don't get me wrong, I'm not complaining about too much work. That would be sacrilege.

I threw myself into the business full throttle and worked all hours, every day of the week, for seven months straight. It was like being on a never-ending movie. Many a night I found myself loading my truck until two in the morning. Sometimes the jobs were stacked so closely together that I would have to pick up the walkies from one set at 10 PM, go back to my shop, check them for loss and damage, recharge the batteries, repack the walkies and deliver them by 5 AM. If it were physically possible I made it happen. I wanted to succeed, but I was running myself ragged. I knew that I was overworked, but I didn't realize how wound up I had become. The sleep deprivation combined with the workload threw me off kilter.

I had a 10-day vacation planned in Colorado. I was meeting an old friend there. This was the worst of timing and the best of timing. Had I not committed myself I would not have gone. I thought the business couldn't live without me. I left with a lot of stress that I carried with me into the vacation. I never needed a vacation as badly as this one; it wound up being very medicinal.

In Colorado, I started to decompress, but it wasn't even noticeable until the end of my trip. After a substantial amount of stress release, I realized how off-the-charts mental I had become. I knew that when I returned home I had to change my approach before I had a stroke. I headed back to Massachusetts with a different attitude. I wasn't getting everything done anyway so I decided to take off most weekends and not work past a certain hour if I could avoid it. It wasn't doing me any good to push myself that hard. It must have been my immigrant work ethic; as you know, I'm not native to Massachusetts.

SCENE 18

The Wreck of the Old 97

A *movie career would not* be complete unless you worked on a Roger Corman movie. Mr. Corman is the king of Hollywood low budget. I hooked into this film, *The Strangler's Wife*, via a fly-by-night film school that cut a deal with Mr. Corman. The devil himself couldn't have made a better deal. Don't worry, there were no souls exchanged. The school approached Mr. Corman, who agreed to put up 50K, which was about 30% of the financing for 100% control. Well, the two producers who put this thing together scratched their heads and thought this was a good deal. They could sell apprenticeships on the movie using Mr. Corman's name and thus make a movie and maybe make a buck in the process.

The first strike with *The Strangler's Wife* was the script. The script was terrible. Terrible would be polite; it may have been the worst script I ever worked on. I had production apprentices, and in my first meeting with them I had to find a way to defend the script. One of my apprentices was very blunt and she said that the script sucked. I couldn't argue about the quality of the script. I did say that as producers this was the movie we were making and it was up to us to make this the best movie we could.

This was a Roger Corman movie, translation: exploitation film. It had a serial killer murdering women. There was gratuitous lesbian sex and a host of hot women. I'm sorry, supposed-to-be-hot women. This is a delicate subject and not to sound, shall we say, anti-feminist, but we didn't have any hot babes. The lead was a fine-looking woman, but she did not fit the bill for this project. Let's just say, she didn't have it upstairs. In a movie where a major selling point is gratuitous sex scenes you need to have something gratuitous to look at. We didn't have that. Casting, strike two.

We never did get out of the batter's box on this one. There was not enough money and compromises were made in too many places. We also had a hard time finding key personnel to work and teach at low-budget rates. Boston was busy because of the impending SAG strike. This seemed to happen about every three years—no strike, just impending. It still scares the movie execs, and they don't want to be caught holding the bag and be forced to shut down in the middle of a production. Everywhere around the country, producers were cramming in the work before the end of June. This scenario had us painted into a corner. It was very difficult to find crew and we were locked into those dates because many of the students were working people and they had made their schedules to fit around that specific time period. Since *The Strangler's Wife* was a non-union show, we would not have been accountable to SAG. If there was ever a time to push a movie back a few weeks, this was it, but those dates were carved in stone and nothing could be done about it.

Not only was the lead actress not exploitive (sexy) enough, she was uncooperative and it turned out that she had all these prior commitments that she had to keep. So now we had to jump through hoops and make schedule changes for the actress. It would have been nice if she'd mentioned some of it up front, but she knew such scheduling conflicts would have lowered her chances to get the role. I didn't mind some of the issues, but she was completely unyielding and I knew she wasn't right for the part from the beginning.

It is not uncommon to have an actor dictating demands on set. On *The Crucible*, Winona Ryder had all guests banned from set, it was a distraction to have too many people around, except for her boyfriend, who was OK. On *What's the Worst That Could Happen*, Martin Lawrence had the camera assistant removed from the set because he bumped into the slate with his head. On *Waterfront*, Joe Pantoliano had to have his lines transmitted by his assistant to his earwig receiver. Apparently he had become so big he was beyond memorizing his lines. He must have heard that Brando worked this way. If you don't know who Joe Pantoliano is, then that just makes my point stronger. It is power, mixed with ego and stirred by success, definitely shaken, and not stirred.

The egomaniacal actor is not just limited to the big show. On another movie that I produced I had a problem with the lead actor: he couldn't handle the pressure. He said, "I need time to get my head together." This attitude puzzled me. Here was his first opportunity to have a lead role in a feature film and instead of embracing it he was freaking out. I wasn't sure if that was the case or if he was just creating a hissy fit so he could have a long weekend. Even though we thought his attitude was absurd, or he was just lying to us, we looked at the schedule and flipped some scenes to accommodate him.

Further into the shoot the director pulled me aside and told me the actor wanted a chair. I said, "What chu talkin' 'bout, Willis?" He went on to say that even though there were chairs on set he wanted his own specific chair. Apparently he had seen too many behind-the-scenes movie making documentaries where the big star gets a big chair with his name embroidered on it. The budget on this baby was $200,000; we usually forgo these types of luxuries at this level. The actor was having a Hollywood moment. So I brought him a chair, no big deal, in both incidents I didn't stand on principle. I did what was necessary to get the movie done and sometimes babysitting is what it takes. By the way, after I gave him the chair he never sat in it. He was too self-conscious.

Back to *The Wreck of the Old 97*, I mean *The Strangler's Wife*. There are many places a movie can be ruined. During production is the most common place, but I have also seen movies destroyed in the editing room. *The Strangler's Wife* never had a chance because of the script. We knew who the murderer was in the first act. There was no tension. It was an exploitation movie without exploitation. We did have some nasty murders, but that was it. Because of a bad script mingled in with poor acting and directing, this movie didn't have a chance to be good. I don't think any of this mattered to Corman. He was getting something for his 50K and through his status and industry connections it was in the video stores. I'm sure he made some money, though the local producers never saw a dime.

Mr. Corman was supposed to grace our set with his presence at some point in production, but unfortunately something came up at the last minute that was unavoidable. He sent his sincere apologies to the cast and crew of his project. That was the cover story and he stuck to it. I don't think he gave a rat's something or other. Either way, the Hollywood Legend did not make it to Boston for his production. We carried on and finished the film for him. In retrospect, the school was put together to make this movie. It was an idea that might have worked, but given the inexperience that surrounded the project, it never had a chance. Shortly after production, the film school folded like an old bridge table.

SCENE 19

Shoot the Messenger

The Strangler's Wife ended and so did all the other productions in town. All the work was drying up in a way I had never seen before. I mean, it was *Grapes of Wrath* dry. Boston became a production ghost town that year. There were driblets of work but nothing substantial. I managed to survive until the last week of August when the docket was filling up for the fall, the busiest time in New England. The fall foliage is, to use the most overused word by people under 25, awesome.

Many movies and commercial companies take advantage of this spectacular backdrop. They shoot here in the fall to cash in on the time-sensitive beauty. I was relying on the fall to make up for the slow summer. Business started to heat up, when the long arm of life took me by surprise and changed my life and many others' forever. September 11, 2001 is truly a day that lives in infamy, a day that caused havoc throughout the U.S., and a havoc that we had never known. I'm not getting out violins for myself. Many more people's lives were destroyed and there were many tragedies in the fallout. I peripherally knew one person who was on one of the planes. Nothing happened to me, or my loved ones in New York, but it had a trickle-down effect on my business. The shoots I was working with were cancelled. I had a deal with the NBC show *Providence* to supply all the walkie-talkies for their excursions east to get local exteriors. They cancelled the present shoot and never came back.

The busiest season here was dead, after an already brutally slow summer. The winter rolled in to create the typical no-work, no-business landscape. Unfortunately, it lasted until April. This was the beginning of the end of my rental business. A year ago, "Everything Was Coming Up Roses," to paraphrase Ethel Merman. She also sang, "There's No Business Like Show Business." I concur.

After 9/11, the economy wasn't doing well, and production companies in New England were going out of business left and right. The commercial business was getting worse every year. Corporations slashed their budgets and in some cases wiped out entire video departments. Companies that had been around long before I arrived in Boston were all going down the tubes. I didn't realize it at the time, but I was also going down.

I had been making a nice living off of small six-figure productions. They shot 16mm film and I would rent them the camera, lights, sound, truck and more. The economy had taken its toll on the business and these little mom-and-pop movies dried up. Along with a downturned economy, the technology was changing and digital video was looking nicer. This became a more viable option for small movies. Mini-budget indies became micro-budget indies, and with budgets under ten grand my rental business suffered.

The summer of 2002 rolled around; the work had picked up a bit. I had an opportunity to produce another movie and jumped at the chance. There was no money with this one, but I believed in the script and thought we had something good. Since I was well endowed, with film equipment that is, I had a lot to offer these young directors. We struck a deal and proceeded.

When I sat in my corner of the set over my soundboard, I would observe and analyze the production and the people. I would spot some screw-up, comment to my boom operator and get back to my crossword puzzle. If I had a screw-up in my department, it was easy enough to replace one person. Managing 30 to 40 people was much more of a challenge. I had produced other shows before, but I had other producers to work with. This was the first time it all rested on my shoulders.

The first thing I learned: you can never have too much help in the office. The core of any movie is the production office. It is the heart all the blood vessels lead to. If the office cannot function to full capacity, then the director and his set flock will not be able to make the best movie possible. I had a couple of great staff members, much thanks again to Dave and Sarah, but I could have used more help. I was also too busy spinning plates that I couldn't keep an eye on the content. When I finally realized the poor quality of the movie we were making, it was too late.

I made several mistakes on this movie. The first mistake was making this film at all. The directors were inexperienced and fell short of the task. I thought the script was strong, but it played out differently from what I'd imagined. The lead character was never likable. And we had no sympathy for her from the beginning. These issues were enough to submerge the whole project, but it didn't end there. The film was plagued with typical low-budget problems that stem from an all-volunteer project.

Here was a rookie mistake for you. I had well over a hundred extras who were playing concertgoers. The only access to the inside of the establishment was for the use of restrooms. We had no other holding area, just a big parking lot. It was a beautiful day and not a cloud in the sky, which certainly worked against us. Most of the extras were dressed in black and they started to wilt in the blazing sun. The only compensation they received was some snacks and pizza for lunch. After the pizza was gone, so were most of the extras.

I had a diabolical production assistant who purposely sabotaged his tasks so he wouldn't be asked to do them again. I sent him on a 90-minute run and he didn't come back for four hours. We had revolving make-up artists, which also caused continuity issues. There were many other departments short on crew some days. I lost an actor right before his scene because he ran into a tree and smashed his face while shagging fly balls at a nearby park. We had to rewrite that scene in a hurry. Naturally, the camera broke down in the middle of the show, and to top it all off when the same useless PA came back from the one and only Starbucks run, he put sugar in my coffee.

In retrospect, I should have fired him on the spot. Some things must be sacred on a film shoot and one of those things is the producer's coffee. Please, don't misunderstand. I know people make mistakes, but this kid made them on purpose and I have always suspected he put sugar in my coffee on purpose. He had to go out of his way to put the sugar in the coffee. I'm not being a conspiracy theorist right now; this was one lone coffee-running man, acting alone for the sake of revenge and rebellion without a cause. This is one instance where it would have been OK to shoot the messenger.

The biggest mistake I made on this project was the age-old error many young filmmakers commit. I thought I could make a bigger movie than was possible. My resources were good and many, but still not enough. The directors were not able to flush out their script and in the end we didn't have enough footage to complete the film. I didn't know it at the time but it was more like producer's boot camp. Even though the film was never completed and our mission failed, it was a crash course in how to make a movie and what never to do again. I cut my teeth here and it helped make me into the producer that I am today.

Finding the right staff is not always easy. I once had a crew member run amok in the middle of the day. I never really understood exactly what happened to this poor lad. He was the first AD on a shoot that was going rather smoothly. The only theory that carried any weight was his abuse of the caffeinated energy drinks at craft service. He left in the middle of the day à la Peter Finch as Howard Beale in *Network*: "I'm as mad as hell and I'm not going to take this anymore!" He certainly had his moment in the sun as he left the set in a blaze of glory.

I had another AD who just froze like a farm boy in the middle of the night watching the alien ships make their landing in the cornfield. It is a very difficult position to fill at the low-budget level. It calls for a lot of experience and that part is lacking on low-budget projects. I found another AD and this time I raised him from a pup, but he still turned on me like a rabid dog. His best quality was blaming his mistakes on others. He constantly tried to cover his mistakes by putting blame on someone who was in the right place at the wrong time. I can't say he is unique in that area. This is a big finger-pointing business. No one ever takes the blame. For some, it is out of fear; claiming responsibility for a set disaster could result in termination. For others, it is survival. They don't have what it takes, so they continue to point the fickle finger of blame at the nearest sucker.

Eventually it came to a head. My know-nothing, ego-growing AD became too big in his own head. His main problem was that he wasn't as interested in the work so much as being the cool guy who works on a movie set. He was not in it for the craft; he was in it for the glory. He liked the idea of running the set and being the AD, and being in the center of the action. He wasn't paying attention to the conversation between the director and the DP, which meant that he didn't know what was going on around him and was often surprised when things changed around him. Many of his friends tried to help him, but he was too full of himself to take advice or criticism. In the end he thought he knew more than I did. That's when we parted company.

Why did I put up with this guy? How did it get so out of hand? Again, you are asking good questions. I spoke to him several times during our final shoot together. I had worked with him for three years and we had become friends. The friendship factor made it difficult to fire him halfway through the movie. I was hoping he would listen to me. By the end of the shoot I realized that he never listened to me and on the second-to-last day we were screaming at each other in the parking lot. That didn't last long; I hate to lose my temper at work or anywhere for that matter. I despise the loss of control and it rarely happens—unless you mess with my coffee, then all bets are off.

With a day and a half left I let him finish, but cut him for the add-on days. If you are a manager for a company and hire someone who does not work out, you can give that person some time to see if the ship can be righted. When you are managing a movie, time is a luxury that is not available. The lesson I have learned is there is no time to work it out. Once someone proves he cannot handle the job, he should be let go immediately. I will never let friendship sway me again. You could say he let the friendship down by not performing his work. He used the friendship to get away with his nonsense. I have not mentioned his name because we were friends at one time, and I know that he's too full of himself to recognize himself in this story of absolute ineptitude. And if you do recognize yourself, old buddy, it is not too late for an apology.

Low-budget movies are filled with kooky moments. Big movies are as well, but for different reasons. Both are about money. On the big show it is the excess of money that causes the craziness and on the low-budget movies it is the lack of money that creates it. I produced another film with a few shoot days in Western Massachusetts and New Hampshire. We shot a scene all night at a dive motel outside of Winchendon, Mass. We wrapped at daybreak and headed north to Keene, New Hampshire for the last week of shooting. I left the set early to make sure that the hotel in Keene was all set for a smooth check-in for my exhausted crew. I left instructions with my production staff to have the lighting and grip truck dropped off at the location. They were to stay with the driver to the location, drop the vehicle and continue north to Keene, where the crew was being housed. The location was less than a mile off the main road. That is why my eyes popped out of my head the next morning when I saw the truck in the hotel parking lot.

I know, you are wondering what the big deal was. The truck was delicate and had already broken down once on the show. I couldn't replace the truck because it was my truck. The truck was one of the many mistakes I made along the way. I relied on someone else's opinion when purchasing it and it was a bit of a lemon. I didn't have the knowledge for such things, so I deferred to someone who did. Anyway, the truck needed to be handled with kid gloves. Well, no use crying over spilled milk. We'll just have to drive it there when we start work.

I thought everything was in order when I left the motel early for the set. Apparently the driver didn't have directions. I don't know who dropped the ball there, and I didn't understand why the driver just drove pell-mell out of the parking lot without them. Instead of heading south toward the set, he and other crew headed north. Cell phone signal was dodgy and I couldn't get a hold of anyone. All I could do was wait it out.

It turned out the driver, truck and crew were lost in some small town that was set in some cell phone–deficient valley. The town was set at the bottom of a steep hill; when they finally realized they had gone too far in the wrong direction, they turned around but couldn't create enough momentum for the truck to get back up over the hill. The boys tried it several times to no avail. Then they came up with the brilliant idea of backing the truck as far as they could up the other hill, the opposite way out of town. They blocked off traffic that crossed horizontally with the main road and the driver let her rip down the hill to gain enough speed and power to get it over the hill on the other side. This could have been a good scene for one of the *Smokey and the Bandit* movies. Regardless of how they found themselves in such a bizarre circumstance, the crew didn't give up. They put the truck back on the road and eventually we were able to get the night's work done. If that's not show biz, what is?

I had another driving incident on the Public Enemy music video. We were shooting Public Enemy at a club in Cambridge until noon. A couple of days earlier, Public Enemy picked up a booking at an all-day music festival at Foxboro Stadium. They were scheduled to go on at 3 PM, which gave us plenty of time to shoot the morning work and then capture the live performance at Foxboro. The driver told me, "There's going to be 70,000 people there, I'll take the back road because it will be a nightmare on the highway."

"Don't worry about that," I said, "the concert started hours ago, and everyone is inside the show already. You'll breeze right in." I bet you can see where this story is going. Sure enough, he did not heed my advice; he took unfamiliar back roads and, you guessed it, he got lost. We had two vans filled with the band and crew roaming somewhere between Foxboro and South Walpole.

Naturally, if I had been in the van I wouldn't have let that happen. I would have been in the front seat with the driver holding his hand all the way to the stadium front entrance. I had stayed back to prep the third part of the shoot for the live show that night at the club. Worry not, for in true movie fashion they arrived with 10 minutes to spare, the band made their designated time slot and we shot the band. Oh yeah, we nailed that one!

SCENE 20

Living the Dream

The year was closing out to what was looking like another cold, quiet New England winter. The phone broke the silence: it rang, and naturally, I picked it up. There was someone on the other end asking for Mr. Monzo, the actual Italian pronunciation. There have only been two people who have pronounced my name like that. One was an Italian American at the employment agency in New York City; the other was the director David Wall. He was about to make another movie and asked me to record the sound. I informed my colleague that I no longer recorded sound, but there were many other ways I could help him. In true Hollywood fashion, we did lunch.

He drove up from the Cape, and we met at my favorite burrito bar that has since burned down. We sat, ate chips and talked about his movie. He told me his producer/AD wasn't coming into Boston until December 20. They were going to start shooting around the 5th of January. I recognized that to be a big red flag. This guy was coming in just two weeks before principal photography. There was no way he could get a movie ready in two weeks over the holiday season. I told Mr. Wall that time was critical and he needed much more of it to make it happen. I also told him that considering the budget, his hired gun was overpriced.

My only motive was to rent him gear and offer any advice I could. While we chatted over refried beans and hot sauce, I never considered producing his movie. I had a personal commitment during the first two weeks in January that was locked in stone. However, when you least suspect it, opportunity strikes. I'm sorry, lightning strikes, opportunity knocks as we discussed earlier. Either way, he offered me the job and we pushed back a month to properly prepare for *Noelle*.

I had $280,000 to put it in the can. That was when you still put movies in the can, now there isn't any cool hip expression where you can put HD. I'd like to tell you where you can put HD. I still have a strong affinity for film and no doubt I was one of its last flag wavers. I would still love to work with film, but it no longer makes sense. Even big Hollywood movies are shooting in HD. It's a digital world now and there is no going back.

With 280K at my fingertips, I was poised to make a movie. I had learned a lot and had a full bag of tricks to save money. I would tell you about all my little money saving schemes, but like a great chef I will take my secrets to the grave, unless I get hired on another feature, whichever comes first. I will tell you one thing: I galvanized a lot of community support in the form of donations from donuts to locations. Many people are happy to support the arts and like I've said, "Who doesn't love the movies?"

A film shoot's mood and experience arise out of the director's temperament. If the director is in a panic, that mood will spread. If he isn't any good, he will lose the crew's respect. Crew people live to work with a good director who knows what he is doing; it reminds them why they went into the business in the first place, to make good movies.

The mood on *Noelle* was wonderful. He respected the crew and in return they respected him and they went the extra mile for him. One morning we had to put colored gels in all the church windows. It wasn't hard, but it was time consuming. Everyone on the crew regardless of department pitched in to help. That couldn't have happened on a union show no matter how emotionally involved the crew was. One is not allowed to cross over departmental lines, and at that level they can afford to bring in enough people to make things happen in the proper amount of time. I don't even expect to see something like that on a non-union show, but on *Noelle* the vibe was right and it just happened naturally. It was actually a touching moment for me.

We had several snowstorms while making the movie, which was great for the big picture since it was a Christmas movie, and it ramped up our production value, but in the midst of the storm it was sometimes trying. One night in late February, a huge blizzard rolled in while we were wrapping for the evening. The lighting and grip truck was giving me some trouble (have you noticed a pattern yet). I wanted to move it to the next location at the end of the night, so if the truck didn't start in the morning, at least it would already be where it would live for the next four days. Everyone kept advising me to wait until morning. It was good advice, but if the truck didn't start it would be a huge setback the next day. I went over to the grips to see how much longer they estimated before we could drive the truck over. As I was standing by the lift gate a huge gust of wind came by and swung the unlatched back door of the truck. A big combo stand (light stand) fell on my head. Yes, it hurt. I was a little dazed, but not confused, but definitely in pain. It was at that moment that I heeded the wisdom of my crew and called it a night. I figured even the truck was trying to tell me something.

It was, of course, the right decision. When we brought the truck over in the morning we had to push up the electrical wires over the truck, which were hanging extremely low due to the snowfall. If we had moved it the night before we would not have seen the wires in the dark, which would have thus caused even bigger problems. We would have lost power for the shoot and I don't know how many other buildings would have been taken out as well. I always felt that was a very cosmic experience, and there was something looking out for me, but that is a topic for another time and a full pot of coffee.

One day on the set the soundman needed a second boom operator. Naturally, I was happy to pitch in for one shot. If something needs to be done and there is no one else available, you have to do it yourself. I have worked with independent producers who would sit in their big chairs and not lift a finger because it was beneath them. It's my movie and if I have to do something outside of my job description, whether it is going to the hardware store or picking up the lunch, I do it. I take that kind of pride in my work when I am at the helm. As I was the most experienced audio person on the set, I figured I should pick up the slack and boom one shot. NOT!!! That was a big mistake. I hadn't held a boom in years. I did not account for rust factor. Besides being rusty, my head was not in the game. It would be like a baseball player without any preliminary training about halfway through the season trying to pinch-hit late in a close game. I bumped the microphone on the low ceiling, I hit the director in the head with the boom pole and my phone went off in the middle of a take. That would be three strikes and I was out. The crew had a good laugh at the dumb producer who left his phone on. I thought it was funny as well. If I was the sound guy on a big movie nobody would have laughed. People would have looked at me like I just dropped the Petri dish with the only cure for cancer.

Another thing that happened on *Noelle* was that my childhood dream of making it to the big screen was finally realized. In all my time in the movie business I had never tried to get in front of the camera. I did have a brush with Korean television. I was walking down the street when I came across a movie crew. I knew the producer and he asked me if I wanted to play the restaurant manager in front of Au Bon Pain. Hey, this was the real deal, I had one very crucial line: "Get back to work, Moon Su!" Even though I nailed it, I had always felt the line would have been more impactful if it was "Moon Su, get back to work." The director assured me the line was fine as written and didn't want me to improv. I went down deep, to a place inside and brought forth the character of the frustrated restaurant manager with pent-up aggression that I held for young Moon Su. His youth and intelligence had always threatened me, which fed into my own insecurities. I thought my job was on the line, and to top it off, that morning my wife and I had fought about the operation my dog needed. It seemed he had torn his second ACL and it was going to cost us another two grand. I became that frustrated restaurateur, I wound him up and he just played.

That was television, but this was 35 mm film, baby! This was the real deal. The irony was I was so disconnected with acting it didn't occur to me anymore. However, Mr. Wall knows talent when he sees it and cast me as the Bus Driver. In the opening scene, after a long bus ride with our lead character who sees apparitions, I drive the bus into the station, look into my rearview mirror and see that he is the only one left on the bus. I say in an implying, yet nonchalant, yet very serious tone, "End of the line, Father." In that moment you just get it all. He has to get off the bus and start anew— very Bergmanesque.

The Bus Driver makes another appearance later in the film, this time with a line that will go down in cinematic history. Our lead character is at the station with a confused look in his eye. I drive the bus into the station and open the doors. He hesitates and I say the immortal line that lives forever on celluloid in my natural Brooklynese: "Are you getting on or what, bub?" If you had heard that line in the theater it would have sent chills up your spine.

It had finally happened, after dreaming the dream, giving up the dream, getting the dream back and then giving the dream up for good, I had finally made it to the big screen with a line, actually more than one. Before we filmed it, I hadn't given it any thought in that context. It was business as usual. As I walked away from the set and back to the office it hit me. It wasn't exactly the big Hollywood movie scenario, but I was finally in a movie. I'd made it. It wasn't the Clark Gable role I had imagined for myself as a youth, but still an accomplishment, which I had given up a long time before. Even though I had put that dream on the shelf, or more like in the trash, I had finally realized my childhood dream and it was fulfilling.

SCENE 21

The Nation

I had an idea that I had been mulling over since the Boston Red Sox won the World Series. I have been living in New England since 1991. I also lived in and traveled to many places around the U.S. One thing that has allowed me to connect everywhere in the good old U.S. of A. was baseball.

I have always loved baseball. I love sitting at the game on a hot summer day with a friend or even by myself, and I love that connection with the past, the relaxation of the game and rooting for my team. Since I'm originally from Brooklyn, I grew up liking both the Mets and the Yankees. There was no conflict for me, as the two home teams never played each other, so I could enjoy both of them. I watched every post-season game in '69 when the Amazing Mets stunned the big bad Baltimore Orioles. I was at Game 5 of the World Series in Yankee Stadium in '78, that day when the Yanks crushed the Dodgers. I also had a ticket in 1986 to see the Mets take the seventh game to beat the Red Sox in one of the most incredible World Series ever. My mother was able to get us into one game during the Subway Series in 2000. We rooted for the Mets, which was the only game they won.

I grew up with baseball, I played it and I watched it. Baseball was a part of my day, my family and my life. But it was nothing compared to what goes on up here in New England with the Red Sox. I never lived and died with my team each season. If they were having a bad year I would just do something else. I never took it to heart; if they lost, that was the way the cookie crumbled, or more accurately, the way the ball bounced. In Red Sox Land it is another story: the team plays a large role in family life, and it is something that is passed down from generation to generation. I would sometimes see a new mother, holding her baby in her arms, say, "There's a new Red Sox fan in the world."

The wins and losses affect the area en masse. It is part of what makes Boston so provincial. The intensity was something I had never seen in any other city. The Red Sox permeate New England culture. If you go back and watch Game 4 of the 2004 ALCS when the Yankees were on the precipice of sweeping the Red Sox and knocking them out for the year, one by one, around the stadium hands came together clasped in prayer for the sports miracle beyond miracles. It played out like a bad Disney movie. If it had been on the screen it would have been thought of as ridiculous. The Red Sox came back that night to beat Mariano Rivera, the game's all-time best closing pitcher. They buried their long-hated adversary, the New York Yankees, and went on to win the World Series for the first time in 86 years. As a baseball fan and a filmmaker I saw an opportunity to make a documentary about the fan base. It was something I knew I could do relatively cheap. I saw that there was a niche market and I thought I would be able to get it out there to the ravenous fan base that seemed to consume all things Red Sox.

It was spring of 2005. I just finished shooting *Noelle* and I was excited about this project. However, my rental business was on the decline and I was losing my workspace in Boston. I had to figure out how and where to manage the gear. I was at the end of the line with the rental business. The production company I had put together was falling apart and the movie landscape in Boston was changing. There were more people in the film equipment rental game, which meant pricing for the filmmaker was getting better. I was on the wrong end of supply and demand. Another era of my roller coaster career was ending. I saw this Red Sox movie, *The Nation*, as a vehicle to make some money and begin producing my own projects.

I put advertisements online seeking fans to be interviewed. There was a great response and I set up a space in my studio for the interviews. I traveled to various places in New England to mix it up a bit. I was also able to secure interviews with the famous Boston sports writer Dan Shaughnessy and the old-time great Red Sox infielder Johnny Pesky.

The interviews came together easily enough, but the big monkey wrench was Major League Baseball, a very uncooperative bunch of people. I tried to get footage and hit a stone wall. The Red Sox were also a dead end. I tried all my connections, but there was no joy in Mudville. I decided that since I couldn't get the footage I would just go with the interviews.

It was tough for me to meet my end-of-the-summer deadline. I still needed to make a buck and I did have some rental business left. I found another rental house that would store my gear and sub-rent it when they needed it. This turned into a huge headache down the road when the owner of the company proved to be unscrupulous. I'll save that debacle for a later chapter.

I wanted to have the final product ready for sale before the end of the baseball season. It took about six weeks longer than I expected. It was lack of funds that slowed me down. In retrospect, it was still pretty quick from concept to final product. I have a meat-and-potatoes approach to filmmaking, in that I don't waste time on what I don't need. Documentary filmmakers tend to shoot hours upon hours of footage and then go through the tedious process of watching every piece of footage to figure what will fly and what will be cut. I understood this before I rolled a frame on my first interview. I didn't want to have so much unnecessary footage to sift through. Many filmmakers enjoy this process, but time is valuable and I understand that transmutation of time is money. There is nothing new under the sun there, an age-old cliché that holds true in our modern world.

I ended up with 40 hours of footage. I could have easily shot another 40 hours, which would have delayed the final product until the beginning of 2006 and I would have missed the Christmas market. Some documentarians take years to make a movie, and although with more time I might have shot a few more interviews, I weighed that against the necessity to get it out there and made the snap decision to move it through production and post-production with alacrity.

I tried to find a distributor, but no dice. I've seen filmmakers wait for distributors until their films were past their moments, so I wasn't going to wait for one. I made a couple thousand DVD's. I picked up some press but not enough. I had been in contact with some of the zealot Red Sox fan websites and sent them copies so they could review the film. Many of them could not get around to watching it. It shocked me a little since that seemed to be a huge focus of their lives. I wondered about these ravenous fans and thought, "How many times does someone make a documentary on you and your passion?" Many of my marketing ideas did not pan out. Many of the people that I thought would at least spread the word about it did not. I had trouble getting people to screenings. I sold some copies, but not enough. I underestimated how hard it would be to sell the DVD.

It was surprising to me because I knew how much Red Sox merchandise was sold, and I couldn't understand why I was having so much trouble getting it out there. The people who bought it and watched it were very happy with it. I had a few people tell me they cried when they saw it. It touched an emotional chord inside. People seemed to enjoy it, yet I couldn't sell it.

I put too many eggs in this Red Sox basket. I thought I had a highly marketable product. I still think it is marketable; I just couldn't get it done at the time. My biggest problem was that I didn't give it enough time. It was only out for four months when a major crisis erupted at home. My financial situation was tanking hard. The bills were not getting paid. I was really up against it financially. *The Nation* had not achieved the desired results and there was a lot of pressure to get some money into the house. I was sinking fast. All of my Ralph Kramden ideas had failed. Such is the life of Ralph Kramden. I was despondent about the lack of success with the Red Sox DVD. Although the marketing had not yet run its course, I had to find work. That is when I came up with the brilliant idea that I could drive a taxi. As mentioned, I have no skill other than filmmaking. I thought I could do this and still sell my DVD.

Once I fully accepted the idea of driving a taxi, my future became quite clear. I didn't want to do sound because I didn't want to go backwards. I felt I had to go anywhere but back to sound. I know how to drive a car and I am quite adept at driving in traffic. I looked at the classifieds to see what my options were. That's as far as I took my newfound taxi career. I could have done my Travis Bickle every day in the rearview mirror: "You talkin' to me? You talkin' to me?" I'll bet that was the first print De Niro impersonation you ever read.

I hate going backwards, but sometimes the more prudent thing to do is head back. I was once walking through the Himalayas of Nepal, when I had the bright idea of heading down the riverside to get to the next town. I didn't speak the language well, but well enough to know that the locals were telling me to turn around. I ignored them. After a couple of hours of walking downriver, the rocks were getting bigger and the river narrowed to the point where I could go no further. This would have been a good time to turn around, but I thought I'd just climb these rocks and go around. After ascending 80 feet or so, I was finding out that this idea was not working out well either. "OK, OK, I'll go back down and head back." Too late, I couldn't do that either; up was easier than down. I was stuck and there was no one around for miles. After much deliberation and finally exasperation, I started to go up. I hugged the rocks and stepped on the protruding crevices to advance. "Protruding Crevices" sounds like a name for a band. I offer that to anyone in the world with no copyright infringement.

At this point, the camera pulls back to see this stupid American trekker hanging by his fingertips. Maybe I should throw in a bloodcurdling scream to set the tone, or just a resounding "Heeeeeeeeeeeeeeeeeeeeeeeeeeeeelp!!!"

Cut back to medium shot of our hero slipping off the mountainside. The music gets stronger to add to the tension. We hear a voiceover of our hero thinking to himself, "This is it. This is your life we're talking about here."

There has always been two of us inside my head. I did not know what to do, so I ad-libbed. My left hand blindly searched for something to grab onto. I felt a plant, close-up on the plant; I grabbed the plant, white-knuckle tight. I gave it every ounce of strength I had and then some. Those roots stood their ground and I hoisted myself up to safety. That was nothing short of a miracle. More about this in *Lenny Manzo: The Lost Years*. I will tell you the ending, though: I survived.

The point is, folks, it is sometimes better to go back than to go forward. I grappled with my decision. This would be a good moment for a montage scene. Medium close-up of Manzo sitting in a café with a cup of coffee; dissolve into Manzo tossing and turning in the middle of the night; dissolve into Manzo driving a taxi down Boylston Street in Boston and crashing into the Old North Church and cut to Manzo waking up screaming.

With my back against the wall I donned my headphones once more. And just like Al Pacino said in *Godfather III*, in his worst moment on the screen (not counting *Cruising*) that lives in infamy among bad immortalized film lines, "They pull me back in."

Once the decision had been made, there was no time to waste. I contacted the local IATSE studio mechanics local 481 (yes, I used the word "local" twice). I had a lovely chat with the office person on Wednesday, I spoke to the sound mixer of the TV pilot *Waterfront* on Thursday, I was hired on Friday, I was working on Saturday. This was the day I jumped on the Hollywood Express train to Palookaville. I was going through another door without knowing it. The train was taking off and I didn't even know I was on it. First stop: Providence, Rhode Island, where I spent three glorious weeks on the never-to-be-seen pilot known as *Waterfront*.

I was grateful for the swift re-entry. I was doing sound, but as an assistant. My lofty days as the sound mixer were behind me. Since I had been out of the game for six years I couldn't get my slot right back. I would have had to work for that again. I would have also had to shell out 20K to update my sound package. The technology had changed: tape had gone the way of the dinosaur. I would have had to learn a new system and I would have had to compete for work that I had no desire to do.

The other thing that had changed was the influx of movie and television work in the area. Years ago, when I started shopping myself around as a boom operator, there was minimal work in New England, and the work that was here was already sewn up. With the current advent of movie production, there was more assistant work available. At this point, it was much easier to find work at the bottom of the food chain. I just wanted to work and earn a paycheck. I could have done without the work, but it does seem to go hand in hand with the paycheck.

And thus my career as the sound utility technician and third man in the department began. This was certainly not the natural order of progression. One often begins his career as a third and works his way up. After 15 years in the biz, I became somebody's assistant. Cut to a lonely man sitting in a dive bar staring into a glass of whiskey for courage. The barmaid comes by; Kitty is her name. "Another drink, filmmaker? What happened, Sugar, fall from glory?"

"How'd you know, Kitty?"

"I've seen it before, chasing the movie mistress is worse than what any woman could do to ya. But that don't mean nothin' now. You gotta pick yourself up off the street, kid, you got talent, you can't let this stop ya."

"I don't know, Kitty."

"As John Wayne would say"—I took off my hat in solemn honor as Kitty spoke—"'Listen and listen good, Pilgrim'—no wait. Let me continue as Clint Eastwood from *The Outlaw Josey Wales*, near the end of the movie when he's giving the pep talk to his adopted posse: 'Now remember, things look bad and it looks like you're not gonna make it, then you gotta get mean. I mean plumb, mad-dog mean. Cause if you lose your head and you give up then you neither live nor win. That's just the way it is.'"

Somehow Kitty's rendition of *The Outlaw Josey Wales* made sense to me. I thought about it for a while. Suddenly, there was a choice: I could wallow in self-pity or put my helmet on, get back in the game and start clawing my way back. She poured me another drink and then we sang "The Sun Will Come Out Tomorrow" from the musical *Annie* three times.

I altered my perspective. Instead of a step backwards I saw it as a side step. I was still in the biz, yes folks, still in show business. Whether I was rationalizing or not, facts is facts. I wasn't doing what I wanted, but I was still connected to the business, which proved to be valuable later, although I didn't grasp it in the moment. I thought it was just temporary. I guess it was, just not as temporary as I thought. I jumped into the roller coaster unstrapped. I didn't know it at the time, but I was digging my foxhole for a four-year run.

At this point, I only had a few brushes with the big show and TV was a new animal. TV looked like the big show; we had a lot of people, a lot of gear, a lot of trucks and a lot of ego. TV was cheaper, it paid less, the perks were fewer and the food was several notches lower. It was also a bigger thrash. The average movie shoots about two to four script pages a day. The average TV show shoots seven to nine pages a day. There are more company moves, which means more loading and unloading. The upside is if the show hits there is job security, but if you want job security you're in the wrong business.

So after a six-year hiatus from crew work, I showed up with a flashlight in my pocket and a smile on my face. I was determined to stay upbeat. I knew most of the crowd, some were old friends and some were old idiots. If you can believe it dear reader, I didn't always get along with everyone. I had a lower tolerance for BS in my angst-ridden youth. Before I stepped onto the set I had buried all my hatchets and knocked off all the chips from my shoulder. I wiped the slate clean and treated everyone with respect. "I don't want any trouble, just put the gun down and everything will be all right."

I viewed this work as my waitress job; I told you I liked the word waitress. I would go from paycheck to paycheck until I could get the producer wheels moving again. I didn't see myself as a sound guy anymore, I thought of myself as a producer and I wasn't losing sight of that vision.

I arrived on set about 20 minutes before call. Getting there early was important. I wanted to be able to ease into the day by just being punctual instead of getting caught off guard. When I was a sound mixer I developed a habit of coming in late. Most indie features took forever to get the first shot off and since it was usually a flat rate I pushed the envelope as far as I could. It was easier to do that when I was in charge. As long as the production didn't wait on me it was a non-issue.

As a foot soldier I needed to be there on time. I was also getting paid by the hour so I didn't need to feel cheated by disorganization and ignorance. There was still plenty of disorganization and ignorance, but they paid me for that. My situation was more desperate; it was touch and go to pay the mortgage. The house was in jeopardy and I wasn't going to make punctuality an issue.

The ship sails at dawn and all must be ready. Tardiness is not tolerated and for good reason. The first part of the day requires all hands on deck to get the show moving. Every department needs every person to start the day smoothly and no one wants to get caught with their pants down. There is a bit of a stigma to having the entire company waiting on you. Lateness is tolerated the least with the drivers. The start of the show depends on the trucks' punctuality. If the gear is not there, there is no movie. There is also a very strong work ethic and sense of professionalism in this business. Let's bring in David Letterman for the last reason. Take it, Dave! "And the number one reason why film crews are always early is ... breakfast is served!"

So there I was, 20 minutes before call time, trying to get breakfast off the truck. I kept walking around, but I couldn't find the catering truck. I asked a woman with a cigarette dangling out of her mouth, "Pardon me, but could you help out a fellow American who's down on his luck." She tossed me two bits and pointed to a folding table with fifty little paper bags.

I'm like, "Seriously? Is that the breakfast? A bunch of cold egg sandwiches? There's no truck? Where's the truck?" You have to understand, it's not that I was some spoiled, entitled filmmaker. My experience had been much different on multimillion-dollar shows. I learned the differences between TV and the movies real fast.

The day began like a college reunion: I ran into people I hadn't worked with in years. They had stayed in their chosen professions and many of them had moved up the totem pole. It was nice to see so many of my low-budget pals working in the thick of the business. I had a great day catching up with some old friends and colleagues. With some people it was like just a few days had gone by, with others it was like we barely knew each other. Time does different things to different people and with some, any closeness that was shared had been washed away by the passing of the moons. They forgot the connection I thought we had. Even though it was a bit awkward with some of the people, the day and shoot went well.

The former name for sound utility tech was cable man/cable person/cable guy. It was the closest name that represented the work. There used to be a ton of cable that had to be run and moved constantly. I was the cable guy on this show, but get this, there was no cable. Everything had gone wireless, which amounted to one cable that led to a bunch of antennas. That decreased the workload by thirty to forty percent. I applauded the new technology.

The job gave me a great sense of relief. My world was crumbling and I was seconds away from putting my house on the market. My brain relaxed and the anxiety meter dropped as I saw a few ducats about to come my way. My stress level had been pretty high and the ability to pay bills was going to make life a little easier. For the first time, I also enjoyed not being in charge. I was happy just to go to work, get paid and leave the work at work.

When I pulled cable on *The Crucible*, I hated it. This time I was embracing it. I didn't want to make any of the decisions here. I just wanted to do the job, get the cash and go home. This marked the beginning of my movie mercenary career.

Night came, and as the 14th hour approached it was clear I needed to make evening arrangements—nothing risqué, just a place to sleep. This is a G-rated book. This is when I found my home away from home, the Motel 6 in Seekonk, Massachusetts, just over the Rhode Island state line. I spent many a night there staring at the barren, pale white walls and watching *World Poker Tour* on one of the six cable channels they offered. Now you know what the 6 means.

We rolled into hour 15 and the crew was getting collectively annoyed. They knew the first day was an indication of how the show was going to go. I donned a neutral face but inside I was dancing like Gene Kelly down Broadway: I was ecstatic to be in double time. This was the reason I signed on to this show, and the more money I could make in a consolidated time the better.

The producer on this show was the most diabolical producer I have ever come across and one of the most despised producers that has ever graced the industry. That was his reputation and he lived up to it. He took advantage of any loophole in the contract to screw the crew. There was no care for anyone in the workplace, and he was universally hated by every crew person in New England.

Later on when the show was picked up, I filled in a few times. The food was so bad I was forced to brown-bag it. On one such evening, lunch was served, and it was the most miraculous succulent spread I've ever witnessed on any show, especially on a show run by El Diablo. The crew rejoiced in the new mouthwatering cuisine. "The caterer is dead! Long live the caterer!"

This presentation was suspicious, something smelled fishy and it wasn't the food. It was too much, the food was of the highest caliber, the presentation was awesome, the catering staff in white shirt and black tie was over the top. I broke out my Sherlock Holmes deerstalker hat that I kept in my set kit and pondered the clues. It was just a little dog-and-pony show for the L.A. execs that came out to check up on things. That was infuriating. Of course he couldn't serve the standard gruel to the L.A. honchos. That just made him a bigger prick because it proved he knew the difference. We cursed his name and feasted that night enjoying the temporary spoils of war.

On the pilot we were run ragged. The nightmare job from hell for everyone on the crew was a blessing for me. But I never worked a job where a little rain did not fall; in this case I mean it literally. The last day on the pilot we were shorthanded. I was forced to bump up to boom. The town was busy and we couldn't find anyone to step in. Missing one out of three guys certainly kicks up the work and stress level of the department. The last day was always a long one. The forecast called for rain. Our last scene of the day was an exterior. Since they knew it was going to rain at some point they decided to make rain so the scene would match when the rain rolled in.

The special FX guys created a beautiful mist that surrounded the talent. In between shots the umbrellas came out for them so they wouldn't get drenched. I boomed the shot and stood 8 feet from the actors. Unfortunately, where I was standing the water was coming down on me like a faucet. I felt like I was in some kind of *I Love Lucy* episode and I was Lucy. I was able to step out of the monsoon and into the mist in between takes. When we did another take I was back in the monsoon. Sometimes the director would say, "Let's go right away, keep rolling." I had my rain gear on of course, but I found out that night it was old and at some point I was soaked through. Aaaahhh, the glamour of show biz!

Two AM arrived and the producer wanted to know if we union folk would waive the meal penalties, in order not to take a second break so we could finish early. As union workers we receive a small amount of money if the production fails to break us on time. This is set up as a deterrent, not as a punishment. Our second meal came due and they wanted us to waive the penalty. As you have already learned we are under contract and as union crew we are not allowed to renegotiate the deal. El Diablo is the only producer I have ever worked for that will sit you down at two in the morning to avoid a $7.50 meal penalty. Usually they get you what is called a "walking meal" and we just keep shooting. Everything keeps moving and you get out earlier.

The meal penalty waiver was shut down before the shop steward could say, "Shove that waiver up your ass." That line potentially moves me to a PG rating. We broke at 2 AM for some Tex Mex. When we went back to work the rain had picked up. We worked another hour or two and then it started to rain harder. Finally, the AD called wrap and the rain was still getting harder. The night and the job were coming to an end. It went well for me except for this crazy monsoon episode. For the rest of the crew it is known in these parts as one of the worst nightmares to ever hit our production community.

As I was performing my wrap duties I asked the script supervisor if she had her headset. The sound department supplies headsets for the crew who need to hear the dialogue to do their work. She asked me in the most condescending, nasty tone, "Why would I have a headset?"

To which I replied, "Because I've been giving you a headset every day for the last 15 days." To be honest I might have been guilty of a touch of sarcasm myself, but it was apropos. We did this every day. It was pouring buckets and I was missing equipment. I just was trying to do my job. A simple "no" would have been fine. A "no" would have been greatly appreciated. I didn't realize that she was looking for a fight. A word about script supervisors: the job is usually held by a woman, who usually has a good attitude and enjoys her work and I have worked with a multitude of them and they are all usually very nice and cooperative. Will Rogers might

have said, "I never met a script supervisor I didn't like." I would have agreed
with Will up until this fateful night.

She proceeded to scream at me at the top of her lungs, "WHY WOULD
I HAVE A HEADSET? I'VE BEEN IN THE BUSINESS FOR YEARS.
WHY WOULD I POSSIBLY HAVE A HEADSET? HOW COULD
YOU ASK ME THAT? WHAT THE FUCK WOULD I BE DOING
WITH A HEADSET? OF COURSE I DON'T HAVE A FUCKING
HEADSET!" This went on until she was forced to breathe and then I just
said, "OK, we're done," and walked away. I left there completely
bewildered. "What was that all about? What did I do to her?" The only
thing that I can say in her defense is that was her natural disposition. She
was always in a bad mood, never talked to anyone unless she needed
something or they were high enough in the pecking order to make it worth
her while. I would surmise that the business and/or life had not treated her
well and it was too much for her. It is not an uncommon occurrence after a
miserable day at work to go home and kick the dog. Apparently she needed
to kick somebody and I was in the wrong place at the wrong time.

At that point, I was totally fried and soaked. The three weeks of this
crazy moneymaker was coming to an end. Some of the gear was wet; the
soundman's mixing board was totally flooded. I'd just been berated like a
schoolboy by the script chick and the rain just kept getting harder and
harder. I stared off the back of the truck watching everyone wrap cables,
props, stands, lights and everything else. There was so much universal pain
on this show. This was my reintroduction back into the biz. I stood there in
utter disbelief, and then I just started to crack up. I just couldn't stop
laughing at the ridiculousness of the entire evening and the entire show. At
times, like this time, when I'm on a job with so many issues and
circumstances that are depressing, but somehow when things go off-the-
charts bad, it actually makes me laugh because of the absurdity. It's beyond
belief and gets me to separate myself from the situation and see things in a
better light. I left the job feeling pretty good, but not before one more kick
in the teeth. It was Thursday morning and I had to drive back home from
Providence through the morning rush-hour traffic. Oy my gevelteshmear!

SCENE 22

There's No Need to Fear, Manzo Is Here!

On the heels of *Waterfront*, *Underdog* rolled into town. "When Polly is in trouble I am not slow, it's hip, hip, hip, and away I go." That was the cry from the 1960's cartoon, which Disney turned into a live-action movie with talking beagles. We used many dogs on this one, with all of the modern-day specs observed to get the industry stamp of approval to appear at the end of the credits: "No animals were hurt during the making of this movie." I heard a story about *That Darn Cat*, the lovely Disney classic with Hayley Mills and Dean Jones. I was talking with an old-timer who had a connection with that film and I asked him how they did it back then. "Well, they killed about 17 cats."

Underdog was already in prep while I was working on *Waterfront*. There were many people jumping over to *Underdog* and a few that somehow found themselves on both shows at the same time, the art of the "double dip," and I'm not talking about an old *Seinfeld* episode. This expression was around a long time before that. It's rare, but it happens. I have never reached such elevated status. There is the legend of the "Triple Dipper," who shall remain nameless, though you might check the *Guinness Book of World Records* for most triple dips by a crew member working on a feature, TV or commercial.

I was not as fortunate as some of my double-dipping colleagues. One job was hard enough to find. The *Waterfront* dough was sweet, but I was far from out of the woods with the bank knocking at my door. I needed to create some options because there was not enough sound work. The sound mixer who just finished *Waterfront* had his regular crew for *Underdog*. I scratched my head for a while, and then when the itching stopped I pondered my next move. I spoke to one of the lighting riggers who was hiring for *Underdog*; he said, "Sure, I'll keep you in mind." I knew that didn't penetrate so I called him a few days later and told him I was serious. In life, sometimes all you need to do is show up, or at least call. He had forgotten about me, but put me on for the next day and told me to bring my gloves. I was about to get my hands dirty without getting them dirty.

Next thing I knew I was laying cable at six in the morning. Surprise, surprise, surprise! I liked it. Hey Mikey, he likes it. I liked it for a few reasons. The money was good and the work was available. I was still in the mindless just-tell-me-what-to-do-and-send-me-the-check head space. What made the work tolerable, and at times fun, was the crew I worked with. I'd known everyone for years, a few of them since they were in film school. As we laid cable and set up lights we talked about subjects that ranged from the topography in China to what was the exact quote in *Scarface*. My friend Tony always knew someone who was online somewhere to settle all disputes and wagers. That was back in the early Stone Age days of Internet, the pre-iPhone era.

The rigging world is another dimension of the movie world. We set it up and tear it down. There is a slight overlap with the shooting crew. We seldom work nights. The 5 AM call time is common, but working until 5 AM rarely happens. Even though the work was hard I didn't mind rigging. A real nice perk about rigging was that I could actually have another life. The days were shorter: 12 hours was an anomaly. I could make plans and keep them.

Rigging in the electric department is physical work. Many of the riggers enjoy the physical end of it. I didn't mind the physical part. I didn't mind hauling the 18 K-watt light. I didn't even mind being hunched over laying cable in the rain. The bane of the rigging department is the dreaded 4/0 (four ought). The 4/0 cable is a heavy, thick gauge cable used to distribute large amounts of electrical power throughout the set. The 4/0 came in several sizes; the most problematic were the hundred footers. This is one nasty cable that takes no prisoners. In *The Ten Commandments* when Charlton Heston was rescued with the Roman General somewhere in the Mediterranean, he was also rescued from his life as a slave laborer. When he passed the entrance where the men were chained to their oars, he looked down in horror at where he'd come from. That's how I feel when I look at 4/0 today.

Though the checkbook was seeing better days, *The Nation* was losing steam. I never could explore all the avenues and potential of the documentary. There were many circumstances that led up to the fall of

Lenny Manzo. That's right, it wasn't one mistake, it was a truckload. They combined with changes in the industry and changes in the world which I could not have pinpointed ahead of time.

I didn't have enough energy to work and to market *The Nation*. I threw myself headlong into the moneymaking machine of the Hollywood film factory. I needed money and they had it, and my back was against the wall. I lost what little marketing momentum I had and I gave up. I don't know if that was the right thing to do. Was it a mistake? I didn't have any energy left. I guess I also felt defeated. I had put too many eggs in the documentary basket. I neglected my rental business: it was something I didn't want to do anymore and it had been going downhill for a while anyway. My gear was getting old and I would have had some reinvesting to do. I lost my space in Boston. Everything was changing. All of a sudden I was working full-time as a freelancer and I gave into it. I figured I would just do this until I could wangle another producing gig. So I stepped into the Hollywood world, and even though I was a day player, I worked all the time.

I hopped back and forth between the electric department and the sound department. I also dabbled in set dressing. The phone rang and it was *Underdog*, asking me to come down and operate the air-conditioning; for some reason, running the AC falls under the umbrella of set dressing. This contraption cracked me up the first time I saw it. The air-conditioning comes on a trailer with a generator strong enough to power the whole set. It comes with tubing 2 feet in diameter. I had to connect the tubing and run it about 1000 feet to the set. Everywhere else on the stage people were melting; on the set it was like a refrigerator. The toughest thing about the job was just setting up and breaking down the tubing.

I was in stand-by mode the whole day until I would hear my name bellowed, "Where's the guy who moves the snake. Where's the snake man, mon? Dónde está el hombre serpiente!" You have to remember some of them didn't know my name. Can you believe it? I had just appeared back on the scene. I was popular in the day, but now there were all these new people who didn't know me yet. Anyway, I became Snake Man for two days and loved it. I would just chill the whole day drinking the great coffee from the art department room. That craft service coffee should have been flushed down the toilet, thank God there were always hot pockets of good coffee on the set. I only worked a week with the set dressers, but I never stopped going back into the art department office to grab a good cup of coffee.

Underdog was the most unique movie I worked on. When I say unique I really mean cushy. Since the heart of the movie was driven by dogs, there was so much downtime; we were always waiting for the dogs. In the meantime, it was like being at a party. We set up shop on the Rhode Island State House lawn, which felt like a picnic. We hung out on the lawn at time and a half waiting for a dog to bark or sit. The producers perked us from time to time with an ice cream truck or a Starbucks run—now that's class. Thanks, Todd.

Conversely, other crew members hated that job. They were bored to tears. They had to keep busy or their brains would implode. It takes great talent to kick back and do nothing, when nothing is called for. I have not known many people who can kick back and coast. However, I was always ready to spring into action: "When Polly is in trouble I am not slow ... "— oh, I just used that line. The main reason I didn't care is because I didn't care. I used to mix movies, I produced movies, now I was just plugging in cables and changing batteries all day. I enjoyed my time, and I was grateful for the work, but it didn't offer me anything beyond the paycheck. I did, however, enjoy the picnic.

There was only one problem with this paid holiday. It set up an awful precedent: I thought this was how many of the big shows were run. I was also a day player, so I was filling in part-time on big days and sometimes they were overstaffed, which meant minimal work. That didn't last too long; reality hit me on the next show and the Easter Bunny was never to return.

SCENE 23

Hitting the Skids

After two months of bouncing around from department to department I had nothing booked and found myself unemployed. Such is the life of a freelancer. I received an email from the union. *Game Plan* was crewing up in the construction department. They were desperate for people, as *Underdog* had sucked up most of the carpenters. I'll have you know I'm not a carpenter. I'm not even handy. I have never had an interest in building or fixing, but that didn't stop me from calling up the construction coordinator. I told him that I was not a carpenter or anything close to it, but I would be willing to do anything that required no skill. He said, "Manzo, you got moxie, I like a man with moxie. You come on down and we'll find something for you to do." He actually didn't say that; that is what he will say when I shoot the movie version of this book, a deal I'm trying to wangle this very second. He did however, hire me on the phone, and all of a sudden I was going out to build a set. I hung up the phone and wondered what I had just gotten myself into.

I showed up to work that sunny morning to start a new day in my jack-of-all-trades repertoire. Did I mention I had no skill for this craft? I want to make this perfectly clear. I know nothing, noooo-thing! Before starting a new job the studios prepare a nice startup package to read, fill out and sign. Just some disclaimers and other small-print stuff to give the studio wiggle room if you are forced to sue them for whatever reason.

I finished the paperwork and hit the shop excited to do something different. I had no idea what to expect; if I had an idea I probably would not have taken the job. I met the foreman and exchanged some amenities, and he told me to jump in with another gent who was taping cardboard to the floor. I thought, "I can do this." I jumped right into it. They were building a stage in an ice rink where The Rock's apartment would be. The Rock has since become more serious about his movie career and has changed his moniker back to his original name, Dwayne Johnson. At this time, he was still The Rock. I guess he wanted to put more distance between himself and his former wrestling world. I don't know if he made the right decision. The Rock, or Dwayne ... The Rock ... Dwayne ... The Rock or Dwayne. I say The Rock. A much cooler name, it carries more weight. Certainly there is nothing wrong with Dwayne, but The Rock has more power. We never did get a chance to talk about it.

We finished that task and my foreman asked me to grab my screw gun, to which I replied I don't have one. He said grab one from the deck. The deck was half built with plywood on top of a lightweight fiberboard. The other half only had the fiberboard. The fiberboard is placed to deaden the sound. Then you put the plywood on top and nail that onto the wood frame. The fiberboard is foam, a substance that you can punch through like superman going through a brick wall. My boss said to grab the screw gun on the deck, so I hopped on the deck and stepped on the fiberboard. Well, my foot fell right through and the leg followed all the way up to my crotch. I was not hurt physically. I was, however, mortified mentally. Everyone looked over at the noise, checked me out and went back to work. A couple of people made sure that I was all right. To me it was like a marching band had come in playing "Seventy-Six Trombones" from *The Music Man*: "Seventy-six trombones and this guy is green, everyone check this guy out now."

The "green alarm" just went off, like Kirk hitting the red-alert button on *Star Trek* and that crazy emergency sound going off. If you're completely green and there is no one to help shield you, there is no way you can hide it and I was St. Patrick's Day green when it came to construction. I knew it would come out and knew I couldn't hide it, but I hoped to blend in a little, at least more than an hour before the entire company knew it. The announcement of my greenness came and went and I was fast relegated to sweeping and throwing out the trash. Yes, ladies and gentlemen, I was now sweeping up the floor, but I was still in show biz.

I swept the whole place, emptied the trash and reported back to my supervisor to inform him that I was done. I asked him what else I should do. He said, "Just walk around, pick up stray pieces of wood, sweep and empty the trash." I did it all again and tried to find something else I could do but he said the same exact thing: "Just walk around, pick up stray pieces of wood, sweep and empty the trash." I caught on pretty quickly and stopped asking him for direction.

On I swept. I swept and I swept. I became so good at sweeping I didn't even have to think about it. I became so good I could whistle and sweep at the same time; I could even chew gum if I wanted to. One thing about sweeping, it gives you a lot of time to think. I thought this was it, I hit rock bottom in the movie business. I had done so many jobs and have had so much responsibility on a set. On *Game Plan*, all I could do to help make this movie was to gather stray pieces of wood, empty the trash and sweep.

One night I was feeling forlorn and stopped off at the dive bar where Kitty worked. Kitty was not from the area, she was from the Deep South and she sounded just like Dolly Parton. "Why Sugar, what is wrong with you? You look worse than last time. I thought you were much better after I gave you my Josey Wales halftime speech. What happened?" She poured the whiskey and I began to tell her about the entire massacre in five-part harmony.

"Well, Kitty, I'm working for Disney as a janitor. I was pushing broom on *Game Plan* and it hit me like a thunderbolt. I've hit the skids. After 15 years in the business I have plummeted. I have mixed sound on many feature films including a mega-million, major motion picture. I've rented, bought or sold every piece of film gear out there from a 35mm camera to a bag of clothespins. I produced several feature films. I have lectured at major universities such as Boston University and Northeastern on filmmaking. With all my vast knowledge of movie making and the movie business the best thing I could put together is sweeping up the stage for a dumb Hollywood kid movie."

She said, "Well, aren't you the lucky one. You are right where you want to be. Things can't get any worse: you've hit rock bottom. There's no place but up now. This is where things start to change for you, Lenny Manzo." I ordered more whiskey.

I got my butt kicked the first week. In the second week my body was adjusting and I was starting to figure out the ins and outs of the job. I was given the low-level task of taking the lunch orders. No carpenter worth his salt would ever do that. That was left to the low man on the totem pole. I embraced this job with all my soul. This was a welcome part of my day. It gave me an extended break from the monotony of the broom.

We had a 15-minute coffee break around 9:30 in the morning. Right after that I would commence the taking of the lunch orders. The gang boss suggested I take the list during the break as everyone was gathered together. Logistically and logically, it was a great idea; practically, it was a rotten idea. There was no way I was giving up my coffee break to do this gofer work. I informed him that I was a union worker and thus, working under the IATSE Area Standard Agreement, I was entitled to the said 15-minute coffee break along with my fellow union brothers and sisters. I stood up for my 15 minutes of coffee.

After the break I had to dig up paper and a pen and walk up and down the stage to make sure I found everyone and be sure not to miss anyone. I then double-checked the money and made sure it was right. You can never be too sure about that. After I knew that I had it all together, I called the eatery and placed the order. Later, when the order arrived about 20 minutes before lunch, I checked it against my master list to make sure there were no snafus. After all, a man's lunch was at stake.

Another thing I figured out was the sawdust. I swept constantly and that was starting to get to me. I didn't mind sweeping; I just minded sweeping all day. I realized there was no real hurry to sweep up the sawdust. I thought, why pick it up at two inches. I'll wait until four inches or even six inches before I pick it up. It won't make much of a difference, no one will care and I won't destroy more brain cells with the inane, dull, drone-like work.

Can I tell you something about the construction department? They don't even know that they're working on a movie, in the sense that on a movie, there is always some downtime. Either you are waiting for them to set the shot or they are shooting and you have to wait while they are shooting to get back to work. There is always some downtime. In construction, there is no downtime. I figured that out pretty quickly too. The gang boss said to me after a week, "You figured one thing out: you don't stop moving." In construction, you are like a shark: if you stop moving you die, or in this case you get fired.

There is also a very strong work ethic in the construction department. It is very head down: don't come up until the work is done. Many of the workers in all the departments have great work ethics. It isn't the same for all the folks above the line. This business is a real slush fest. The top dogs are raking it in and getting perked with a ton of amenities. This mentality trickles down to the crew who get perked and housed and given extra money if they are in demand. Everyone is getting some piece of the pie and there is plenty to go around. The slush fest comes to an end in construction. It is strictly meat and potatoes, work and go home.

A man can do a lot of thinking while sweeping a floor 10 hours a day. What did I think about besides the next break? I'll tell you what I thought. I thought, "This is not how my movie career is going to end. I was going to figure this thing out. I didn't know how, but to paraphrase Scarlett O'Hara, 'As God is my witness, I'll never sweep the floor again.'" That emancipation felt great. It gave me hope and my spirit didn't break. I held my head high and continued to sweep.

I was working on *Game Plan* for several weeks and things changed; I really got into a groove. The crew tripled so my lunch order was taking up half the morning, and the guy who was supervising me left due to a family emergency. I actually had nobody to answer to. I was still fetching wood and keeping the place clean but I was no longer receiving extra mind-numbing tasks, like the day I had to clean all the construction coordinator's personal rusty tools that had gone to seed.

As I got to know the carpenters, some of them started to teach me stuff and let me do more wood work. I was starting to learn about building things. After being in that environment for some time I embraced the work. I lost a few pounds and I was feeling pretty good physically. I was glad some of the guys were taking an interest in me, and letting me do some work that required more skill. I was using tools and getting a real feel for this work. I really went through some type of transformation. I told my father all about it and he was quite shocked. My father was a construction worker himself for some time, but was unable to pass down his skills to his disinterested son. At 45 years old I was finally learning some basic building skills and appreciating it.

There I was, pounding nails, carrying wood, sawing wood, sweeping it up and strangely enough, I liked it. Work was ramping up; we were doing 12-hour days and went from working six days to seven days a week. At the height of the job the foreman called us in for an early-morning crew meeting. "First of all, I want to say what a great job y'all been doing, a great job." I thought here it comes, I knew we were way behind schedule, we had already gone to a seven-day week, I thought we were going to be ramped up with even more overtime. "Yesterday, during rehearsal, The Rock tore his Achilles. We are in an official holding pattern. Don't build anything, don't cut anything and don't hammer anything. Just hold off until I get back to you."

The silence was so thick you could cut it with a knife. I know it's an old cliché but what else do you cut thick silence with? Anyway, "Wow! What's going on?" I'll tell you what was going on: we were on our way to the unemployment line. I thought of every Achilles injury I had ever heard of and it was an injury that would bench an athlete for the rest of the season. What a turn of events. The whole crew was just blindsided. Now with absolutely nothing to do, all that we could do was talk, and talk begat speculation and speculation begat rumor.

One of the carpenters started a rumor that The Rock was holding out for more money and he was convinced The Rock, or rather Dwayne, was faking it. That idea was preposterous since he had already cut a multimillion-dollar deal playing the lead role in a family movie that he was using to change his image. It was great to watch the rumor mill in progress. The carpenter mentioned that to me as speculation; a few days later, I heard others passing it off as fact. Rumors fly around in this business and people love to chat and gossip. It's like the telephone game you played as a kid. Information is passed; facts are watered down or left out, changed, stirred and shaken, then spat out as unsubstantiated, full-bodied rumor.

So under orders we did nothing. I wasn't into the movie folding, but I was going to enjoy *The Last Days of Pompeii*, doing as I was told: nothing. I took out a book and sat in the sun. After a while, I came in for a drink and there was one carpenter in the back of the stage working. Then the other guys start mumbling to each other, "What's he doing back there."

"I think he's working."

"He's working?"

"He's working."

"Yeah, he's working all right." Then here it comes: "Maybe we should be working too."

"Yeah, if he's working, we should be working."

"Let's work then."

This blew me out of my socks. Here we were under strict orders that came down from some head honcho at Disney to cease and desist all further work. What part of that was unclear? All these guys started to work again. Therefore that meant yours truly had to go to work again. This was ridiculous beyond belief. They continued to build a set that we were going to have to start tearing down in a couple of days.

Ultimately this is not my kind of work. I don't need to work for work's sake. I realized that these guys and many other people that I work with go out of their minds if they are not kept busy. Downtime is only handled well by a few of us professionals. If I have to help build a wall for the apartment, I build it. If I have to move all the cable because it's in the shot, I move it. If the set has any debris on it, I clean it, and so on and so on. The one thing I can't take is busy work; creating work to fill the time. I feel I can manage my own free time. I don't want to fill it up with idle nonsense, especially idle nonsense like building sets that are going to get torn down.

After a couple of days it was clear that The Rock was down for the count, and the show was on hold. The location was only rented through the summer. It was going back to a skating rink in the fall. Even when The Rock—excuse me, Da-wayne, when Dwayne got healthy they were going to have to find a new location. So we had to take apart the stage and number everything so that we could put it back together when the time came. A third of the stage was useless because we just poured fresh concrete two days earlier. This had to be broken apart and put into the dumpster.

I learned some new skills and I am 10 times handier around the house. I did a few more days on construction later that year but it was even worse. It was demolition. Demolition is nasty work. This is sledgehammer work; just think rock pile in those old prison movies, that's demolition. That was it for construction and me. Some things are just not meant to be. I worked about three more weeks on *Game Plan* before it closed down. I jumped back on *Underdog*, which was still going on. Many of the guys were either moving on to other projects or vacations, so I was able to carve out a slot on the last five weeks of the show. I was there to the very last day the company wrapped and had a great time picking up the mountains of cable all over Providence.

SCENE 24

What I Really Should Do Is Direct

It was the fall of aught-five and movies were coming to town. It was so busy for me that I had options coming out of my, ahem, ears. Due to a huge tax incentive, Rhode Island was luring many movies to the Ocean State. Massachusetts did not have one on the books yet so it was still a movie ghost town with tumbleweeds and dust storms. The Seekonk Motel 6 was officially my second home. It was the closest thing to a prison cell I have ever stayed in. It was clean but this hotel chain is the king of no frills. It is the barren white walls that give it its correction facility feeling. After being put near the laundry and some other poorly placed rooms I found one that was fairly quiet and I nestled in there for about two years on and off. There is a multiplex cinema right across the street that I never saw the inside of. I was always too tired to go to the theater. It was just me and the remote, holed up on the outside of Providence watching the *World Poker Tour*, History Channel and an occasional movie that caught my eye.

I'm going to tell you another little secret about yours truly: I don't have cable at home. There, I said it. I said it and I'm glad. I have a very philosophical view about it: TV sucks. Shall I clarify? It's a great invention that has been abused since its inception. It is a big time suck and more often than not there is nothing on the mega-amount of channels I want to watch. I sit in the hotel on my third or fourth pass through the repertoire of stations and realize nothing is interesting to me. Since I am on the tail end of the baby boomer generation, I grew up with free television. I never could make the crossover to paid television. It is no small sprinkle out of the income; most people are paying around fifteen hundred bucks a year for their entertainment packages. This is my small way of protesting the industry ripping off the people; just call me a media tree hugger.

The area was heating up, and not unlike a baseball free agent, I had my choice of more than one place to play. A slot in the sound department was open on the film *Evening*. This was a drama that could have been viewed as a "chick flick." It was star-studded with big actresses. Claire Danes was the lead, and she was supported by Meryl Streep, Glenn Close, Toni Collette, Vanessa Redgrave and Natasha Richardson. It had a stellar cast, mediocre script and novice director. The movie speaks for itself. It is a dull, slow-moving, pointless film that crashed at the box office.

The director was foreign and spoke with an accent. I noticed several times some of the bit players would just nod their heads as if they knew what he was saying and repeat the same action he was trying to have them avoid. This gave me a little comic relief. Comedy had become the glue for me in this business, especially in the Hollywood world. There is always some real-life satire going on in the back bowels of a movie set.

Working as a sound utility technician, script approval very rarely comes into play as a deciding factor for working on a movie. I ask myself one question: Do I have anything else booked for that time frame? If the answer is no, I take the job. If I have another option I take the higher paying job. If they are the same pay I seek the better conditions. It comes down to simple math. *Evening* was also my first full feature since my crew comeback. I had eight weeks of solid work and in the movie industry we call that a full-time job.

There was a shift taking place inside of me. It was on *Evening* that I began to tire of the day-to-day work in the Hollywood trench. On one hand, I was grateful for the work; on the other hand, I knew I had other skills I could utilize. It was just six months previous I'd been happy just to have a job and happy for the comfort of not having to think for a while. Being in business the last few years and having it crash around me made the daily grind of just going to a mundane job great. Once, I was washing dishes in Aspen, Colorado. I was in tough mental anguish at the time. I just needed to go to work every day to make some money and figure out what I was going to do. I washed dishes six days a week, sometimes seven. After three months solid I looked up and said, "What the hell am I doing washing dishes?" I finally snapped out of my depressive trance and realized quite abruptly that I was wasting my valuable time cleaning silverware. That's exactly how I felt on *Evening*.

We did many nights on *Evening*; the title was a dead giveaway. The nights could be pretty cold in Newport, Rhode Island, even in the fall. We also had our share of rain. One night, there was a huge storm and we were slated for night exteriors. There was no way under the present conditions we could get anything done. For some reason, there was no backup plan that night. The production staff deliberated for a while and closed down for the night. Twenty minutes into the wrap, the storm stopped. They had shut down a little prematurely. The cast and crew have eight-hour minimums. The wise thing would have been to wait it out for several hours as they were on the hook for a day's pay anyway. Who am I to argue with the great minds of a movie production staff? This was, however, a welcome break for the staff and we went home very early that night.

I was in a difficult situation; the work was fast becoming boring and painful, heavy on the painful. I had no choice. With my family obligations I had to keep on working. The last six months had been good, but I still struggled. At least I was on a good path. I had accomplished the task of bringing money into the house, but I wanted to find better work. The salary was good, though more money never hurts. I either wanted fewer hours or more control of my hours. I wanted more freedom; I did not want to be ball-and-chained to the set of somebody else's movie. I wanted more freedom. Yes, Freedom. (Follow along now with Aretha Franklin's "Think": "You better think (think), think about what you're trying to do to me, yeah, think (think), let your mind go, let yourself be free." Put the book down and run around the room singing à la Blues Brothers circa 1980.)

We did have one truly magical night on *Evening*, at least it felt that way to me, and it was rather Felliniesque. There were balloon lights throughout the woods. Helium-filled balloons that lit the night sky, a great soft light that looked brilliant in the woods. There were multicolored E-Z UP tents all over, covering people and equipment, which added to the festive look. The craft service was in high gear with an array of food from sliders to deep-fried turkey. The smell of beef permeated the air and everyone was eating into the wee hours of the morning. The moon was three-quarters full, which added to the overall beauty of the night. The cast was in full party, high-society 1940's garb, which heightened the elegance of the night to create a world that seemed to exist in that moment. Two 1946 Buicks in mint condition rounded out the visual text. It was one of those nights when all the elements came together to manifest a unique experience that went beyond movie making, an evening of magic that was serendipitously created by light, costumes, props and people. Something unique and beautiful came together through a multitude of factors on a semi-warm evening in the fall in Southern Rhode Island, a rare night when the Hollywood magic affected my soul.

It was on *Evening* that I had my grand epiphany: I was ready to direct a movie. I had been in the biz for over 15 years; I knew I could do it. I learned it by osmosis. I had been kibitzing on the side for my whole career. I analyzed everything on a movie set; whether it was the hero's death scene or the inefficient shuttle system to lunch, I picked apart the movie machine constantly.

Glenn Close had a small part and played Claire Danes's love interest's mother. She heard the news of her son's death and she started wailing like a widow at her mobster son's funeral. I thought it was the wrong direction and explained it to the set dresser that was standing next to me. "She needs to have a more subtle approach, she is from New England, she's proud, she's a strong woman. We should see this and she should struggle to contain herself and crumble inside."

To which my esteemed colleague said to me with an edge of sarcasm, "Maybe you should direct the rest of this picture Len." He was joking, but I didn't disagree. I realized I could do it. Between years of watching movies and years of working on them, I had the knowledge to do it. I was confident about it, but at the same time I hadn't a clue what I could or would do about it. It is tough to find a producing gig; the director's chair is much more elusive.

After years of operating from the peanut gallery and offering my two cents to whoever had a handy ear to bend, I was hit with the brightest light bulb since starting on this crazy adventure called show biz. I stood on the set in awe of my new ability and saw the light much in the same way John Belushi saw the light in *The Blues Brothers*. I heard an angelic symphony and saw visions of deceased directors in my head: Cecil B. DeMille, John Ford and Jean-Luc Godard. Godard was useless in this vision—I couldn't understand a word he said—but the other two bastions of cinema urged me on. The music changed and I was in the middle of a 1940 Busby Berkeley musical. The whole cast and crew started to tap dance around me, while the grips and electricians jumped into a nearby pond and kept the rhythm while doing synchronized swimming. I walked over to the pond to get a closer look and started to get wet from the splashing. It was at that moment

I realized that it was actually raining, and it was time to come back to earth. I grabbed a tarp to cover the sound gear.

I came to the conclusion that I could direct. I knew how to do it. So what was I going to do about it? The short answer was nothing. Given my present circumstances of house, wife and kids, there was no practical way to pursue it. While I was still struggling for grocery money, it was preposterous to try to segue into directing at that point. As bright as the bulb was, it was impractical and farfetched for the moment. I continued chiming in on the sidelines and pontificated to anyone with the interest or patience to listen.

SCENE 25

Boxing Day

Evening ended and I wasn't too worse for wear. I hustled a few days here and there where I could get them. I picked up some commercial work booming and filled in with the riggers here and there. I was called for a night on *Dan in Real Life* with Steve Carell and Juliette Binoche. The utility person needed a day off so I headed back to Newport for the evening.

It was near the end of the shoot, in the middle of the evening, that the entire supporting cast including Dianne Wiest and John Mahoney were wrapped. After huge applause by cast, crew and everyone in between, the actors proceeded to hug each other. They were all quite moved by the artistic experience of the filmmaking process. They seemed to have deeply touched each other. It was quite a large display of emotion, all led by a highly emotional director who was bawling his eyes out. This guy was a faucet of emotion. When I arrived on set I was informed that he wept daily.

They were all having this beautiful experience while the rest of the crew was just waiting around for it to be over. Very few of the crew watched what was going on. It was clearly a time that one could spend a few moments smoking a butt or grazing at the craft service table. After watching the biggest end-of-summer-camp display of emotions I had ever witnessed, I realized how deep in the sand the line was drawn that separated the above-the-line and below-the-line factions.

It was an educational moment for me. I thought about it for a few minutes. Should I hug the various actors? Should I start to cry and sob and hug the DP and hug the director? Just jump right into it? Practicality stopped me from making an idiot of myself, but the fact does remain, in this capacity I am clearly not seen as part of the collective force when it comes to the process. I don't really mean me specifically, I mean the collective crew me. I mean the crew in general. It felt as though we crew people were supporting the creative team as they stood on top of a massive drink tray on our backs. It is similar to the servants of a wealthy family working on Christmas Day to help create the joyous moment for their employer at their own expense, never being allowed to participate in the experience. A separate humanity exists on the film set; the director, producers and actors create a wall around themselves and the below-the-line crowd is not permitted in.

On the set we have what is known as "the video village." This is where the muckety-mucks hang out on the set. They sit under an E-Z UP tent, which protects them from sun. The sides go up to protect them from wind and rain. Heaters are brought in if it is cold. Why not, hell, they're paying for the whole thing. It is just an odd thing to have this upper-class island in the middle of a blue-collar neighborhood. In most towns the rich folk all live on the hill with big mansions, away from the working class. At a major company, the corporate offices of the executives are very plush and down the hall. On the film set the executive suite just happens to be right in the center of everything.

It is odd because depending on who they are and who you are, or more likely what your job is, they don't even see you. There are many producers, directors and actors who you see and work with on the set that will not talk to you because you are so low on the totem pole it would waste their time.

On my first introduction into the business I was unaware of the gap. Since I broke in on independent low-budget movies, the line was thinner. Many of the actors had not made it yet. Also, as the sound mixer, I had daily contact with actors as I had to interact with them about the sound. While wiring the actors, we would discuss placement of the mikes or we would talk about baseball, movies, France or whatever. There was more contact naturally. When I was a third, the actors rarely interacted with me. Many avoided eye contact or ignored me altogether. Does being a highly paid artist put you at a higher status in the world? We know the answer to that is yes. Hollywood actors are today's royalty. Society has put them on this ginormous plinth if you will, from which they are adored and envied. I believe it is the envy that keeps them so high up there. Everyone craves their 15 minutes of fame and more if they can get it. Society has led us to believe that it is the new American dream. Follow it to the floor of *American Idol*; with Simon out of the way I'm sure it's a piece of cake.

And thus ended my first year in the movie trench. This movie work was different for me. I was no longer in charge. Even if I wasn't in charge of the production I used to be in charge of a department. In the beginning of the year, I was under such mental pressure that I appreciated the neck-down work. Not that you don't need to have a good head on your shoulders to do this work; in fact, the film business bottom-feeders are a highly educated bunch. Neck down in the decision making process only. The stagehand salute is similar to your standard military salute, except you salute outwards from the neck. After hand and arm are fully extended you drop the hand briskly, accentuating the neck-down aspect of your job.

The year was bittersweet. I had managed to keep my head above water due to the steady flow of work. The house was no longer in danger, which decreased my stress and made the home life smoother. However, my body paid the price for the financial success. I tore some muscles in my back from the dreaded 4/0. I spent the whole year at the bottom of the food chain, where one's opinions are better left unsaid, and had some nasty nights working till dawn. Even though I managed it well, it wasn't what I wanted to do. At times, I thought about my fantasy taxi job. I do recall they have heat in most of the cabs.

SCENE 26

Kobayashi Maru

The winter blanket fell over New England and with its usual punctuality the New England film community shut down for 2006. Producers prefer not to shoot here in the winter. I prefer not to shoot here in the winter. I hate working here in the winter. I can go on at great length about New England, winter, work and my natural repulsion toward it.

This time, the slow winter was helpful to me. I was free to pursue other work—producing work, that is, swimming pools and movie stars. I turned over some rocks, made some calls and put out some feelers. I checked out all the film-related work sites, looked at Craigslist every day. Finally, a call came in from WGBH, the flagship for public television. They asked me to come in for an interview.

I arrived to find out that it would be a conference call as the director/producer was out of town. This was a first, but it was fine. I was in the room with another GBH producer and an associate producer. We were all hunched over this little box on a glass coffee table. After yelling into the speakerphone for 20 minutes, they said, "It sounds good, we'll get back to you." It was a step up from "don't call us, we'll call you." Actually, I was very confident; the interview went well and I felt like they were going to hire me.

My instincts were correct and I was hired. I was content with the rate and ready to rip into the job. Now the bad news: they handed me a preliminary budget of $2.5 million, and I had to slash 40%. That's right, I had to cut a million bucks out of the budget. "Well, a ... OK ... uh ... yeah ... uh ... I'll get started."

This was the GBH version of *Star Trek*'s Kobayashi Maru, the test for all future starship commanders where they are set up to fail, although I didn't know it at the time. They weren't consciously setting me up to fail, but the task was insurmountable. My only mistake on this job was that I tried to comply with their wishes.

I hope you have been able to keep up with all the *Star Trek* references. I have seen every episode from the original series at least 10 times. I watched it in its first run. My mother and I watched it every Friday night at nine. It was a sad day when it was taken off the air. I've seen all the movies up until they killed Kirk; they could have left him in the Nexus. It was tough to see my hero go down after all these years. All the answers in our troubled world can be found in many early *Star Trek* episodes.

The GBH show was a low-budget project pretending to be bigger than it was. They already had several producers on the project. Now they were hiring somebody else to do the work they didn't know how to do. I really thought it was odd that they needed a line producer. Wasn't there anyone at GBH who knew how to budget a film? The short answer was no.

The task was impossible from the start. They had a massive CGI (computer-generated images) budget, which they refused to cut. That was the biggest problem with the show and they weren't going to budge on that. They hired two directors for the same project. The first one was also a producer and the writer, and was experienced in documentary filmmaking. GBH felt that the project called for a second director to handle the narrative portion of the movie. These were re-creation scenes with minimal dialogue and they didn't want to take a chance without an experienced helmsman. That question certainly can be debated, but the additional expenses of the second director, an assistant and his air and hotel arrangements were weighing heavily on this little old would-be $1.5 million budget. It didn't end there because he insisted on using his L.A. casting director, where there was no negotiation on rate, which trickled down to out-of-town actors, who also needed flights and housing. It was hard for me to believe we couldn't cast this thing locally.

Even though I knew it could not be done unless they decided to make some major cuts they were married to, I did the best I could to augment what was in my control. I waded through the script with a fine-toothed comb. I took out my hacksaw (calculator) and went after the money. I slashed, I cut, I carved and I shaved. I sliced, diced and made some julienne fries. I scheduled and rescheduled this thing, trying to eliminate as many shoot days as possible. I worked night and day to make this thing happen. I eventually finished the budget and met my deadline. I presented it to the executive producer and we set a meeting with the execs at GBH. To my astonishment they could not meet with us for another week. I was flabbergasted. When I started the project time was supposedly of the essence.

I still had plenty of other work to do. There were more arrangements to be made and the crew needed to be hired. I knew finding a crew was an issue, because Boston had a lot of production in the pipeline. I carried on until that fateful day at the GBH office, where we had our budget meeting. I showed up about 10 minutes early and then my producer showed up. Then the big guy came out of his office and asked if I wouldn't mind waiting while they just chatted first. Of course I said, "Yes"; it wasn't really a question, just a polite way of saying, "Wait outside." I have to tell you, that felt like a bad omen. Maybe you don't believe in omens. OK, it was a bad sign. All right, you don't believe in signs. Well, it wasn't good. I knew something was wrong immediately. Naturally, since this meeting was about my budget and I wasn't invited to the meeting, the only thing I thought it could be, after I applied some basic grammar-school math, was that my job was on the line. "This is not good" was the phrase that was churning around in my head.

After about 40 minutes, I thought, "This can't be just about me, this is bigger than me." That started to make me feel a little easier. Another 20 minutes went by, then my producer came out of the room. I was right, it wasn't about me, and it was indeed about something bigger than me. It was about the whole project. They decided after dragging their feet and making an unrealistic budget to pull the plug on this creative team, cut their losses and figure it out from scratch.

Wow! What a storm! And a storm that I did not survive. The worst part about it was that I didn't even get to speak to the executive producers about the budget. They hired me to bring the budget down. I would have thought that we could have at least discussed it. I had not lowered the budget to the desirable number. I also did not have the authority to change any of the creative aspects. This was the proverbial rock and a hard place, which was later replaced by the phrase, book and movie of the same title, *Catch-22*, or damned if you do, damned if you don't. Caught behind the eight ball? They got you by the balls, would be stretching it. Let's just say in good old-fashioned American English, I got screwed.

They fired me with dignity and gave me two weeks' severance pay. I was back out on the street. Wait a minute, the phone rang! "Who is it?"

"It's the crackerjack producing team over at GBH."

"Really? What do you want?"

"The show's back on. Do you want to come back?"

I said, "Is the Pope Polish—I mean, German? Put me in coach, I'm still ready to play." Hey, I'm back in biz!

"Let's talk tomorrow and we'll go over the details."

Ring, ring, the call came. "Well, we have good news and we have bad news, first the good news—oh, there is no good news. The bad news is we changed our minds again. Forgive us, Len, for we know not what we do."

I have to say, when the initial ax fell on yours truly, I handled it pretty well. I had just missed out on a production manager job two months prior, a two-million-dollar movie on Cape Cod. I knew the line producer and I had a great interview. I counted those chickens way before they hatched. After all, I knew the line producer and the production manager was his right arm on the movie. He succumbed to pressure from higher up and hired their "recommendation." I was depressed. I thought that was my job. When I snapped out of my mental agony, I decided that I would approach future jobs as if anything could happen and that nothing should ever surprise me enough to devastate me emotionally.

After I was sacked from GBH I just rolled with the punches and moved on. Even though I lost my job and didn't get the other one I was in the running for, I felt like I was at least in the game. I was getting interviews and hired, so there was progress. Always the glass half-full guy, even when there's just a sip in the glass.

That was my brush with public television. What is it about this business that makes it so hard to do right? It does happen, people do it right. It's just rare. So I was like Humphrey Bogart in Paris looking for a job. There were movies shooting already: *21* with Kevin Spacey and a TV pilot that just pulled into town called *I Am Paige Armstrong*. If you are wondering why you haven't heard of it, it is because 80% of pilots do not get picked up. A network will do about 10 pilots in the late winter and early spring. Only two or three will go into production. A pilot will run about three to six million. They'll drop about 50 million and pick three shows. The other pilots go into the trash—I mean, archives.

Paige called and asked if I would help out in the lighting department. There was no hesitation, I grabbed the work and headed down to

Providence. So I kept up the false bravado until I was on the job. I was forced to leave my nice cozy heated office, with the sweetest little coffee pot you ever did see. If that wasn't enough, there were three cafés and a Starbucks within walking distance. Once again, man is forced to leave paradise.

What I missed more than the coffee, if you can believe that was possible, was the heat. I love heat, did I mention how much I love heat? Now, I don't need it to be a sauna or anything, but a nice warm office with a coffee pot sends me halfway to nirvana. It was cold outside. Did I mention that it was cold out? I tried my best to just pick up the pieces, but being forced out into the elements, and the reality of losing four months of work in my specialized craft with the possibility of taking that momentum somewhere else, devoured my psyche.

I was chained once again to the oar of my captor's boat. The reality of another year in the trench was setting in. I would like to define the trench. To begin with, the crew trench is really a personal perspective. There are so many people lining up for these jobs. Most crew don't see it as a trench. Most people who work on movies generally like their jobs. Many are happy with the pay and the perks. They like what they're doing and they like the lifestyle attached to it. I would be happy if I were doing what I wanted as well. As a producer I give every ounce of my 110% to the project. I can't say I have that kind of zeal when I hold a boom or set up a light.

I thought I'd taken the job loss with a grain of salt. When I arrived in Rhode Island to work on another dumb pilot, I slipped, or rather fell—no wait, I nosedived—no, that's not it either, I collapsed, yes, I collapsed. Thank you for bearing with me on that one; I do try ever so hard to find the right word. (Here's a secret I'll share: I sometimes, yes sometimes, but only sometimes, use a thesaurus.) Yes, friends, I collapsed into a depression. I went downhill so fast, like Calvin and Hobbes on a snow sled. I plummeted like an overpriced stock.

In the blink of an eye, I went from landowner to slave. It was tough; it was so bad I dropped my Lenny Manzo poker face. Yes, dear reader, I left the happy hat on the windowsill and I wasn't going home to get it. A co-worker noticed that something was wrong: "Are you all right? You don't look like your usual self." It was a rare moment for me to let my guard down publicly. I usually would save that for the ride home. As Bogie says right before he sends Mary Astor up the river for life in *The Maltese Falcon*, "I'll have some rotten nights ... but that'll pass." I knew that I wasn't going to need just a few days to shake this one off.

This job was only a week. It came, it went and then I found something else and was looking at another year of the same stuff. I want you to know that I don't stay down for long. I do hit rock bottom emotionally from time to time, but I don't stay there. This would be a good time to insert the song "Tubthumping" by Chumbawamba. Feel free to sing along: "I get knocked down, but I get up again, you're never going to keep me down, I get knocked down, but I get up again, you're never gonna keep me down, I get knocked down, but I get up again, you're never ever gonna keep me down. I get knocked down, but I get up again, you're never ever gonna keep me down!" It is really much better with music.

When I was a young single man, I always had the option of quitting and starting anew. If things were not working out I could change my circumstances. It is not as easy with a family. My options have decreased and other things become more important or at least take precedence over things as frivolous as what you really want to do with your life.

Moving up in this business is hard. There are many people already ahead and many others at the same level as I am. Then there is a huge population of other wide-eyed people either behind me or coming up with the bright idea of getting into the film business. If that is your case, you can call me. I do consulting at reasonable rates. I'm trying to model my ads similarly to Hulu's: quick and hopefully not too annoying.

I finished *I Am Paige Armstrong* and picked myself out of the gutter and crawled over to see Kitty. Even though Kitty had been tending bar most of her life, she was a hidden sage amid the backdrop of the restaurant. This time, she said, "Now sweetie, every time you have a setback you just fall apart. This is show biz, baby, you can't give up now. Look how far you've come already. Now I'm no tea-leaf reader, but I think you got something, something inside worth getting out. Remember it takes years to become an overnight sensation. Longevity is the key. Who heard of Tommy Lee Jones before *The Fugitive*? He kicked around Hollywood for years. He lands a colorful role supporting Harrison Ford, next thing you know he's the biggest thing since French toast. For God sakes, don't make me sing another chorus from *Annie*!"

The GBH job was gone and nothing was going to bring it back to life. The coffee machine was gone, the heater was gone, the neighborhood cafés a stone's throw from the office were all gone, the steady paycheck was way gone. After being thrown out of Kitty's place at 3 AM I realized that she was right. I woke up the next morning and like Jackie Gleason in *The Hustler* I threw cold water on my face and jumped back in the game.

SCENE 27

You Meet the Same People on the Way Down

The next stop on the big-budget bandwagon was the Showtime episodic TV show *Brotherhood*, an Irish *Sopranos* set in Providence, Rhode Island. This is ironic, because Providence is known for its Italian population. Fortunately, with show biz we have what we call the suspension of disbelief, a fancy term for smoke and mirrors. You watch, accept the situation, and more stuff gets piled on top.

Brotherhood was a temporary staple in New England production work. They shot the pilot and all three seasons here. I didn't get a regular spot, but it filled some days. I didn't mind doing this one part-time; it was always a thrash, but you already knew that since it was television. One of the allures of movie making is the different locations and interesting places you could wind up. *Brotherhood* was the antithesis of that. We shot at the stage several times a week and the same bars and houses in Providence. It was a dull job, and yes, bad food.

I was getting fewer and fewer days on *Brotherhood*, and then one lone feature rolled into town. It was *27 Dresses* starring Katherine Heigl, who was riding the wave of success from her hit show *Grey's Anatomy* and was just making her move to movies. She has a great flair for comedy on and off screen, which worked out for me. I had my boom pole extended about 14 feet and I was adjusting my cable. As I was wrapping the cable around the pole I lost my grip for a second. Ms. Heigl was having a casual conversation with Judy Greer and Edward Burns. You can see where this one is going, or rather where the boom was going. It came straight down and just grazed her forehead. The three of them just started cracking up. Fortunately for me, no one else saw the runaway boom pole. Of course I apologized and she just waved it off. If Katherine had a nasty disposition I could have easily been fired.

Since I am coming clean with my misadventures as a boom op, there were a few other close calls that I have kept locked away and never told a soul about. On *Surrogates*, I was sitting on top of a 12-foot ladder and the same thing happened: I just missed the head of Bruce Willis and caught it before it hit the glass table, catastrophe narrowly averted. I did clip Ben Affleck in the leg, but that wasn't serious; he didn't even notice. Hollywood is a much safer place now that I have hung up my boom pole.

Getting on *27 Dresses* was a double-edged sword. Yes, I needed the work. The big issue for me was working with an out-of-town mixer. They always sound great over the phone, but I knew I couldn't trust that. When I was first mixing movies in Boston, I worked with a budding DP who used to tell me, "You're not like most sound guys." At the time, I wasn't sure what that meant. Actually, I didn't know what that meant. I was afraid to pry. Now, I'll tell you what he meant. The average soundman in the motion picture business is a highly trained, well-skilled professional, and for some reason many of them are the uptight anal-retentive types. There is some type of paranoia that many mixers seem to have in common. Many of the guys I worked for are overly fastidious and overreact to minutiae that doesn't make a difference. It only makes a difference to the utility tech, because he is the one dealing with the sound mixer freaking out. After working and observing quite a few of these guys, I would say they are the most anal people on the set. That says a lot, because the camera people are also wound up tight.

So the out-of-town boss is always a wild card. It never worked out for me, which was the case on *27 Dresses*. A day didn't go by without the sound mixer yelling at me for something, either something I missed or something that had nothing to do with me. One minute he's thanking me for my work, the next minute he's flipping out.

Another bad omen—as you can see, I do believe in omens and signs. I am, however, not superstitious. I see something and it gives me a feeling of what is about to come, the proverbial writing on the wall. This time, the foreboding feeling was the resemblance the mixer had to my grandfather. I'd worked for my grandfather when I was a kid and it was no picnic. He also had a crazy temper; nice guy for the most part until something went wrong. He always had a quick joke for his customer or passerby, but when something didn't click he would blow his top. This initial connection made me feel uneasy, especially since he had been dead for 20 years. At first I thought it was an apparition. An apparition would have been better; this was real.

I had my back against the wall and nowhere to go. I had to suck it up for the eight or so weeks of an awful work situation. It was a shame because otherwise this was one of the best shows I've ever worked on. The producers were friendly and nice. As I mentioned, Ms. Heigl was lovely and Ed Burns was one of the friendliest actors I've ever worked with. This was the first big show where the director knew me by name. Believe me, that is impressive. Thanks, Anne, you were a peach.

It was also the first big-budget comedy I did. I learned quickly that comedies are the best shows to work on; everyone is in a good mood. Humor is the goal and it makes for a nice light working environment. The mood of the film usually transcends to the workplace. A drama is heavy on and off camera. Everyone takes it so seriously; it's like walking into a funeral parlor with an open casket.

The production was perking the crew with on-set baristas or ice cream or something pleasant every few days to show their appreciation. It was one of the few big-budget experiences where I felt involved in the project. I felt part of the group instead of being just a cog in the wheel. All the actors were nice and friendly and the line between above and below was thinner. I only had one problem. My job was a nightmare. My boss was driving me crazy and the Steadicam operator was up my butt. I dipped into his holy frame and he laid into me. He was used to working with guys like Frank our New York boom operator, who never made an error and understood every lens, and knew where every reflection and shadow was on the set. Frank was an absolute pleasure to work with. He taught me some stuff and he treated me with respect. I can't say that about the camera guy. The ironic thing was that it wasn't my fault I dipped into the frame; usually it is, but not this time. I was caught in a situation where my boom was under Frank's. If I had raised it I would have hit his boom and compromised the sound. It can be a lose-lose business at times.

Murphy's Law applies in movie making. I had words with the cameraman. I felt I had to stand up for myself. I did this for a while. Then it hit me: Why did I think I needed to even defend myself to him or the sound guy who was riding me constantly? It was on this show that I learned something intangible that has stuck with me. Why did I let these people upset me? Why did I take it personally? It wasn't about me. It was about them. They were the ones with the problem. Even if it was my fault, there was no reason to treat me in such a demeaning fashion.

It was during *27 Dresses* that I stopped letting people have a negative effect on me. I learned to look at such people as if I were watching television. It was like watching a bad sitcom. This had been something I'd dealt with throughout my life, and in the past it would have frustrated me and eaten at me. I finally learned how to let it roll off my back. I decided it didn't matter what other people thought of me. If they felt the need to yell at me, then so be it. It made no difference to me anymore. I had my reasons for being there and I needed to stay. I couldn't lose my job over something as trivial as speaking up to a person who wouldn't hear me anyway. I took a lot with me as I left that movie. I had always had a problem working for an overbearing boss, which fueled the fire of my indignation over abuse of power. Since then it hasn't been an issue for me. I'm just not fazed and ironically I haven't run into that kind of thing anymore.

Things finally came to a boil between me and the mixer with the famed cotter pin incident of aught-seven. It was my moment to push back. I was using the hand truck to move around gear. Upon finishing my task I noticed the cotter pin was missing. That was used to secure the hand truck when it was folded up. I informed my grandfather's doppelgänger that the pin was missing. Naturally, he yelled and pointed the finger of blame at me. Even though I'd had my epiphany about others reprimanding me and I was having a more Buddha-like attitude when it came to sticks and stones and blah blah blah, I was incensed about being the fall guy every time. It was my turn to lose my temper and I just yelled back, "I didn't lose your pin. I'm telling you because I noticed it is missing!"

Yelling at him seemed to calm him down and he started to reason with me. "OK, go back to the truck and look on the ground and see if it fell out while you were loading the truck." I went back to search the parking lot, and sure enough there was the little old pin glistening in the sun as if it were mocking me. I'm just kidding; I didn't think much of it, picked it up and told him I found it. That was the last we spoke of it.

I know what you're thinking: "A-ha, it was your fault, Manzo, you dropped the pin while you were working, in fact Grandpa was right in this case." In a manner of speaking, maybe. I didn't lose the pin, it fell out. While I was loading the truck I wasn't staring at the pin to see if it would fall out or not. Yes, your honor, I was wheeling the aforementioned hand truck with the cotter pin in question, but had no knowledge of it popping out of its holder. I was an innocent bystander in the world of faulty equipment and a hysterical sound mixer. I throw myself at the mercy of the court.

Another bad omen was the second Barry walked off the truck. Barry was the stills photographer on *The Crucible*. *The Crucible* was such a bad job and I knew there was some correlation. Don't worry Barry, I'll keep all the nonsense that happened between us. I told Barry, "Twelve years ago, you met me on the way up, now you're meeting me on the way down." The old adage is indeed true.

There was indeed a connection between *The Crucible* and *27 Dresses*. I was forced to deal with authority in a different way. On *The Crucible*, I had options and I was able to confront the situation. On *27 Dresses*, I had no options, my situation was more desperate and I was forced to suck it up.

Throughout my life, I would get jobs with overbearing or downright stupid bosses. It would invoke my indignation and most of the time I would express myself and not care about the consequences. With two children, consequences mattered, but on this show I did something different: I didn't take it personally. I let the guy blow off steam and paid no attention to it. I let it roll off me like water off a duck's back. I refused to let it bother me. It was no skin off my potato. Rather than feel like an abused child, it gave me strength. I had developed a thicker skin over the years and such things didn't bother me anymore. It was liberating.

SCENE 28

The Velvet Hammer

One afternoon on *27 Dresses*, my brother electricians cornered me at lunch. They wanted me to be the shop steward for the show. This is the crew's rep to speak to production if there are any infractions thereof and forthwith. Most people don't want to pick up this gauntlet. It is an extra responsibility that involves ticklish situations that need to be addressed. I have good communication skills, I hope you would agree at this point, and I was able to interact with the production staff quite smoothly. It was on this show that my buddy Jack McPhee dubbed me The Velvet Hammer, for my abilities to achieve soft justice.

It seemed natural that since I had my own superhero name I should don the proper outfit. I wore a purple V on my chest with a scarlet cape. Of course I had gloves and tights to match. I would wait for a call and dash over to a back room in the wardrobe department, change into The Velvet Hammer and zip over to the production office to fix any would-be union issue. Upon reprimanding the producers and making them promise never to break the contract again, I would say, "My work is done here, I must go now and return my watchful eye over my union flock." I would run with a huge burst, jump out the nearest window and fly around the set.

The crew would yell, "There he is, The Velvet Hammer, fighting for justice on film sets throughout New England. Hail The Velvet Hammer! We love you Vel!" It was usually at that point I woke up from my lunchtime nap.

The Velvet Hammer moniker stuck and I wound up being the shop steward on most of the shows I worked on. Even though I was shanghaied the first time, I liked doing it. It gave me a reason to talk to the producers, and it perpetuated my learning experience. Since most people didn't want any extra burdens attached to their already filled day, I was able to continue to live out my superhero fantasy.

The summer passed and Massachusetts was heating up. The tax incentive was sweetened and the studios were taking advantage of it. *The*

Women, My Best Friend's Girl and *Pink Panther Deux* all rolled in at the same time. I figured I could easily land one of these babies. I figured wrong. The younger bucks landed the work and I was left out in the cold. That was certainly an eye-opener. This only reinforced the fact that this work is always so tenuous. It was also illuminating to realize where I stood as a cabana boy for the sound department.

There is a constant fear that lies in the hearts of even the most sought-after freelancers: the fear that the phone will not ring again, the fear that the work will go away and the fear that no one will hire them ever again. Many people hole up in their living rooms thinking, "What am I going to do? What am I going to do? What am I going to do?"

Not everyone is afraid. I'm actually not afraid. Something always pops up and just in time. It's hard for some to remember that. It is almost like clockwork here in New England: the winter sets in and after a few weeks of unemployment the people collectively freak. I often wonder what drove them to freelance work in the first place.

As luck would have it, the Local 11 stagehands union needed help with conventions and concerts and my movie background made it easier to wangle some work. I wound up plugging in audio cables for them on and off for a year. I also was able to step into the exciting world of rock and roll for about five minutes. I did a big show at Gillette Stadium. Jimmy Buffett called and wanted me to help load out his concert. I checked out the tail end of the show until it was time to go to work. There were over a hundred of us and I was put on a team of eight. I was clueless; I just swam with the fish, as opposed to sleeping with them. If you did not get that last reference you must see *The Godfather* again.

We were on a four-hour minimum, so the crew was amped up to beat the clock. They not only worked fast, they were buzzing like mad bees. They tried to push the pace, which made everyone seem like they were on some type of amphetamine. I must clarify that they were not actually on drugs, it just seemed that way. I don't want any trouble with the boys at Local 11.

We continued at this highly frenetic pace for two hours until everything on the stage was crated and ready to go. After working at breakneck speed, we had to stand around and wait for the truckers to pack the trucks. No matter how fast we off-loaded the stage, putting it on the truck could only go so fast. We wound up waiting another hour to get everything on the trucks. The amount of time saved was negligible. They gave me a Jimmy Buffett t-shirt and that was my first and last brush with loading out a rock and roll show. I can't say I miss it.

Even though I didn't get a full run on a movie, I stayed busy enough day playing. Day playing is great if you get into a groove. It's a nice wave to ride with the right amount of work and time off. I caught the last days of *Brotherhood*, wrapping up the stage, where I overheard *My Best Friend's Girl* was short on set dressers. I put in a call and was hired. The location was a charming condo on Commonwealth Avenue in Boston. It was a nice place that had to be redressed with practically the same furniture they originally had in there. Not an uncommon practice.

I arrived and was immediately put to work. The name "set dresser" is really a euphemism for furniture mover. The boss left me the notes, which were basically to unload the entire apartment and another dresser would arrive shortly to help. "Shortly" was about four hours later. The other set dresser got lost and said he couldn't find his way to one of the most popular, centrally located and most famous streets in Boston. After we were working for a couple of hours, he told me that this was his last day on the job and he was leaving the state. He certainly sounded convincing when he told me he'd gotten lost.

For a while, my appearance on the set was accompanied by, "What are you doing today Len?" Some people have a second craft, but I was turning up in a different department every week. It made no difference to me whether I was plugging in lights or whacking some actor with my boom pole; it all paid the same. I liked the idea of the versatility and it cut down on the boredom, but I decided that set dressing was not my thing and I did not seek the pleasure of dressing a set again.

Steve Martin needed my services on *Pink Panther Deux*. He told me there was a hole in the schedule and wondered if I could manage to come in a few days a week laying out some 90-pound cable. "Sure, Steve, I'm here for you." I didn't get a chance to talk to Steve much on that show. He was very busy with this one. You want to hear something really cool about Steve Martin? He doesn't work nights. The word on the street is that he puts it into his contract. That was music to my ears. Steve, from everyone over on *PPD*, thanks.

I had a small milestone on *Panther*: I turned 47. I kept it a secret. Birthdays on a movie can mean lunchtime cake and song with the entire crew singing the standard "Happy Birthday" jingle. I dodged that bullet. I want you to know that I'm not some type of birthday Scrooge. I didn't know half the crew, and I was going to let this one go unnoticed. A few hours after lunch, I did tell one of my buddies in my department and told him why I didn't mention it. I was glad it was over and I didn't have all these strangers singing to me.

At the end of the night when I went to the truck to get my bag to go home, the lights went off, the best boy brought out a cupcake with a candle and sang to me along with two genny operators and five lamp operators. They gave me a card, a few gag gifts and a bottle of bourbon that I immediately cracked into. For me, there is only one way to drink whiskey, and that's straight up. I poured the cups and the boys toasted me. It was a special moment for me. Even though I was put on the spot, I enjoyed this a lot better than the entire staff singing out of obligation. The surprise party lasted about 20 minutes. I was touched to the core. Hey guys, thanks again for the whiskey and making me feel alive—even you, Bernie.

While I was on the job, I received the official word that *Noelle* was being released in 200 theaters nationwide. This was great news and I was very excited; that is, I was very excited until I heard the date. It would be released on December 7. For those of you who are unaware, that is Pearl Harbor Day, and that day lives in infamy. I'm not a superstitious guy, as we discussed; I could read the writing on the wall. It wasn't just the inauspicious date that triggered the bummer hotline, it was also very late in the Christmas season to be released. *Noelle* was a small independent movie—a good one, but still a small one compared to the films it was up against opening weekend, which were *I Am Legend* and *Alvin and the Chipmunks*. The cumulative gross for both films opening weekend was about 125 million. There were some great film minds that had come together to figure out this release date. *Noelle* should have opened in fewer places with more push in order to gain success and momentum; it needed time to build up steam. It should have been released in mid-October or the first week in November at the latest. It might have been the little Christmas movie that could, if it had gotten a chance. The distribution had been botched and there was nothing we could do about it. The distributors had thought that people who had seen their previous films would come out to see it. I scoured the Internet for reviews and articles and there was nothing. There was barely any press. They put about a million into prints and did little advertising. We were left hung out to dry.

Before we signed a distribution deal, we had made a print and had run it ourselves on Cape Cod where it had been shot. We'd sold out all the shows for 10 days straight. You can get your cousin, your brother-in-law, Joe who runs the deli and Mabel at the hairdresser's to come, but friends and friends of friends run out after a couple of days. People were seeing this movie and talking about it and passing it on. People who came to the film liked it.

After failing to get the movie into the end zone, the field goal was blocked and the movie was pulled from the theaters. Before the month was over, the film had left the box office, completely taking my hopes and dreams with it. This was not one of my better moments.

The theatrical release is not an easy accomplishment, but it doesn't do much good unless people come to see the movie. This was the problem with the distributor: once the deal was cut, we had nothing to say about what was best for the film. We watched from the sidelines as the film plummeted away. It was at this point I noticed I was spending too much time over at Kitty's place. There was nothing else she could say that could help. Even her beautiful southern accent was lost in my depression. After a few weeks of crying in my beer, I put it behind me and threw myself back into work. Being depressed is like being stuck in the mud. One can get comfortable in depression and it is easier sometimes to wallow in it than to pull out of it. One can even get comfortable languishing in the mud. The toughest part is taking the initial steps out of the mud; that is when it is most uncomfortable.

All this was happening while I was engaged on *The Box*. It was December and *The Box* was going to take me until the end of January. At least I was employed. I don't know if that made it better or worse. I was down again, and with nowhere else to go, I appeared at the home of my childhood friend, Oscar Madison. Several years earlier, Madison's wife had thrown him out, requesting that he never return. Can two divorced men share an apartment without driving each other crazy? I was feeling a little like Felix Unger at that point, though not as devastated and certainly not suicidal.

The Odd Couple is my all-time favorite TV show. It ran for five years almost in obscurity. It had one of the worst slots of the week, 9:30 PM on Friday night. I was still a kid so I watched it every week. It became a hit in syndication. The movie with Jack Lemmon and Walter Matthau was excellent, but Tony Randall and Jack Klugman took it to another level. It is a show that has influenced my comedy and if you can find the other *Odd Couple* references in this book, my hat goes off to you.

SCENE 29

I'll Never Wash This Cheek Again

The Box is a Zombie/Alien/Horror/Thriller. This movie never knew what it really wanted to be and it had bomb written all over it. My words rang true at the box office where it settled at the bottom of the sea. On its generous $30 million budget they only pulled back half, which probably didn't even cover its advertising budget. I predicted the ensuing nosedive, and one of the PA's owes me a latte to this day. I bet that this flummoxed attempt at filmmaking would head south fast and would not break even at the theater.

The Box was no walk in the park. It doesn't get gnarlier than this. We started in November and pushed through to the end of January. Strap in folks, big storm coming, figuratively and literally. I had my worst day ever against the elements on this show. It was one long, cold, nasty night at the old mental ward in Medfield, Massachusetts, the same place Scorsese shot *Shutter Island*. A ferocious blizzard hit us in the early evening and we shot through it until the sun came up. It was the worst combination of extreme cold, wind and snow that I had the displeasure of working through. Four fleeces, thermals and a coat didn't hold up to that crazy night. There was nowhere to go, nowhere to hide. We worked until dawn, which was about when the snow stopped.

There was, however, a huge bright spot in this job. The fact that there was a job in the winter was a miracle in itself. In the pert near 20 years in the biz, I have never worked more than three winters. The L.A. crowd works all year round. This was new for us who lived in the East Coast Tundra. It is usually a natural fade to black, but this year the town was also popping with *Hachi: A Dog's Tale* and *The Maiden Heist*. I caught a big break not getting on *The Maiden Heist*. Everyone who worked on that show got burned by the payroll company going under. The paychecks were good but the health benefits never were paid. The union is still fighting that battle.

We shut down for the holiday break so we can all enjoy our respective holiday, be it Chanukah, Christmas, Kwanzaa or Festivus. This time of year is an industry détente, when most of the business shuts down and hibernates for two weeks. It feels like a freight train pulling into the yard on its last leg just before it breaks down. I survived another year in the trench, this time with only a quick break to patch my bones.

The final leg of *The Box* was all on the stage. The last three weeks were going to be inside on a nice cold stage, which I was delighted about. It was about 55 degrees in there. It wasn't warm, but it wasn't outside. The workload decreased and I began to feel the blood in my veins again. I was elated to get out of the elements. Several of my colleagues hated stage work because it was on the dull side. I knew the alternative was back outside, fighting off frostbite.

Even though the conditions were bad, I was still having a good time on this movie. Cameron Diaz was kind enough to provide a private barista for the cast and crew. When I saw Nick, Spielberg's favorite barista, the first morning on the street serving coffee, I jumped out of my shoes. He then told me he was going to be there every day. It was a good thing I hadn't put my shoes back on because I would have jumped out of them again.

Cameron gave everyone a mug in an effort to save on cups going to the landfill. I had several cups a day and enjoyed the daily espresso with an occasional chai or hot chocolate. At the coffee stand, Nick the barista kept track of the crew's statistical consumption. The more drinks you had with your cup, the more paper cups you saved. The most cups saved would win a prize furnished by Ms. Diaz. That was all fine and dandy. It looked like I probably would win the prize. Nobody on the set could drink free espresso like me. There was a Teamster who kicked back as much coffee as I did. We went down to the wire, neck and neck, and it was close there for a long time, but the winner and newly crowned Espresso Drinking and Environmental Champion of the New England Movie Community was— you guessed it, dear reader—me.

I'd like to thank the good people of Warner Bros. for having me on their winter debacle. I'd like to thank the Academy—scratch that, there is no Academy. I'd like to thank Nick the barista, for hooking me up seven times a day, and most of all, I would like to thank Ms. Diaz again, for the barista, the coffee, the coffee mug and the lovely card created and written in her own hand. She also gave me a lovely gift and best of all, upon receiving the prize, I seized the moment to hug Cameron and plant one on her left cheek. Even a jaded crew guy could not miss the opportunity to kiss the lovely Cameron Diaz.

SCENE 30

Golden Time

In 2008, there was no rest for the weary or for a guy who was nervous about losing his spot. The movie world has a short memory. If you start turning down a job because you want to take time off, then you leave a door open for someone to come in and take your spot. Like a fireman when the bell rings, you go to work. The next train to leave the station was *The Clique,* a teenage bestseller going straight to DVD.

This little 23-day movie had cakewalk written all over it. The leads and supporting cast were all minors, which meant restricted work hours. It had to get done efficiently to meet its deadline. The law requires a nine-hour day, which includes three hours of school and rest periods. It never had a chance to turn ugly.

The director was a Hollywood journeyman, Michael Lembeck, who started out as an actor and began directing 20 years ago. His father Harvey Lembeck was in *Stalag 17* and played Eric Von Zipper in the Frankie Avalon and Annette Funicello beach movies. I'd seen all of them. I thought it was amazing that I was working with the son of Eric Von Zipper.

I observed Mr. Lembeck at work as I observe every director I work with. I also pay close attention to the production team and the actors. I analyze every movie to glean some tidbits that I can take with me. I learn something on every shoot that makes me a better filmmaker. Michael Lembeck was one of the most efficient directors I ever worked with. He also knew how to get the most out of his actors and finessed the scenes constantly for the better without wasting time. It is rare to work with a director who can do a good job and get it done on time. Besides his excellent skills in the craft, he was great to work with and treated everyone around him with respect. I always feel the need to point this out because it is an aberration and not the norm.

The Clique was indeed painless. Before I knew it, I was at the wrap party with a single malt scotch in my hand. I should mention I'm not a heavy drinker, though I have had a few in this book. I do enjoy the occasional shot or beer. Alcohol is always good for a little color in any story, book or film. I would like to say at this time to everyone out there, when drinking, act responsibly.

Paul Blart: Mall Cop rode his Segway into town right after *The Clique*. I was barely able to brush my teeth before I jumped onto another feature. *Mall Cop* sounded good to me: six weeks at the Burlington Mall, translation: six weeks of warm interiors at the end of the winter. I love interiors. I love heat. I loved it before I was in the movie business. We go way back, me and heat. I have a new fondness for it. I wrote these very words in the heat of my office. I can't say enough about being warm. I think it's my thin blood, yeah that's it, my thin blood. That's my story and I'm sticking to it.

Naturally, it wasn't all interiors. In the first week, we were shooting in Quincy, Massachusetts at the State Trooper Training Facility. It was located on an isthmus far from the center of town. It was a cold, cold day and having water on two sides made it twice as cold. I don't know how you calculate that in degrees. So, if it is 20 degrees, does subtracting another 20 degrees constitute twice as cold? Then what if you are at 0 degrees, what is twice as cold then? Think about that for a while.

As we were off loading the truck, the sound mixer scoped out a place indoors for us to set up. We had enough cable to run our antennas, so we were in business. I was spared a very nasty day outdoors. I thought to myself, "Isth-mus be my lucky day." You'll have to forgive that one; I just couldn't resist. Hey, even Johnny Carson wasn't spot on all the time. You'd give him a pass. Johnny had a great technique with a bad joke. As soon as it died, he would move away from it in an obvious manner. He'd make fun of the joke. Then he was making a joke about his bad joke. He berated it and insulted it until he was as far away from it as possible, then moved on. He was actually the master of the making-the-bad-joke-better technique. Isth-mus be the delivery.

They played a game on *Mall Cop* called "Who's Directing the Movie?" There was a constant discussion over what was what and whose vision we were following. As if it mattered. That was one stupid movie. Kevin James is a funny guy and he does some funny stuff with some great sight gags, but it was a stupid movie. Someone could argue the point as it grossed over $180 million worldwide. That's not the point. I knew this movie would do well. I didn't predict that it would be that much, but that's another cup of coffee I'm trying to collect on as we set the under/over bar at 65 mil. I took the over, of course.

I thought it wouldn't be good, but I knew it would be successful. It had what the people wanted: something light with some funny stuff. It didn't have to be intelligent or have a plot that made sense or a believable romantic situation. Poor pathetic loser saves the mall and gets the girl. There's that American fantasy that keeps popping up on the big screen. I remember a time when the studios used to make funny scripts into comedies. That's right, they would actually use humor to make a comedy.

As we were preparing to start *Mall Cop* we were getting ready to leave it. That is, the rest of my sound team and I. The mixer received a better offer on a $120 million sci-fi show with Bruce Willis. There was no choice in making that decision. Your status as a key crew professional is determined by the size of your, ahem, budget. If you start out making movies on million-dollar shows, then getting to the 5 million mark is your first hurdle. You can't get that job unless you've done one before. Then you might ask, "Well, how do you get a job like that?" That's a very good question. And thank you for asking. It is usually circumstance that helps you make the jump, or if you know somebody, if you have worked with someone else in the office who could vouch for you.

When coming up in the ranks, the first barrier to break is the 5 to 15 million. Once there, you can eke up to 20 million, but 30 million, that is another story. The 30-to-60-million-dollar range is a tough nut to crack. As you get into higher budgets, there are fewer movies made at that level and there are people who are already established who get called first. Years ago, they would never have thought about hiring a local New England sound mixer for a $120 million movie. It just did not happen. You might ask, what changed? Perfectly natural segue. The production companies tightened the belt. After some re-evaluation, the brain trusts realized that you didn't have to live in L.A. to know how to place a microphone or dress a dining room. To save money, the studios started hiring more keys locally. Eet ees not, ow do you say eet in your langueege, ro-ket sur-jhe-ry.

If they bring in crew from out of town, they must fly them in and put them up at a hotel and also give them a per diem. The rates for the out-of-towners are usually higher, presumably because they are big gunslingers and big names for their respective positions. When the key of the department is hired from out of town, she invariably wants to bring in her second, so you're not flying in just one hired gun, you're flying in two. They also start their day on the clock from the time they get into the shuttle van at the hotel. Conversely, their day ends when they return to the hotel. A local will work a little cheaper to get the job. If she demands too much, it might be enough to pull the trigger on the out-of-town person even though she will still cost a lot more.

In the sound department, a soundman never goes anywhere without his boom operator. A successful sound team will be spending more time with each other than with their spouses. In the sound department, it is almost like a marriage. Even though there is a third person, the relationship between sound and boom is sacred. There is a ceremony much like for the Cosa Nostra—uh-oh, I've said too much.

Another place where production companies squeeze the penny is the studio or the stage. When you see movies about movies they are shot in these fancy soundproofed rooms on the lot in Hollywood. That luxury does not exist on location. Many cities throughout America do not have big soundstages. The cost is astronomical and there is not enough work to make it profitable. However, they still end up building sets, and that is usually in some cheap, dilapidated warehouse that they get for a song. One of the biggest dumps I've worked in is located in Chelsea, Massachusetts. That dust-ridden building with the tin roof was in the landing pattern for Logan Airport. In that poorly ventilated box, they shot *Pink Panther Deux*, *21* and *The Town*, to name a few. Chelsea is a long way from glamour.

Since we had a solid offer, we told *Mall Cop* we were going to bail six weeks into the show. My boss gave them an opportunity to hire someone else; they stuck with us and I kept working continuously. Since the jobs overlapped, I was the one to go to *Surrogates* to do the location scouts. Before every job, the key people head to all the locations to make a plan of attack and interface to figure out their needs for the movie. It's a fairly pleasant experience, usually about a 10-hour day with plenty of snacks on the bus. This business does nothing without food.

One day, we were at an old mental institution scouting one of the locations. We were outside on a fairly nice day. The director was discussing the scene. He said, "This tree is in the way, we're going to have to lose the tree." Lose the tree? Lose the tree! It never would have occurred to me to take out that tree. I would have shot around it or found something better than cutting down this huge 100-year-old tree. I guess it is all about how you view the world. To him, the life of a tree meant nothing; in some parts of the country, people protest for the life of a tree. I guess I'm somewhere in the middle. I couldn't say anything about it without jeopardizing my meal ticket, though I never would have cut it down.

Surrogates was the quintessential Hollywood piece-of-crap movie. It didn't start out that way. The graphic novel was pretty good and making it into a film was also a good idea. When I read the script I thought it could be OK. They took a meat ax to the budget and slashed 40 million off the top. You would think you could still make a good movie with 80 million. However, most of what was cut was the special FX budget, which is odd because it was a special FX–driven movie. As we were shooting it, I realized it never had a chance. Maybe that was the way the studio felt about it. They were already cutting their losses in production.

On the third day of principal photography, our star Bruce Willis arrived. When the actors arrive on set, they block the scene, which is a preliminary run-through so everyone can get their bearings, cast and crew alike. The stand-ins replace the actors and then the crew prepares for the shot. The process was delayed because we had to wait for Mr. Willis to get off the phone. I'm sure it was an important call. I hope at this point sarcasm is easily identifiable. This moment symbolized and solidified the way this show was going to go, and the production was going to revolve around Willis and no one was going to say "Boo." It was clear from the start who was running this clambake and it wasn't the director. This was the classic Hollywood situation where the actor was totally in charge. At first it seemed like a power play; after working a while, it was apparent that Bruce was doing it for his survival. The director didn't seem to know what he wanted. We would arrive to set every day and nothing would happen for half an hour. It was very festive in the morning with enough time to eat, drink a casual cup of coffee or have a smoke or two. There was no sense of urgency. Why should there be with 80 mil to play with?

We started with a week of overnights. At that time of year, there were only 10 hours' worth of night. We found out quickly that Bruce didn't like to work nights. He put his foot down about that right away. He would stay until we broke for lunch at midnight. In the movie biz, the first meal break is always called lunch no matter what time it is. The second meal is always called second meal. You can call it dinner if you like but you never call lunch dinner even if it is at 8 PM or midnight. We also say "good morning" when we come in at night. If we worked the graveyard shift every night, that would probably fade. Because we go back to days fairly quickly, we never really adjust to the nights. If and when you do adjust to night work, it's usually time to go back to days.

So Bruce didn't like to work nights. Who did? We all hated nights; he just had more clout to get out of them. But unlike on *Pink Panther Deux*, we forged through until dawn. There was still enough night work to be done without Mr. Willis. On *Zookeeper*, they started the show with six weeks of straight overnights. It drives people over the edge. I know a few people who cracked and didn't finish the show.

We shot a club scene that called for a technocrane, a huge crane with a long extendable arm, and it ain't cheap. It has to be driven up from New York the day before and comes with a highly paid guy. After all is said and done, it could run about three or four grand for the one shot they need. Getting this piece of machinery inside this particular location wasn't easy. The door was tight and it was up a flight of stairs. They needed a huge forklift and it took about an hour to get it into the building. We never used it. It sat there all day collecting dust. The day was so poorly scheduled we left several shots on the table. On the big shows, they keep these high-priced pieces of gear around like toys. If they don't use the machine, oh well, we didn't have time to get to it. No sense in crying over spilled technocranes.

Another expense production pays no mind to is the extras. They will keep them there until the bitter end, whether they need them or not. They are viewed more as props than people. Nobody is sending any props home early and certainly nobody is sending extras home early. The repercussions are too great if you send them home and then you need them later. If the director gets whimsical he can pull a scene out of his bag of tricks—after all, it does say on the call sheet that there are 30 extras that day. In this business, nobody wants to be caught holding the bag. If the extras are signed on for the day, that is the end of it, they go down with the ship. No one is pinching those pennies. The only red flag is if they are approaching their 16th hour, then their whole day goes retroactive to triple time, aka "Golden Time."

That's when the extras hit the radar screen and are dismissed before the bonus money kicks in.

A word about the modern-day extra, who is no longer referred to as such. They are now called "background" or "background artists," if you will. There are many different types of BG'ers. Most of them are actors or would like to be. Some background players do it as a part-time job. They come out for a day or two when a movie is in their area and enjoy socializing, indulging in the craft service buffet and getting two or three free meals. The background artists are not allowed to have the same privileges as the cast and crew. They do not have freedom of movement and are limited to the holding area, where there are usually chairs and tables and snacks. As the budget goes down, so do their amenities. On low-budget independent movies, they try to wrap the extras by lunch so they do not have to be fed. You can ask Robert Rodriguez about that one. I have done many a trick to save a buck, but I haven't resorted to that one. As a producer, the depth to which one can plunge to pinch a penny is infinite. A producer should set a line of how low he will sink in order to retain some self-respect. That line is not clear-cut, but you know you've crossed it when you are universally disliked.

For some professional background artists, it is their livelihood. They go from show to show as background only. Many stay toward the back of holding so that they don't get picked to be featured in the shot. They don't care about being featured, they just want to be brought back the next day. If they haven't been seen already, they have a good chance at being asked back for another day's pay.

Then there are the deluded dreamers who believe they are going to be discovered and get their big breaks out of holding. They never take acting lessons or try to perfect their craft. They think they are going to get pulled out of the crowd and rise to stardom. Few people go that route and the ones who actually get a break like that can actually act. A speaking part is rarely given on looks alone. You still have to deliver the line. There are many actors who have no idea how bad they are. Today, many of them can be seen on YouTube in poorly directed skits. There is a lot of talent that is still waiting to be seen, but there are an inordinate number of untalented actors out there as well. These are usually the people who crane their necks at the camera when they get the opportunity and thus ruin the shot.

The best background artists are the ones who are aspiring actors who are working at their craft daily. They either have studied or are currently taking classes. They approach it in a completely professional manner and do what they are supposed to, nothing more, nothing less. They pay attention, listen and keep quiet on set. By cooperating, their silence speaks volumes. Over time, they get noticed and are often featured, and they are the ones who may get a chance to say a word or two. Not the Lucy Ricardos of the group. That only works on 1950's television.

The crew people are deathly afraid of getting cornered by an extra. If they are being cornered it is by one of the crazies who will tell his life story to anyone he can pin down, thinking if he keeps talking to people he'll be making a connection that will propel him to fortune and fame.

One morning on *The Town*, I hopped in a shuttle van going to the set with some crew people and one extra. The AD told the extra to take the van to holding. As we approached the set, the driver asked us where we were going, to which our lone extra replied, "I don't know, nobody told me where to go." He didn't listen and kept yakking at length about how he was there to do the robbery scene and how he was a firearms expert and his knowledge of pyrotechnics was massive and he thought they might use him as a liaison between actors and the special FX people. I informed the driver to take him to holding and told him again where he was supposed to go. I was on the street a half hour later and saw him being escorted by another AD to holding and he was telling her how no one had told him where to go.

Another time, on the set of *Brotherhood*, the driver waited for an extra in the parking lot. I felt trouble instantly. She did not have her act together and was fumbling with the wardrobe accessories she brought with her. She finally came over and had a hard time getting into the van. Of course getting off the van we went through the same trip again. Somehow this tornado whirled in front of me at the breakfast truck and caused a huge delay there. I finally unleashed myself from this storm to resume the flow of my day. I still see her on sets from time to time kicking up dust and causing a minor commotion.

Now, where was I? Ah yes, I was ripping the director on *Surrogates*. It makes me wonder how someone can get such a high-paying job without really understanding what to do. He had directed *Terminator 3*. I guess the studio figured he could do it; the conversation probably went something like this:

"What do you think Harry?"

"I don't know Sid, what do you think?"

"Well, he did *T-3*."

"Oh, so he knows how to do a robot picture. How did it go at the box office?"

"Over 400 mil worldwide."

"Not too shab-o."

"He's also the only robot-picture-making director that is available right now."

"Does he know what he's doing? Is he a good director?"

"He made 400 mil at the box office."

I don't think this is an exaggerated presumption on my part. Did you see *Terminator 3*? It was lame, and it certainly lacked something that its predecessors had. It was a big break for the director to be part of a franchise that was an automatic moneymaker. My sister could have directed *T-3* and it still would have been a moneymaker—no offense, Sis. My other suspicion is that there is some type of buddy/nepotistic situation, which rules big time in Hollywood. On one hand, it's always a drag when you lose the job to the boss's nephew who knows nothing, but the other side of the coin is that there is something to be said for a sense of loyalty. You might say nepotism is Hollywood's best quality.

SCENE 31

Baked, Fried and Oiled

Surrogates was a long, tedious job. I had some good moments but the boredom of assistant audio work was making me ill. I was like a bored child who couldn't support his own body weight. The work was getting to me. I was also on the longest feature run of my life and it was making me loopy. In the past, I'd always had some time in between jobs to decompress, but this run had been nonstop for 10 months and I was working fairly steadily before all these back-to-back shows. I was burnt and it showed.

During the middle of this job, I knew that life could not continue like this and even though the money was good, it was a dead-end job for me. I had left the audio world once and with good reason: I was tired of it. I knew I couldn't continue in this vein endlessly. I started to get my mental wheels turning a bit and began to consider some alternatives beyond driving a taxi. I'm not putting it down; heck, my Dad drove a taxi in Manhattan for 25 years. At one time, I asked if I could drive it part-time. He told me it wasn't for me. He was saving me from myself, or a little nervous about me driving his cab—maybe a little bit of both.

Since my recent entrepreneurial ventures had failed, I developed CFS (cold feet syndrome, not be confused with chronic fatigue syndrome) and I was a little fearful of diving into something new. This wasn't altogether a bad thing, because it made me examine my options more seriously before I jumped into something. It was not clear as to how I was going to change my life because I had a lot of baggage. I had a family to support and an overinflated mortgage due to my rental business's demise. I knew it wasn't going to be easy and I also knew that I might not succeed. I had tried many ideas and I had plunged in with total abandonment. This was also a problem. The point is that I had failed several times and learned that a good idea did not necessarily amount to success. Even without success guaranteed and with the prospect of beating my head against the wall for the rest of my life, I made the only choice a semi-sane person could make. I was going to escape from the Hollywood foxhole. I was done. Beyond the hours and tedium of the job, I could never let go of having control over my own destiny. I could not let the chains of society fetter me forever. The alternative of giving up would be a death sentence for me. I had no choice but to push on.

In a Sisyphean manner, I kept going. I'm not punishing myself; I hope to one day get the rock up the hill for good. Now that I was done with *Surrogates*, I had some downtime to collect my thoughts, but I couldn't come up with anything concrete. I had been working my butt off in the trench for three years and I had no solid direction in which to proceed. I decompressed from *Surrogates* and enjoyed some time off. I was astounded at the lack of ideas floating in my head. In the past, I had so many ideas they were a detriment to me.

The problem with ideas, especially good ones, is that ideas spawn other ideas, which leaves you with a nest of ideas. Ideas are like unplanted seeds: they have the power and possibility to grow into something real and beautiful. Ideas are in fact a little more delicate than seeds. They need much more nurturing and care; they need more work. If you have too many ideas, you have a bunch of plants that aren't getting the proper attention each one deserves. They grow a bit and then die without being given the opportunity to bloom fully. This, however, was not my current problem. I did not know how to proceed. I was a bit shell-shocked from the last 18 months of work and felt lost.

Another problem I was having was that I was trying to close the door on my old business. I had a bunch of film equipment that I wanted to sell. Unfortunately, it had been hijacked by a colleague and former friend. The name shall be changed to protect the guilty. Mr. Hijack had taken my equipment to his shop in the spring of 2005. We agreed that he would take it, use it and pay me for it. During this time, I realized I was not getting all the rental money I should have been, but it was better than nothing, and I had lost patience with this business. In January of 2007, he was evicted from his space and he put all my gear into a trailer. Monsieur Hijack did this without telling me; I needed my gear for a project and had a hard time accessing it. I also wanted to have it back so I could begin the liquidation process. He gave me the run-around and before you knew it, I was working again. Being on a feature precluded me from getting any other work done. This bamboozlement continued well into 2008. He gave me back dribs and drabs until one day I had to finally go see Joe Friday. I went down to the local cop shop and explained my predicament, and I filed the necessary papers.

All I can say is thank the good Lord himself for granting me the foresight to buy insurance. I was able to recoup a decent amount of the cash, it came in one sum, and I didn't have to take the time to sell it. In every storm there is always some ray of light. On a lighter note, that chiseling, hijacking, low-down varmint has since gone out of business. If I'd seen it on the big screen it would probably have given me more pleasure. Actually, it did bring a smile to my face when I heard the news.

Surrogates ended and I took to drinking. Well, I wanted to, but it's too fattening. I say this because I was shell-shocked. I always feel somewhat shell-shocked after a movie, but I had been constantly working for a year and a half. I was baked, fried and oiled. I didn't get a full-time spot on *Edge of Darkness* with Mel Gibson and I was fine about it. If they had called I would have gone like a lemming over the mountainside. It was a blessing that call didn't come. I had become a shell of my former self and was down for the count. After a couple weeks, my synapses started to reconnect and I recovered some motor skills, like walking and chewing gum, but not simultaneously.

After some more time, the haze started to clear and I noticed I was still living with my family. The convenient movie amnesia vehicle dissipated and I re-introduced myself to them and we began to get acquainted again. I had wondered if there were any more people living here and my wife said it was just her and the two kids. After spending some more time at home, I got to know these strangers called my daughters. They turned out to be very nice people. I drove them to school again, went to some of their sporting events and saw them every night at dinner. I started to think that this is how most people live; they go home at night, eat dinner and see their families. I thought there might be something to that kind of lifestyle.

Recovery came quickly and as the gears were getting lubricated in the brain and the machinery was warming up, the fire started and smoke came out of my ears. You could see light bulbs pop up over my head.

It was at this time that I took a look at my writing and thought it was a lot better. I have been writing for 30 years. There was no previous goal except for the act itself. I had kept a journal on and off; I wrote some poems and a few songs, but nothing that I cared to go public with. It was in September of 2008 when I finally decided to write something more than a diary. I was still a little perplexed over in which direction to proceed. I went to the café every day and drank coffee and experimented with different ideas, but nothing really moved me yet.

The work was already dying down and all I could do in the fall was piddle around on various jobs that came my way. But when *Opportunity Knocks*—I mean literally, *Opportunity Knocks*, a game show that never saw the light of day—came to town for a few days, I jumped on board. This had the makings of a vaudeville show run by carpetbaggers. It was a traveling game show that stopped all over the country to put Mr. and Mrs. Front Porch and their families on TV to win cash and prizes. They set up the stage on the street right in front of the contestant's house.

The first thing the company had to do was cut down the only tree on the family's property. The front yard was not big and they had built a brick wall around the tree to showcase it. The tree was about 12 feet from the house. In came the buzz saws, which hacked the lone arbor on the property. I bet you are starting to think I'm some sort of tree hugger. First off, I'm not the type of guy who hugs a tree and tells. Secondly, it's about unnecessary waste. The tree was alive and beautiful and doing a service to us by brightening up the neighborhood and pumping out oxygen. I would say that one would need a good reason to chop it down. Maybe it was a deal breaker. The carpetbagger producer probably put it to them thusly.

"Look folks, we really want to use you, but that tree of yours—and don't get me wrong, it's a nice tree and all—but it's smack dab in the middle of our set. Now if we can't take it down, weeeell, the Billingsworth family up the street has already agreed to pull up their prize rosebushes. Sorry, folks, my hands are tied. So we either lose the tree or you lose the chance to win cash, prizes and television immortality." Well, you already know how that story ended, mostly. I guess they were able to keep what they won that night unless there was a clause in the contract that stated the show must air to collect, because this episode never did air. The show ran for two weeks and died.

More day playing for me and I found myself working with Mel Gibson, so to speak. We were both on *Edge of Darkness* but we never actually crossed paths. I was so busy on this show I just never had a chance to chat with him. So Mel, forgive me for not making it over from second unit to shuck and jive, but as we both are consummate professionals, I knew you would understand that my focus could not have been interrupted as I brought the high-power electrical cables affectionately known as 4/0 from the truck to the street. Please accept this as a formal apology and you are welcome to stop by for dinner any time you are in town. Just give me a little notice so I can have the wife rustle up something nice for you. (Note to all feminists: That was a joke.)

While I was day playing, a call came from a commercial mixer in town to boom a couple of days for him. In the old days, a commercial was a piece of cake for a boom op. They would do quite a few takes in a row but they were short and sweet.

"Tastes great!"

"Again please."

"Tastes great!"

"Again."

"Tastes great!"

"One more."

"Tastes great!"

"One more time."

"Tastes great!"

"Again."

"Tastes great!"

"Give me one more."

"Tastes great!"

"Again."

"Tastes great!"

"Just one more."

"Tastes great!"

"Cut."

Now that's what I call a good day on the boom. "What changed?" you might ask. Well, aren't you the inquisitive type. Technology. With film, there was always a need to think about it from a financial standpoint and also the max time on a camera roll was 10 minutes. Now with the wonderful advent of HD, there isn't a care for the expense, because there is none. It is outputted to a card and downloaded. How long they can shoot is unlimited, and for a boom operator, an aging one at that, a commercial is no longer a day at the beach.

My commercial boom career ended in a debacle. Today, I make a public apology to Bill Cucinello for dipping into his frame at least 30 times in the course of two days. Any other DP would have probably had my head on a platter. Bill just said, "Can you bring it up, Len? Len, you're dipping in. Len, you're in again, Len, just a hair higher, just bring the boom up a tad." That was the day I took myself out of the loop for any future boom work. It was a very embarrassing day at the office. I was like a pro athlete who played one season too many. Ask Brett Favre about that.

In November, I picked up a little electric work on a four-million-dollar debacle in Gloucester called *Hatteras Hotel*, shooting only 15 minutes from my house. Shooting right on the water in New England in November, yes, that is right, dear reader, it was cold out. I informed my boss of my seasickness issue and he thankfully kept me off the boat and the dock. I did make it down to the dock once during a hurry-up fiasco, when we needed all hands on deck. I did get a little woozy but held on. I was later relegated to refilling the generators that sent power to the lights on the 500-foot breakwater. It was nasty out on that breakwater; cold took on new meaning.

During the evening, I was scheduled to man a backlight about a half-mile from the set on the beach. It was only my years of experience that saved me from a cringing disaster that evening. There was a place to pull up my car as I awaited instructions from the gaffer. I was able to hang with the heat on and the tunes cranked while I waited for instruction. Every hour or so, the walkie would go off and I popped out of my car as I heard, "Move it to the left, a little more, too much, back again, a little more, that's it." It seemed to be in the original spot, but who was I to argue? I made the adjustment and hopped back in the car and sat for another hour before another tilt was necessary.

At the end of a four-day stint in this locality, my buddy Tony and I had to go all the way out to the end of the breakwater and bring the gennys back to base camp. As Tony says, "Lenny, we'll always have the breakwater." How true, how true. There is nothing like a hellacious experience to bond two human beings. We carried this heavy generator over the rocks and back to dry land in the freezing night air with gusts upwards of 50 miles per hour. It was no picnic. We survived of course and yuck about it every once and a while. Tony caught on a while back and found himself a day job at a local university teaching America's youth. He does movie work part-time and is constantly reminded of why he went back to school to teach.

One day we had a company move, and while the truck was still moving, the gaffer came over the walkie screaming at us to unload the truck. The direct quote was, "Losing the light, we're losing the light, unload that truck even if it's still moving! Losing the light! Losing the light!" Where do you even go with an order like that? I can imagine what the Teamsters would have said to us if we'd started off-loading with a truck still in motion. You may ask, "What causes this type of behavior?" I just want you to know I appreciate the highly interactive nature in which you are reading this book. Well, I never did done get my sheepskin in psychosocial graces, but I can tell you that there was something wrong with the picture. We just looked at each other, mouths agape, and shook our heads in disbelief.

Another drudgery of this particular job was the 50,000-watt soft sun light known as the Death Star, which took eight of us to move. Actually, it is a very stupid light to have around. It does give off a lot of power but offers no flexibility, and it is very expensive. The production would have been better served by three 18,000-watt substitute lights that could have been set in the same direction if needed and also used separately.

The worst thing about the Death Star was that it was damaged one night. The production was on the hook for the repair and they were down 50,000 watts of power for a while. It was a toy that the producers were conned into using. There is always a game that goes on with every department between wants and needs. The keys want to get more than they need and the producers want to cut out more than they should. In the end it comes down to who can outsmart the other guy. With the crew person always putting out the final disclaimer, "I can't guarantee it will be done right if we don't have such and such to do it with." The relationship is based on fear. As I said, nobody wants to be left holding the bag. One day on *Underdog*, we had 18 extra hands in the lighting department and I'm sure the gaffer had said, "I can't guarantee getting it done on time if I don't have enough guys." So fear is put into the heart of the production manager, the tug of war goes on, the budget dance begins and in the end, some compromise is made, either giving in to excessive man days that cost the production too much money, or shorthanding the crew and creating extra overtime that costs the production too much money. They get it right sometimes; that occurs usually when the team has worked together before, and there is some trust established.

During my four-day stint in Gloucester, I witnessed a lovely little incident at the craft service table. I was just standing there gobbling down a poppy seed bagel with cream cheese, and staying warm in the process, when the discussion between the producer and director began to, shall we say, escalate. As I was enjoying my bagel and coffee with a fellow lighting technician, I was compelled to turn around when I heard someone yelling.

Since I was a day player I wasn't privy to the players of the production team. My colleague informed me that it was the producer, who was indeed reaming out the director in front of several cast and crew. I have never seen this on a Hollywood production; this kind of thing usually happens behind closed doors, but it is not uncommon from time to time for one of the above the liners to blow a gasket in public. I was surprised, but I must say I enjoyed the live soap opera as the producer said, "I can't believe you didn't take care of that!" No response from the director. "You should have taken care of that!" Still no response. "YOU FUCKED ME ON THAT! YOU REALLY FUCKING FUCKED ME ON THAT!"

To which the director replied, "You're out of line."

Producer: "I'm out of line?! I'm out of line?! I'LL SHOW YOU WHO IS OUT OF LINE, I'LL SHOW YOU WHO THE FUCK IS OUT OF LINE!" He yelled at the top of his lungs for all to hear and did not care who heard and didn't notice who was in the room. All the director could do was walk away, and in true grammar-school fashion the producer said, "Oh yeah! You better walk away!" The guy sounded like he was totally off his nut. However, I had no idea what he was referring to. He actually never confided in me. I wondered if it had anything to do with the movie. It was like they had something else happening on the side. That is pure speculation on my part. I'll tell you one thing, though: the director did not finish the movie. Coincidence? I don't think so.

Even though I was feeling that my days were numbered with this type of work, it was one night on *Hatteras Hotel* that sealed the deal. After several days of work and after being on my feet for 11 hours already, the hardest part of the day kicked in. It was after midnight and we had a huge wrap.

Our truck was several blocks away so we had to load up a stake bed truck and bring it back to the main truck. It is not a cost-effective system; essentially it is double work. We had to load and unload one truck and then load the big truck, and we had several trips with the small truck. The reason it is done like this is because sometimes we can't get the large rig near the location. I wondered about that at the end of the night when there was so much parking in the business district. It is just easier to make that decision instead of figuring out how and when to move the truck. It adds up to a lot of overtime for crew and drivers. These are the decisions that slip through the cracks all the time. That is the way it is done so that is the way they keep doing it. The machine is set up in such a way that no one wants to do anything out of the ordinary. Once line items are signed off, there is no looking back, especially if the production is on budget. Most production managers are not trying to save extra money, they are just trying to do their jobs and don't want to upset the apple cart.

After picking up the infamous 4/0 cable—by the way, "infamous" is one of the most misused words in the English language. It means famous in a bad way. "Irregardless," which is not even a word, is another one. "Regardless" is quite sufficient, but many people feel inclined to make a larger point of regardlessness—also not a word. So, after picking up the goddamned 4/0, and all the other cable that was on the street, we loaded it onto the stake bed and brought it back to the other truck. I looked at my watch, or should I say my phone? Either way, it was after midnight, and there was still a boatload of gack outside the truck. I was in serious pain and every time I lifted something I felt the pain in my already injured body. My shoulder was damaged from the hospital shoot that I had boomed. It was kicking up big time as it was a fresh wound; it was giving me trouble all the way up to my neck, out into my arm and down to my lower back. The left side of my body was out of whack down to the back of my knee. This was also triggering an old injury from 1987 that only acted up under serious duress. Everything was out of alignment and I was exhausted on top of it all.

At one point during the wrap, I was so unconscious that I just relaxed up against a poll. Then after about 30 seconds, I jumped up and hoped no one saw me just totally lose my focus at an important time when everyone was busting their butt and just wanted to get out of there. I was unconscious, though. I did not know what was going on. I could have crawled up against the curb and gone to sleep on the streets of Gloucester. The last hour of the night was like the final minutes of a football game on the losing side, or a defeated boxer just trying to stay on his feet out of pride. I was delirious and broken. I was really pushed beyond my limits after an already hard week. I thought, "If I'm 48 years old now and can't do it, how can I do it at 51 and 55?"

Naturally, I had to recover again. Once the healing process started and I felt a bit rested, it allowed my brain to start working again. The rat's wheel started to spin and I thought about my situation over the last three years. Even though I didn't like the work I was doing, and what it was doing to me, I really wasn't being proactive about changing anything. I did check out a producer's lead from time to time, but I hadn't tried to create an option for myself. After a lot of contemplation, reflection and genuflection, I moved toward some small epiphany. I felt like the universe beat me up on the job for my own good, as a way of pushing me out of the business. Yes, folks, more writing on the wall and it was in plain English: Get out now!

My head was still confused and I couldn't think straight. I thought about spending 40 days in the desert to clear my head. After much deliberation, I decided that the desert idea was not practical. I had too many other responsibilities. So with the desert idea shelved, I turned to my old haunt of inspiration. No, not Kitty's; I turned to the café. During my downtime, I would spend a couple of hours a day writing, and as the days passed, a book was coming to me, in this case a novel. I had an idea that incorporated my travels from years ago. I knocked out about 40 pages but it was still scattered and I was still learning about writing. However, I was getting some good stuff down and liked the direction I was heading in. Then the phone rang. "Yes, this is Lenny Manzo, what can I do for you?"

"We need your soul for three weeks, is it available?"

"Well, I did sell part of it to some other Faustian producer, but there is still a piece of it left that I can give to you."

The double-edged winter job rolled into town in the form of a TV pilot called *Bunker Hill*, starring Donnie Wahlberg. The money was welcome, but by now you know how much I hate the conditions. This one was all about the elements: we were outside every day except for the last day. There were interiors, but they were never big enough to get the gear inside. We were forced to set up on the street. I definitely froze some of my extremities off.

By union contract, TV can pay you less money than features, and they do. They are deemed a lower contract because they don't have as much money. A TV network does not have much money? This is something I still scratch my head about. The networks are loaded with money. All they have is money. They are huge companies that own other large companies. In fact, many are even owned by even bigger companies. If there is one thing they are not short of, it is money. Somehow they have been able to play the low-budget card with the union and get away with it. At least the union holds them to a standard; without the union we would be raked over the coals. Let's all sing together:

Look for the union label

When you are buying that coat, dress or blouse

Remember somewhere, our union's sewing

Our wages going to feed the kids, and run the house

So look for the union label

It says we're able

To make it in the U.S.A.

Sing loud, sing proud. I will now get off my apple box and return to our regularly scheduled program.

This time it wasn't just me; the mantra on this show was "Thank God, it's only for three weeks." If this had been a feature the cyanide would have been passed out. The shortness of the job is what made it mentally tolerable; we averaged 15 hours a day. The highlight of this job was the last day. The weather caused an impromptu wrap party. We were hit with a blizzard and everyone was put up at the Marriott. They were over a barrel and didn't want to risk the crew driving on the road. When there is a big risk of liability and being sued, the production always does the right thing.

The job finished, winter began and there was no work on the horizon, and I felt fine about it. I went through the holidays in a fog and somewhere around the beginning of January I put some deep thought into what I should do next.

"Hey, why don't you get back to your book?" Thank you, Peanut Gallery Member. It is a fair question. I decided to shelve the book (now that's comedy). I shelved the book because it could not have been written with interruptions. It would have taken me months to get a first draft. There was a lot to figure out and I didn't have the full vision. In time I could have done it, but it wasn't time I had. I would be working before I knew it.

The year 2008 came to an end, but a new year was right behind it and with it a sense of urgency was upon me. I was three years deep into this portion of my career and I was pressed for change. I'd had a hard time over the years finding a job as a producer. I had been pigeonholed as a soundman and even though I had produced for six years most of my work had been with one company. Throughout the last three years, I'd applied for some jobs. The old phrase "don't call us, we'll call you" is still invoked. I was way sick of pounding pavement, concrete or cyber. The traditional methods were not working for me. After some deliberation, the light bulb turned on in my head. It was not exactly an idea, it was the idea that I needed an idea. Technically, it was an idea, but that was an old idea; still, I needed an idea. Basically, I had the great idea that I needed an idea, so at least I was on the right track.

I wanted to stay in the business, but I needed a new direction. I had to dust off my entrepreneurial skills one more time and get back in the water, create my own destiny and be my own boss. Naturally, I thought about producing a movie, but the landscape of distribution had changed. In the old days, money was raised to make a movie and a distributor bought the film. It was an expensive process, but if you produced a decent product, there was also a decent chance you could get it distributed. In modern times, this is no longer the case. Modern independent producers are distributing their own films. They must identify their audience in advance and connect with that audience as they make the film, keep them in the loop until completion and then get them to buy it or come to a screening.

It is much harder today to have an independent movie picked up for theatrical release.

It doesn't necessarily matter if you have a good movie. The chance of getting anything picked up and paid for by a distributor is slim. I knew that whatever I was going to make, I was also going to have to distribute by default. I approached this problem from a practical standpoint and asked myself, what could I make that could be done low-budget, not need stars and could sell if done right? The answer, my friends, was horror. It's an age-old tradition for jump-starting a career. Horror can be done on the cheap.

Find a spooky house in the woods and you are in business. One location, minimal gear and crew, non-union actors and you're on your way. Stars are not needed in horror because everyone is going to get killed. It is one genre that absolutely does not require expensive name talent. I had several levels of budget, all of them low. I just needed to raise the money, which was a problem. The budget, although low, was in six figures, which is ultra-low by Hollywood standards, but still not chump change for an investor. I had not raised that much money before and it would be a challenge.

I like writing and my soul resonates when I can get my creative thoughts out in an eloquent manner. I've never had a flair for business writing, such as resumes or business plans. It was taking me forever to hack out a business plan for the horror movie. It was tedious, boring and my work seemed so flat. It didn't seem to have the passion to capture an investor's attention enough to make him fork over a couple hundred K.

As fate would have it, I ran into a colleague who was just finishing his movie and it was getting ready to go out on the market. I had supported the shooting portion of his movie while I still had equipment. He showed me the final cut and I was blown away that anyone could make such a good film for 10K. The wheels started spinning—that was either my brain or the hamster in my head, I still haven't figured out which.

Camera is on a close-up of a man's face in deep thought. Camera dollies back to reveal the man at his desk. In one hand, an incomplete business plan for a project without any momentum; in the other hand, a completed movie sans box art. He pensively stares at the disc. Looks back to the business plan, stares intently, back again at the disc and nods slightly. He again looks back at the business plan, crinkles his forehead and winces. One more glance at the disc and smiles. He gets up, walks to the file cabinet, files the business plan and exits camera left out the door.

Upon finishing the scene, I re-entered my office and quickly went to work. I contacted the producer-director of *Life, Love & Loss* and told him I wanted to help distribute his movie. He was up for it and we hacked out a deal and went to work. Distribution is the key to the success of any independent film. This seemed like the best course of action. I could get my feet wet with a film that was ready and we could try to tackle the market. If I was successful here it could pave the way for my own work later. I had learned a lot about distribution and marketing since my Red Sox doc. I was ready to apply it. The movie needed some final touches, the box art needed to be created and the website needed work.

While I was knee-deep in distribution land, ABC rolled into town bearing pilots. I snagged a couple of weeks of work that was fairly painless. ABC tried to pull a fast one in an attempt to jerk me around over a $52-a-day housing allowance.

I had been working on and off in Rhode Island for three years and the union contract states that any union member in my local that lives more than 60 miles as the crow flies from the production office qualifies for a housing allowance. Shows come and go and I get the housing allowance in Rhode Island. Where does the breakdown come from? Someone over at ABC somewhere fairly high up in the chain of command gets a bug in his ear that ABC can sidestep this clause by saying they are making something else other than a pilot. One of these well-paid monkeys convinces some other monkey that they can save some dough by screwing a handful of blue-collar slobs out of their housing money. Someone bites on that biscuit and says, "That sounds great," and they proceed to dance around the housing clause. "We don't have to pay that, we're not a pilot."

The union business manager inquires, "What are you, then?"

"We're not a pilot."

"What do you mean you're not a pilot?"

"We're not a pilot."

"It says right on the pay stub, pilot."

"We're not a pilot."

That was the party line and the production manager stuck to it. The housing allowance was left out of my check. This was ridiculous. I knew without a doubt the union would get my money. After much litigation, ABC was forced to honor the black-and-white contract they'd signed, which meant they had to re-open the books and pay another accountant to go through the whole thing again, thus costing more money. That, ladies and gentlemen, is show biz. It works in a manner similar to government.

I finished these shows and went back to work trying to manifest the distribution business. Again, there were some more roadblocks and the movie was still having post-production issues, and before I knew it, Richard Dreyfuss and Blythe Danner needed me on Cape Cod. I had heard about this movie and it sounded like an impending disaster. I had no desire to work on the beach. Movie multiplied by low budget, multiplied again by beach, usually means trouble. They called and I went anyway. As you know by now, we are programmed to never say no. Now hold on, I bet you think I'm going to complain again. Well, I'm not; the job was a pleasant surprise. I was called to work in the lighting department. The last week was exteriors and the sun did most of the work. It actually turned into more of a vacation. I made a few bucks and pondered my distribution thing that wasn't going anywhere.

Over two months had passed and it was going slow. I realized that one of the main problems was my lack of control. Another issue was all the work I was doing to promote this movie. I felt that I should be doing this type of promotion for myself. I still wanted to distribute the movie, but more on my own terms. I didn't want to put a lot of effort into this project and end up back at square one. So I put the food in the hamster cage which allowed the wheel to spin again. I was happy that the wheels could spin again.

More time passed and after several months of working on the distribution of *Life, Love & Loss*, I had not moved along very far. Things were moving slowly and the film was taking much longer to complete. I moved away from the project and went back to the drawing board.

Even though the distribution deal did not work out, I was getting a better sense of what it would take to get a product out there. The biggest problem was that we were understaffed. We needed more help. It's an uphill battle; creating buzz from nothing takes time and effort, heavy on the effort. The most important thing I learned from this and the Red Sox documentary was that coordination of the events in a timely manner creates the most bang, and then you can roll with the momentum. When I released *The Nation*, I was so strapped that I didn't have time to form a plan. I just started selling it. I also didn't have enough time to keep it moving. There have been some hard lessons in this dog-eat-dog movie business. I secured another certificate toward my entrepreneurial career. Every failure is best viewed as higher education. After you finally learn everything you should not do, success is almost guaranteed. "Almost" being the key word in that sentence.

Raise the Clown Flag

I *had not always made* the right choice in the past. The biggest issue was not thinking things through. I would get an idea and think, "Wow, what a great idea! I'm going to do it." I would dive in headfirst without thinking about all the factors involved. This time I didn't want to rush into something, but at the same time it left me gun-shy. I was in a difficult spot; although I wanted to proceed prudently, time was passing and nothing was changing.

I knew at the heart of any venture there would be a website. I could either showcase my work, or use it as a tool to sell products or distribute movies. I tossed my future around for a month and then in the merry month of May I put the hammer down. I debated whether I should have pulled the trigger over putting the hammer down. In the end, it seemed like putting the hammer down was the way to go.

So, with the hammer down, good buddy, I pushed forward and I bought the domain name LennyManzo.com. I thought about the site and all the things I could do. I was happy to get back on the entrepreneurial horse, and thus LennyManzo.com was born, or maybe conceived would be a better word. Well, if not conceived, I would at least say inseminated.

Once I finally made the commitment to do it, I threw myself into it all the way. I contacted a friend and colleague at Generation Productions, a talented web designer who agreed to do the work. We began the process of creating and launching the website. We went through many ideas, discussions, back and forth. We were making progress when my movie mercenary alarm went off. I looked to the sky outside my penthouse and saw the Mercenary Man Signal bright in the sky (very similar to the Bat Signal). "Holy low-budget feature, Mercenary Man." I slid down the pole to the Manzo Mercenary Cave and strapped in for another feature film. I followed the light in the sky until it led me to a little indie feature called *Valediction*. Since then they changed the title to *Locked In*. It will always be *Valediction* to me.

It was a soft year for work. I was not able to get a day on *Grown Ups*, which was shooting only five minutes from my house. That is the sad, ironic tragedy of the business. Any day I went to work from April through August, I passed the crew parking lot on the way out of my town. It mattered little to me which Hollywood bomb I wound up working on, as long as the checks cashed. There is no justice, especially in the movie business. One mustn't dwell on it. When the movie gods toy with your existence you must not pay attention to them. If you ignore them, they will go away, but if you curse them, you fuel the fire and they wreak even more havoc upon you.

The movie gods are the former Greek gods. They seem to have been out of work for a long time and they pick up a gig now and then. They moonlight as baseball gods in the summer. It's a pretty busy gig as the home-run prayers mount up by mid-July. They do like drama; that's why they pick up some work in the movie world. They're out there making it rain and doing whatever they can to push your endurance. They also have a great sense of humor, which was made clear on *Valediction*. This movie was packed with drama, on and off the screen.

Valediction had shut down once already. Just three days before principal photography and without warning they closed shop and left town in the dead of night. This is also one of the double standards of the business. A producer will cancel you at the last minute and apologize, maybe. If the crew person does it, a producer makes it a personal assault, or act like it's one. If I ever leave one job for another, I consider whether it is worth torching the bridge behind me. The people at the top of the pecking order do it all the time and get their asses kissed as they head out the door. It's a bigger game for the people without clout or who live below the line. The idea is not to burn any bridge and keep all avenues open. It is not always that smooth and easy, and sometimes things get nasty. These days I often take a tunnel instead of a bridge; I've never heard of anyone having to burn a tunnel.

Valediction closed abruptly and went away into the night. I never gave it a second thought. The independent world of cinema is even flightier than the studios. A few weeks later, it reared its ugly head and claimed it was going to fly in less than a week. They had to start on Monday, June 8, 2009 because they had to be finished by July 3. The director was getting married on July 5, in London. I guess that's a good excuse. Our star Ben Barnes also had the same drop-dead date. He was running to Australia to shoot the next sequel in the *Narnia* franchise. This movie did not have any breathing room. We were shooting six-day weeks; they were walking a thin line. We have an axiom in this business: good, fast and cheap, pick two. Fast and cheap will not get you a good product. Good and cheap needs a lot of planning and will not be fast. If they want it to be good and there is no choice but to do it fast, it is going to cost them.

With the train running and no brakes, we steamed headlong into production. It was a beautiful day for a lovely June exterior. The first day was easy enough, but I knew it was the calm before the storm. We had scheduled 23 days out of the next 26. Sunday would be our day off. There was no room for error. A smart producer will leave herself some extra time, in case some unforeseen circumstance arises and she is forced to add days. That wasn't going to happen here. If we were going to go over—if, HA! If we were going to go over, it would be daily. There was nowhere to put an extra day unless they took away the day off, which was not impossible.

Our truck had not yet arrived so we were temporarily working out of a box truck until the camera/sound truck arrived. Due to poor planning, the truck arrived after wrap, and both departments spent an extra two hours loading the new truck. If it had arrived earlier in the day, we could have made the switch during the day, thus saving 14 hours of combined double time. If they could have picked it up a few days earlier, they could have saved renting two trucks on the same day. This was just the tip of the iceberg.

All jobs are relative to time, need and situation. I hadn't worked much and this was only a four-week job, six days a week. Because of the length of the job it was easy to handle the hours. Also, I was in need of cash so I welcomed the compact overtime situation. The best part of the job was that it was in the summer. The elements were right and it wasn't too hot either. I donned my Velvet Hammer outfit and took on the shop steward responsibilities, and on this job I had my work cut out for me. There was drama galore on this one, starting with the fact that they possibly would not have enough money to complete the film. Now logic would dictate that if one had come this far and spent all this money, there would be enough money to finish the film. Not necessarily the case.

Since the production had shut down once already, they were on thin ice with the unions, and they couldn't be trusted. The unions and the payroll company were forcing the production to put up a bond to guarantee the payroll for an extra week. They would also not be able to touch the money until the unions were satisfied that all debts had been paid. The deadline was Friday, the 12th of June. The union told them, "If you don't come up wit da dough, see, the plug is gonna get pulled, see, ya get me, no more mista nice guy. Either come up wit da scratch or take your act on da road cuz we ain't gonna take it. You got dat, bub?"

There was a lot of tension among the crew. As much as people complain about a bad job, a bad job is certainly better than no job. As the week ended and D-Day was in sight, the crew became pessimistic. The production seemed to be stalling. The show was in huge jeopardy.

As the shop steward, the on-set liaison between the production and the union, I was in the thick of the financial fury that was taking place. If the money did not hit the union coffers by the end of the day Friday, the movie would be shut down and the entire crew would have to walk off the show. Friday came, and most of the day passed with no word, the ubiquitous question, "Have you heard anything yet?" on everyone's lips.

"Oh yeah, didn't I tell you? We're all going to be unemployed on Monday. I don't know how it could have slipped my mind." Actually, in that situation I held my sarcastic tongue. It was a bit nerve-racking for many of the crew. I must have been asked at least a hundred times that day about the fate of our little movie. There was nervousness and fear that permeated the set at the abandoned hospital in Malden, Mass. "As soon as I know, you'll know." This was information I was not going to keep close to the vest. The minutes kept ticking off the clock and with them went any optimism; most people felt the whole shoot would fold. Do they have the money or what? Are they this stupid to go this far to let the whole thing blow up with only a quarter of the movie in the can? I knew they were stupid but the other answer was undetermined.

Finally, in the eleventh hour, the phone rang. Well, actually, it vibrated; one can't leave the ringer on while on the set. The phone vibrated, I picked it up: "Yes, this is Lenny Manzo the shop steward who's been waiting on pins and needles all day with his fellow crew people to find out if we're all getting sacked. What's that? We can keep our jobs? Huzzah! Huzzah!"

With employment secure, there was a group sigh of relief, and then it was business as usual. We went back to the craft service table and made another Starbucks run. This movie was the closest thing to camp I had experienced since *Underdog*. The director would do these long closed rehearsals, which amounted to a mass coffee break. Then there would be a rehearsal for key personnel that I was not privy to. That would extend my coffee break. After the rehearsal, my boss would dole out the game plan, we'd set up for the shot and then break again while the lighting guys set up.

Valediction took downtime to another level. With a little more application on my part I could have studied for the bar exam. There were oceans of downtime. This was an area where I could thrive. Outside of my usual set banter, I was making rather good use of my time. Even though I didn't go for a correspondence school course degree, I was working on my future. I was writing articles and reviews for my new website and trying to develop my style.

It was at this time I decided to join Facebook. I had held off from making the plunge because it had seemed odd to put so much information out to the public. I also knew that it was a wormhole to the past and I wasn't sure if I wanted to open up those doors. I deliberated for months. Since I was going to be a public person via my website, my Facebook misgivings did not matter anymore.

I knew that when my website was launched I was going to have to deliver content daily. I thought this would be a good way to get started. Facebook permits 420 characters per status post, which allowed me to write a paragraph daily. Even though it was only a paragraph, it created a discipline for me. I would come home from work, sit a few minutes and form my words to describe the day. Humor was certainly the goal. I am always cracking jokes on set and wanted to transfer the spoken word to the written. Facebook was the perfect vehicle to write in an unpressured environment. Co-een-ca-dinc-al-ly enough I was engaged on a project that had so much fodder to write about. I began my introduction in the Facebook community with a daily account of the escapades on the set. Here are some of my first posts.

June 10, 2009

Valediction, Day 2, the storm arrives!!! In the form of a 15-hour overnight, spaghetti and meatballs at dawn. I Love Show Biz! We left the location without a call time or location for the next day (this was a first, check your email while you sleep). The ship has a hole. I would never point a finger, but something is gumming up the works.

June 13, 2009

Flash: 2nd unit gets busted circa one o'clock this morning. The process trailer towing the hero car gets nailed due to lack of paperwork. Permeets! Permeets! We don' need no stinkin' permeets! Who's running the asylum?

June 14, 2009

Valediction has been berry berry good to me. Besides the nights, the rain, the long hours, the bad food and the incompetence, it's a great show. Funny, it is very similar to the last show I worked. It could be worse; it could be … TV aaaaahhhhhhh!!!! (Add *Psycho* music here.)

June 15, 2009

The fireworks continue when the producer and accountant go at it in the middle of the set. After being coldcocked on the production floor the accountant bites the dust and is now standing in the unemployment line. A ringer is coming in from L.A. on the red eye to right the ship. The crew is laying 6 to 1 on early dismissal. I say the big bird she flies. Daddy needs a new pair of shoes.

June 16, 2009

As the smoke cleared and the dust settled, another day on *Valediction* has passed. Production and crew mended their relationships (the back pay helped). We wrapped at a reasonable hour and everyone stayed to roast marshmallows by the bonfire, which was made by setting the honey wagon on fire. There was a group hug and tears were shed.

June 17, 2009

The Kumbaya moment has passed and things turned ugly once again. In a desperate act to save money, production is cutting PA wages by 50%. There are rumblings of a mass walk. Even yours truly was let go early tonight to avoid double time and meal penalties. This show is on thin ice with everyone wondering if the payroll company will have the money to write the checks. I don't know about you but I'm on the edge of my seat.

June 18, 2009

Fourteen hours, a ton of rain and no checks on payday. Things are coming to a head and it ain't pretty. Zero hour is coming, if payroll isn't met, life as we know it on *Valediction* will never be the same. On a lighter note Starbucks is only nine minutes away from the set. Life has a way of balancing things out. I guess I'm just a glass half-full kind of guy. Find out tomorrow if Manzo gets paid!!!

June 19, 2009

You can sleep easy tonight; there is joy in Mudville. By some miracle in the 11th hour payroll has been met. Although I don't think we're out of the woods yet. We did 15 hours tonight and the schedule does not get easier. There's no breathing room for this production with hard outs for the lead and director. Starbucks becomes even more critical. There's always a silver lining.

June 20, 2009

The cast and crew will be meeting at the production office at 9 PM tonight to watch a rerun of Dr. Phil. Dr. Phil's guest is Tom Cruise, who talks about similar problems on *Risky Business*. (This was the first production where the group hug was employed to mend the internal problems happening on the set.) Ladyfingers will be served.

June 21, 2009

Another 12-hour day, it's like bankers' hours. I can't say the same for my fellow crew members who are getting a tad beat down. It can't always be a walk in the park. Film, she is a fickle mistress; you never know how she will treat you (repeat line with French accent for proper effect).

June 22, 2009

The week begins with another 4:30 AM wake-up. My clock doesn't go off and it is 5 AM. The *Mission Impossible* music goes off in my head as I scramble to get out the door. A quick rinse in the shower, I don't shave and I grab my laid-out clothes (good pre-pro there). I push the speed limit a little, but not enough to lose all the marbles. I land on set with two minutes to spare. Still enough time to order breakfast off the truck.

I did take poetic license with many of my posts. Fisticuffs were never exchanged, but there was a screaming match in the middle of the set. The rumor mill churned and the accountant was going to be fired. It sure looked like it. One knock-down, drag-out screaming match wouldn't necessarily be enough to lose your job, though. This is a business that thrives on drama. The shouting match in the middle of the set left us uneasy. Anytime there is trouble between the accountant and the producer it is cause for alarm. It wasn't clear what transpired. The set grapevine moved rapidly, and it was hard to differentiate fact from fiction. Another accountant was supposedly hired, then the original one was back on the job. The fate of this feature was uncertain daily.

Every movie has its own personality. On the second day of *Valediction* it was already set. We shot at a swanky joint called the Whiskey Bar, in the Back Bay of Boston. We did not get the first shot of the day until five hours and 23 minutes after call. Even for a big movie that is a long time to prepare for a shot. Some might go as far to think this is unacceptable. I guess if this were a normal business it would be unacceptable.

You usually know within the first several days of shooting how the experience is going to be. Even by the end of the first day you have a rough idea what you are going to go through. Some movies run like clockwork. They create schedules and stick to them. If something goes wrong they figure an efficient way to work around their problems. That is, however, the anomaly, not the norm. The norm is that stupidity rules and *Valediction* was far from the exception. Fortunately, it was summer and the conditions were good. Put this movie in the middle of one of our bleak New England winters and it would have turned into a nightmare.

Even though the movie was overworking us, I didn't care. I was glad to have the job. It was only a month and work was becoming tenuous. I embraced it for the money train it was. I just did my best not to kill myself. I mean that literally. The problem comes on the way home when I'm nodding off at the wheel. I have a 40-minute commute and in the wee hours it is hard to stay awake. So the last 20 minutes I'm fighting for my life. I open the window, chew gum and drink water. Many times I have been only 15 minutes from my house and was forced to pull over to sleep.

I can't say enough about shooting a movie in the summer. The night exteriors take on new meaning. This is when it really gets good, on a balmy summer night after midnight. I'll enjoy the warm breeze on my face as I watch the lamp operators set up the big lights. I'm usually having iced coffee about this time. At this point, I get the urge to break out my chaise lounge to really soak up the ambiance. I haven't been on a show yet where I felt that could actually fly.

Even though production had met the bond demanded by the unions and the payroll company, it was still uneasy. The bond covered a week of work and though we knew the week's pay was guaranteed, if they didn't come up with it weekly we could still be derailed at any time. I was feeling optimistic. I thought this fly-by-night production company held together with rubber bands and Murphy Oil Soap would eke it out, stay afloat and help me make my mortgage for another month.

Due to limited pre-production, the dam was leaking everywhere, and due to the time constraints, the only way to plug the holes was with cash. At that point, mistakes could only be rectified by the all-mighty buck. So, I witnessed one of the sleaziest things I've ever seen any production company do. Acting out of desperation and unscrupulousness, they slashed the wages of their production staff and they did it retroactively. "By the way, you know that money you made last week, well, we can't give you what we said we would. I know you'll understand because it is for the good of the movie, and that's the only important thing at this point, so buck up, suck it up and have a hearty lunch. Oh yes, we'll be working late tonight so make sure you are all ready."

They couldn't do that with the union workers who were under contract, so they cut the salaries of their production staff. The PA's were totally getting screwed. Many of them asked me what they should do. I advised them to walk off the job. If they all walked off the job it would mean a lot of trouble for the production, and with this reputation of not meeting the payroll, the production would be hard-pressed to fill the positions quickly. The PA's would have them over a barrel and the producers would be forced to acknowledge their original agreement. They would be forced to keep their word.

It's not that they ignored my advice; they were afraid to walk. They had odd ideas that they shouldn't walk off a show and they might be blackballed or something like that. It was naïve to think that, but there is a lot of fear about getting a bad reputation and being unemployed. If one walks off a show for justified reasons (a retroactive pay cut would fall into that category), far from being blackballed, you would be respected for your decision to walk, especially if it was in a unified front. It would have been a wild scene to see the production staff walk; it would have made great theater.

This new wave of shafting the little guy created a bad mood on the set. The injustice aroused the crew indignation and lowered morale. This job was caving in for everyone, except for little ol' me. I was having a great time. My workload was light and they let me off early several nights. The saving grace was the longevity of the job. It was quick, four weeks; I could do that standing on my head.

In the meantime, my Facebook posts were taking on this crazy tone. I didn't know what to expect when I first started this Facebook thing. I received some great feedback; people were really getting a kick out of my writing and were encouraging me to write more. The phrase "Lenny, you should write a book" was bandied about. I still wanted to write a book, but hadn't found the proper thread. I gave it some thought but the idea hadn't hit yet. I continued to write on Facebook, and I kept writing articles for my future website.

Facebook was an excellent workshop. I stretched my poetic license, mixing up fact and fiction to create something humorous. I was having a good time with it and so were my co-workers. I also found out that others in the film community were really eating it up. They felt fortunate to be on other shows and hearing the daily horror made them happy they weren't on *Valediction*. It's always funnier when the other guy slips on the banana peel.

June 23, 2009

It happens a lot on *Star Trek* when they stun the whole planet. Similarly, the energy on this movie is at a standstill. My friends, we are experiencing a malaise. Starbucks is closed and there's not a ginseng peddler in sight. Tomorrow morning everyone is voluntarily coming in an hour earlier for athletic boot camp. Yours truly will be sergeant at arms. I take my inspiration from *Full Metal Jacket*. Now, where did I put my medicine ball?

June 24, 2009

Athletic boot camp was a huge success, with a 97% turnout. The crew then approached the day's work with an unprecedented ferocity that I have never seen in my 18.75 years of filmmaking. The warp speed work effort was so successful that producers and the unions are already talking about making it a mandatory part of the workday. The only question is: Will it be on or off the clock? Leave it to money to ruin something as righteous as the movie business.

June 25, 2009

A man passed by our catering line today at lunch and inquired if we had to pay for lunch. He was told no. Then he asked if you had to present a ticket or a voucher. We also told him no. He seemed to think that some form of exchange had to take place. He was not satisfied. Then an electrician replied that you had to pay with your heart. I said, "Not unless you want to go to the top, then you pay with your soul."

June 26, 2009

The real story: I was walking down the street one day; a guy came out of nowhere and asked me, "What is the capital of Bolivia?" I hesitated; all of a sudden two other guys jumped me, hit me over the head and knocked me out. I was shanghaied! Next thing I knew I was shackled to a sound cart booming low-budget, independent movies. Had I answered La Paz, my whole life would be different today.

June 27, 2009

The unthinkable happened on the set early this morning. My colleague placed her Starbucks coffee in a corner and went about performing her movie making duties. Upon her return it had vanished. An overzealous locations assistant threw out her "Hot" cup of coffee. This sent a ripple through the production. Is there no sanctity in the world when a cup of coffee is no longer safe on a movie set?

June 29, 2009

Our lovely night exterior in downtown Quincy at the swank President City Inn, is slowly being washed away. As the Doppler says there is no way out of this one, with a torrential downpour on the way. No doubt we will be *Swimming to Cambodia* tonight. On a lighter note the crew calendar is being planned. I'll be photographed as Mr. February. Just call me the Gangster of Love.

June 30, 2009

Wrapped @ 4:18 AM, driving off the road @ 4:37 AM, in bed @ 5:15 AM, asleep @ 5:16 AM, lawnmower guy @ 9:14 AM.

July 2, 2009

It is our fourth and last day in our South Boston location. It couldn't come any sooner as the tenants are fed up and the landlord throws a fit. Didn't production grease this guy? I guess they're feeling inconvenienced. Can you believe it? After all, who are we doing this for? What would they do at night if not for the altruistic film industry? We'd be in the dark ages! People would be forced to read a book & maybe even talk to each other!

July 3, 2009

America can sleep easy tonight knowing that there is another movie in the can going straight to cable. My job is done here. I walk away with pride and joy knowing I've done my part for the sake of art. Stay tuned this summer for *Further Adventures of Lenny Manzo* as he hops from feature to feature to make further contributions to the motion picture industry. As long as moviegoers still eat popcorn I pledge my allegiance to the Cinema & everything it stands for!

I was enjoying Facebook, especially the instant reactions. It allowed me to flex my writing muscles. In between status posts I still worked on content for my website. You can catch up with me anytime on Facebook, where I'm still doing one-liners. Now back to our regularly scheduled nonfiction book.

With massive overtime, we made our days. However, the scenes later in the day seemed to be compromised by lack of coverage. With no sense of urgency, we meandered throughout the day collecting meal penalties and double time. It was hard to figure out what was causing this; mostly we couldn't figure out who was in charge. The executive producer showed up every day but disappeared into the night. There was no one steering the ship, at least not on deck.

The production tried in vain to get us back to days by wrapping us early one night, which took us into "splits" (noon to midnight shifts). The days were so long that we eventually went back to nights. They were in fact so long we wound up going into reverse splits with a call time of 9 PM and a wrap time of 11 AM. As my friend and fellow soundman Anton Gold once told me, "When you go into reverse splits it's time to raise the clown flag, because you fucked up!"

SCENE 33

Benny and Me

Saying good-bye to *Valediction* was not hard. Even if I'm enjoying the show it is always good to finish. I was looking for a little time off before I started *Zookeeper*. All of a sudden the wind shifted and manpower needs ramped up. I was supposed to get two weeks in between movies. That didn't happen. This is an all-or-nothing business: when it rains it pours, feast or famine. Whatever metaphor you like it is always the same, either too much work or not enough.

Life moved on, but *Valediction* didn't. They must have spoken to that exec over at ABC who was trying to screw me out of my housing money, because these people were trying to stiff me out of my holiday pay. I wasn't concerned since the union still held a huge bond, and they were not giving it back until every nook and cranny of that shoot was audited. The union keeps Hollywood and any other would-be filmmaker on the up and up and makes them keep their end of the bargain. Without the union, I don't know how badly conditions would deteriorate. I'm going to take a break now and sing the union song again.

I picked up a couple of weeks on *Zookeeper* with the riggers. The movie took over the Franklin Zoo and I was called on once again to distribute electric cables. I was back to day playing. I prefer jumping around from show to show; it is easier on the mind and body, but tougher on the wallet.

The summer continued and I hooked into *The Fighter* with Christian Bale and Mark Wahlberg. It was great to be reunited with my old colleague Mark Wahlberg, who I hadn't seen since 1999, when our paths had crossed on *The Perfect Storm*. That was exactly what happened: he was heading toward his trailer and I was heading to the craft service table. I do remember a slight nod of recognition. You take your brushes with fame when and where you can get them. On *Mrs. Winterbourne*, it was Ricki Lake who was coming from the craft service table when our eyes met and locked on each other. We both kept walking slowly, never losing eye contact. Then my left foot slipped ever so slightly off the curb, our focus was interrupted, and she said, "Oops." It is an evening that I shall never forget.

On the set of *Surrogates*, Bruce Willis bumped into me as he was chatting on his cell phone. Like any honorable man he took full responsibility for the incident and said, "Oh, I'm sorry." On my only night working on *My Best Friend's Girl*, Kate Hudson and I road an elevator together; I believe we were going down. It is these moments that make it all worthwhile.

I bounced around *The Fighter* from department to department. The real bummer about *The Fighter* was that we shot in Lowell, Massachusetts. I have nothing against the town of Lowell, an old mill town that gave birth to Jack Kerouac and the home of the *Lost Eden* debacle. It has tried to make its way in the modern world, but when it comes to espresso, it simply has not hit the mark. There isn't even a Starbucks! The local cafés were extremely disappointing and I absolutely refuse to go to that other chain that claims to have good coffee. I don't know how, but I survived.

It was on my first day of *The Fighter* that I knew this was a serious operation. I knew they were doing things right when I saw real maple syrup at the breakfast buffet. Unfortunately, I didn't spend much time on this one, a few days here and there. I did have a minor incident with a bee and the director, David O. Russell. Sounds like a short story for kids: "The Bee and the Director."

The year was 2009 and the date was significant, because every 10 years since 1979 I've been bitten by a summertime bee. I don't know the meaning of the 10-year bee bite cycle; I don't know anyone else it happens to. So the bee incident of aught-nine was no chance meeting. The power of fate worked its mighty hand. Destiny awaited me on *The Fighter*.

There I was, moving equipment, enjoying the sunny day and perhaps I was whistling. In the movie version, I will no doubt be whistling. That is, the actor playing me will be whistling. I still have not settled on the lead yet. I am now considering either Damon or DiCaprio. These are some tough decisions I will have to face, but on with our bee movie.

As I was moving equipment, I was bitten by a bee. The director came up to me and insisted something should be done. "You should tell someone! Tell the producers! Let's get them to get rid of these bees!" I told him it was OK. He went on, "Who takes care of this?! What union takes care of this?!

What union kills the bees?!" I did appreciate his zeal for my health and well-being, but I told him I didn't know any bee-killing union.

I landed a full-time job. Ben Affleck had asked me to work with him on his new film *The Town*. There was no way I could turn Ben down. I read the script and offered my notes to him and his staff. They loved my ideas, but they weren't sure if it was the direction they wanted to go in.

Yes, that was the movie version again. The unglamorous version is that my boss from *Valediction* was hired on the job and he brought me along. My boss was interviewed while we were on *Valediction* and the process lasted most of the summer. In the end he was hired, which meant I was hired. It had been a lean year and I needed this one. I met Ben while we were prepping. He came over to me and introduced himself. I actually recognized him from the movies. I thought this was auspicious; usually the director doesn't give me the time of day. Actually, his whole staff was congenial and very professional. It was a welcome change from some of my past adventures.

It was late August when I hooked up with Ben Affleck. He enjoys returning to Boston to shoot his movies, and it only made sense that we finally connected. The word on the street was that Ben liked to do a lot of takes, a philosophy on which Ben and I do not agree. I like to get what I need and move on. It just increases the work later to labor through all the other takes. Then again, I've never worked with such a large staff. For everything I've made I've had to go through all of my own footage.

There were also a number of times he didn't cut which left me hanging out there holding a boom over my head for 10 minutes. I did manage 12 seconds of rest while the actors reset. That is one thing I am not going to miss. As I grew older, booming went from "this is fun" to "this is not bad" to "this is uncomfortable" to "this is really painful" to "I'll never do this again."

Besides pushing my back to the brink, Ben was good to work for. The first good sign was having Tony's Catering on the show. I hadn't seen Tony's since *The Perfect Storm*. Tony had a stellar reputation, and was at the top of the list for a wonderful set meal experience. If I mention Tony's I have to mention Peter over at Magic Hat, who always went out of his way to make me a vegetarian meal.

The show was well run and a good work environment, though we still did our share of 16-hour days and never missed a long one on a Friday. This is just something that cannot be avoided in the biz, at least when working below the line. You never know how it will go and must be prepared for anything. As they say in Egypt, "Trust in Allah, but tie your camel."

About two-thirds of the way into *The Town*, I was ailing inside. It wasn't that I was depressed; it was that my brain was becoming completely numb due to the boredom and tedium of the work. I would forget stuff that I would do every day. I was tired of fetching cables and batteries. I was in pain daily. It had been almost 20 years since I'd first put a boom in my hand. I wore a younger man's clothes then. Everything was catching up with me at the same time. It was the last days of disco and I knew it. This was going to be my last rodeo. They were going to have to find someone else's soul to whittle down, which wasn't a problem because there was a long line of souls waiting for my job.

Another life-altering event happened. I had a big birthday on this show: I turned 49. Forty-nine, Len? Really? What's so big about that? I was just about to tell you, honestly, I do appreciate your participation and I'm so glad you've made it this far. If you've come this far I know you certainly want to see how this thing pans out. And there is a cliffhanger, so be ready.

I am not one to think about birthdays and old age. I accept the process; it certainly seems to be the same deal for everyone. I don't think I can change the current system and I'm not looking for any fountain of youth or alchemical elixir. Birthdays have come and gone, some with fun and fanfare and some very quietly. This was a quiet one; I spent it on the set and didn't get off early enough to go to the House of Blues that night. The main thing that hit me at 49 was that I was going to be 50. I know, real big revelation, historically 50 has always followed 49. However, once I hit 49 I zeroed in on 50 immediately. It was like the countdown started. I'd hit the big zero ages before. Twenty was a piece of cake and quite frankly, very welcome. Thirty was sweet; I passed that moment in India. Forty came and my family threw a surprise party for me. Forty caused some reflection, but had no major effect on me, and I took it in stride. Fifty is something different; it feels different. It is a mark of time in everyone's life. It is important to figure yourself out by 50. Fifty was going to be a reality fairly soon. I pondered it all, my life, my family, and of course my work.

I wanted to get off this merry-go-round ASAP. I felt a little like Olivia de Havilland in *The Snake Pit*, just your standard story of a sane person locked inside a loony bin. How much longer could I go on? This was a defining moment for me. I ran over to the craft service and grabbed a carrot from the table, dropped down on my knees and in true Scarlett O'Hara fashion said, "I'll never pull cable again!" Excuse the repeat performance, but it fits so well. If you didn't get that reference, you really need to contact me and I can give you a list of about a hundred must-see movies; *Gone with the Wind* would make that list.

Even though *The Town* was a very demanding movie to work on, I enjoyed the environment. This film didn't have a lot of the nonsense that most Hollywood features come with. The environment was always professional. The only problem with that is there are no juicy anecdotes from this one. I could tell you about the night they shot through a storm, while the leads played a romantic scene on the river, but I can't because I missed that night due to a personal commitment. It was such a bad night that the production made hats that read, "I survived scene 57." The real tragedy of that scene: it never made it into the movie.

SCENE 34

I'd Like to Thank the Academy

We finished the film a week before Thanksgiving. I went into my usual post-feature decompression mode. I relaxed and enjoyed the holiday. Then it was right back to work. I called my web guy and put the final touches together for LennyManzo.com. While he was getting the technical end together, I was spending my nights drinking coffee and writing content for the site. I was working just as many hours as if I was on a feature. I was extremely motivated to make something happen and create an alternative to avoid going back to the Hollywood dream factory. I was never an assembly-line kind of a guy.

I wanted to get my website up and running, make it popular and make a living off of it. I had a stream of ideas. The tough part was figuring out the best course of action. I thought about selling my own work. I had learned about distribution and wanted to distribute other films. I also wanted to write and had to create my own forum.

In the first week of December, I thought of an idea for an article for the site. It was about my first days in the biz. I wrote the first page and it hit me like a thunderbolt, much in the same way Michael Corleone felt when he saw Apollonia the first time. Though I was not in love, the effect was the same. I knew immediately what I had written. Yes, dear, lovely, loyal, glorious reader, it is this very book you have in your hand now, or in your Kindle. I saw the whole thing in my head. I knew I had all these stories and I knew I could write them.

I dug in with a frenzy I had never known before. I stayed up all night writing page after page. Drinking coffee until two in the morning. During the following three weeks I batted out the first draft. I had been writing on and off my whole life, but never with this much conviction. At the same time, I was still writing content for the website. On December 21, 2009, I launched LennyManzo.com.

The reality of the website coming to fruition was a major accomplishment for me. I had been working on it all year and at some point it seemed unattainable. I didn't know if I was ever going to complete it. Yes, there were moments of doubt, but I pushed through and made it happen. That New Year, I had a lot to be grateful for and a lot to celebrate. It had been a month since I'd left Ben Affleck and company. I was at the height of personal production. It was the beginning of my most prolific period. I could feel life was changing again. I entered a new phase of my career. I wasn't sure where it would take me. The difference at this juncture was that I was creating my own work. I was following my instincts and exploring my own creativity. Out of all the things I'd ever done in my career, this current phase of writing movie articles, writing reviews, discussing the business, writing my quippy Facebook posts and, most of all, writing this book was what felt right. This made sense to me.

My final Facebook post of the year went something like this: The year is done and I make my last post of aught-nine. I'd like to thank all the wonderful people at Facebook for making this all possible. I'd like to thank my colleagues, my friends and family, who never stopped believing in me and never doubted me. I want to thank all the folks along the way who have put a hand out to help Lenny Manzo. I'd like to thank the Academy for making this all possible. (This might be the closest I will get to an Oscar speech; I wanted to do it at least once. I've been rehearsing it in some form for 39 years.)

SCENE 35

My People's People

The 2010 New Year was a festive one. My children were older and we had our first New Year's Eve party at the house. It wasn't anything elaborate, just some friends to bring in the New Year. At the party, a friend of mine said that he had just hooked up with a group of investors and that they back movies, and do I have anything.

"Do I have anything? Do I have anything?!" Does ice melt? Does coffee have caffeine? Does Donald Trump have the worst hair for any multimillionaire? How does his hair person keep that job, anyway? Don't get me started.

I told him I had two projects with scripts and a director attached, one for six million dollars and the other for a million. He went on to explain that his people never fund the whole project, they only do half the money and we would have to come up with the other half. I asked him why they only do half; he said, "That's what they do, they only do half, they're half-the-money guys."

That knocked the six-million-dollar project off the table. We didn't have three million; if we did we could just make the smaller project. That left the million-dollar show for discussion. He said, "Send me some info about the project and I'll present it to my group." I contacted my director. I didn't think much of this and it didn't sound real to me, but no stone should be left unturned. I called my colleague and we both agreed that these half-the-money guys would most likely come up empty, but we sent them the package.

In the meantime, I had a second draft to write. I figured that since I'd knocked out the first draft in three weeks I could probably have a finished product by spring. I don't know if you got that, but that was a joke. I thought it was true at the time. I had no idea about the mountain of work that was ahead with rewrites. It didn't take too long to see that the book was not around the corner. I was undaunted. I felt that this was one of the best things I could do and something I could get behind.

My course had shifted a little. I was still able to write for the website, but what I couldn't do was marketing. The book and the articles took a lot of time. I was doing some marketing, but it wasn't driving streams of people to the site. I decided that out of all my ideas, the book was the best course of action, and I was going to stay with it. I put most of my energy into my book and let the site grow on its own.

One afternoon in mid-January, while I was pounding away on the keyboard at a local café, I received an email from my friend about the half-the-money guys. He wrote, "Right now they are saying that they would like to do multiple 'mainstream audience films' in a slate—so, unfortunately this is too small and does not fit the criteria." A slate is a bunch of films and often when people tell me they want to do a slate it means they just like talking about doing a slate. Funding films is difficult enough without trying to fund multiple pictures at once. I'm not saying it is not done; it is just a red flag.

When it comes to talking about raising money to fund projects, this is an area where you can't trust anything anyone is saying. On the surface everyone seems interested. It is the natural way people act. They always act interested. People always like to talk a big game, and down the road that project they were "interested" in might be on the table again with others who are sincerely interested. It was good and necessary that they feigned interest the first time they heard it; since it is taking off, they can get back on it, since they were always interested.

Funding is the toughest part of the movie making process. That might be said of any business, but movies are risky and funding independent cinema is not an easy task. There are two main reasons people get into funding films. The first is the huge lottery-type payoff that comes at the end of the rainbow with a smash box-office hit. The other reason is the allure of show biz. Everyone wants to be involved in some way. Not everyone can juggle or do impersonations and the rich folk are not going to learn how to light a scene. They invest to put some glitz in their lives. They want to be attached to a movie and mingle with the celebs.

The bright side of the "I can't help you" email was that it inspired me to write a short movie. I wrote a nine-page script in about 20 minutes called *My People's People*, and if I do say so myself, it came out great. It was funny and it spoofed the industry. I looked at my work with pride. I liked what I had written. The question was what was I going to do about it?

My first action was to think about it. I knew I could get it done cheaply enough. I had enough friends and colleagues that I could call on for a favor. It was the time factor that concerned me. I was so busy with the present manuscript you're reading and creating articles for the website, I didn't know if it was practical. Now that's funny! There is nothing practical about this business.

I tossed and turned about it for a month. Perhaps we can go to a montage of me having sleepless nights, pondering the script over espresso, sitting at my desk making phone calls and climaxing with me jumping out of bed, screaming, "I'll do it, I'll do it!" I had to do it. I had stood idly by on set after set watching directors go through the motions or just not knowing what to do. I was no longer going to be a kibitzer. This movie was written, I only needed a day to shoot it and I had all the crew and gear I needed. I put the green light to *My People's People* and began the process of bringing it to fruition.

My first phone call is always to my DP Beecher Cotton; I find out when he is available and go from there. I had a lot of support from my friends and colleagues, and most of the pieces quickly came together. The only thing I didn't have was a location. I needed a restaurant and I needed it for free. I didn't have much money to shell out for this project. I began looking for the location in the usual way: I called some colleagues who scouted for a living and asked if they had anything. After several weeks of effort and nothing to show for it, I shared my plight with my computer tutor. Computer tutors have replaced therapists in the modern world. He liked the idea and had a lead on a nice place in Lynn, Massachusetts called The Blue Ox, an excellent restaurant in downtown Lynn. I spoke to the owner and he put me in business.

Now that the location was secured it was full speed ahead. It was time for the auditions. I had been at auditions before, and I had a voice at some of these events, but this was the first time I was in charge of the casting. I put up ads on various websites and posted the auditions on Facebook. I had about 30 replies and eventually set up 25 auditions for one day. I made only one mistake: I forgot to schedule a lunch break for my co-producer and me.

Fortunately, many actors are flaky and a few didn't show up, so I was able to squeeze in lunch. Everything was falling into place.

I had sent out the page-and-a-half excerpt from the script. It contained a very tongue-twisty monologue. I had everyone read for that part. It was the hardest part of the movie. I needed to find someone who could nail that. The biggest eye-opener at the auditions was the lack of preparation by many of the actors. They all had the script well in advance but many of them did not have a good feel for it. Very few had it memorized.

Most of these actors were non-union and needed projects like this. It is essential for actors to land some roles to move their career along. I was blown away by much of this cavalier attitude toward their art and potential career. Here was a chance for a lead role in a short movie and many of them were unprepared.

I let all the actors have a crack at it with their own interpretations, just in case there was magic in the air and to see if they could hit the high note on their own. Sure enough, that didn't happen. That was fine. I really wanted to see how they would take direction. I gave them the notes, you know, a little more of this and a lot less of that. Some of them were amazing. They did it the exact way the second time without any augmentation. That made my job easier.

After round one, I was not bowled over, although there were some contenders. I invited back 10 gentlemen. I gave them another page and told them to memorize both sides of the dialogue. Anyone who could not remember the dialogue was not going to get the part. Since the script was nine pages, it would take a full day of shooting. Normally, nine pages are too much for a shoot day. But since the movie was two guys talking without action or location moves, I knew I could get it done in one day if the actors were well rehearsed. If they were not prepared it would make for a long day dealing with line flubs.

I brought the guys back and set them up in pairs so they could read together. The first two up were Chris McCabe and B.J. Ray. They had it down, they blew me away and it was highly coincidental that they were paired together. There was chemistry between them and both actors had prepared and it showed. This was a great feeling, knowing I already had the parts potentially cast. There were a couple of other contenders, and some were eliminated by default: they were still working off the script.

With the actors cast and the location secured, I rounded out the crew. I rehearsed the actors thoroughly and this was the key to making it happen all in one day. We shot nine pages in 11 hours. That is great by anyone's standards. Everything was smooth as silk, or to use a more modern expression, it went like butter.

I had two coffee pots blazing at all times. We did have to hold on one take due to a loud percolation incident. That was the biggest faux pas of the day. We did an average of four takes per shot. Since the actors were rehearsed there was no need for extra takes that would have created more work in the editing room. The editor and I knocked out the post-production in four editing sessions of four hours each. The toughest part was the music. Then good old Tony from the breakwater stepped up and put something together for me. With minutes to spare, I FedExed the movie to Robert Redford and company at Sundance. *My People's People* is currently playing at my website.

Even though it was only a seven-minute short, it was a great personal accomplishment. I knew I could direct, but knowing and doing are two different things. I needed to go through the process once. I am ready to move on to the big time. I have started my first script for a feature film, and I'll tell you one thing about it: it's a comedy. You probably could have figured that out on your own. You'll hear about it soon enough, unless you fancy yourself an investor. Then by all means feel free to contact me and let me bring you down the yellow brick road of movie making.

As far as my decision to stay in the Hollywood trench, it was taken out of my hands. Even if I wanted to stay on this bandwagon, I would have crashed with the rest of my colleagues. The movie business in New England dried up like burnt toast on a Vegas buffet. The governor of Massachusetts decided to cut the tax incentive from the budget. Another bureaucrat made it his personal mission to get it off the books. It was in danger for several months. In that time, these fly-by-night production companies pulled up stakes and hopped over to the next state that was giving handouts. The producers didn't want to shoot in a state where the incentive rug could be pulled out any minute. All the films slated for Massachusetts left in the middle of the night. By June, when it was clear that the incentive was not being taken off the books, it was too late. Disney, Sony and all the other big companies were gone and the state lost all that momentum.

Some of the A-list, first-called players have managed to stay alive with the one movie and a TV show that graced New England in 2010. The production outlook is already looking better for 2011. There seem to be several movies coming here in the spring. Eventually, it will pop back. It always does.

As for me, the timing was right. Even if I wanted to stay on humping cable and pushing a boom pole around and practice the art of not conking actors on the head, I could not. The work slowed down like molasses in wintertime. Melted away like an M&M on the craft table in the blazing sun. Slipped away like a _____. I figured I'd let you try one.

The universe is speaking to me and the seas have parted to lead me down a different path. But of course folks, I'm not leaving show biz. I'm just getting out of the biz to get back into the biz. For better or for worse, I'm a lifer. All of my eggs are nestled tightly in this show biz basket. I'm in it for the long haul. Once again, I've recommitted myself in another facet of show biz. My career is in its fourth incarnation. I've left the technical world to embrace my creative urges again, of course nothing risqué. In a way, I'm back where I started, following my dreams. I still have a lot to accomplish. I am on the other side of 50 and I'm still pushing my way in the world. The future feels brighter than ever. There is a strong wind of change blowing and there is no going back. Especially after my self-confessed boom antics.

SCENE 36

The Road to Oprah

Well friends, filmmakers, countrymen, what have we learned? I hope you've learned some things about the movie industry and I hope I've brightened your world somehow. As for me, what have I learned? I think it wasn't enough to want to see Uncle Henry and Auntie Em ... and ... if I ever go looking for my heart's desire again, I won't look any further than my own backyard ... Oh, I'm sorry, that's what Dorothy learned.

The most obvious thing I learned was how to make a movie. I also learned not to trust men with product in their hair. It is not across the board, but it is right there with men in white shoes. The biggest thing I learned was about the expectations of others. I no longer put that pressure on anyone. Many people fail, many are afraid, and some are just screwed up. I don't hold anyone to any standard. I take people as they come. Most of all, I don't take anything personally anymore. It is a big life lesson for anyone. Once you let go of the attachment to others' thoughts and words, you have taken leaps and bounds toward personal freedom.

I've been through the mill now, but I've come out on the other side. The dues have been paid, and then some. This last year has been so refreshing. I've been able to work on my projects and explore my creative juices. I'm living in the present doing my own work, with an eye toward the future. I am in the midst of the biggest change of my career. I have taken myself out of the technical portion of the business and I am only applying myself to the creative end. I may be a little late getting out of the gate, but what I really want to do is direct. Is that funny or what?

After getting burnt out many times, being pushed around by the industry and making many mistakes, I'm ready to go for it full steam ahead. As long as I breathe I will never give up on what I want to do. I have always known I am an artist. It's just taken most of my life to figure out how to express it. I won't settle or give up on what I think is important. The only thing that could change is my idea of what is important.

My art is humor and I will continue to express it through voice, film or keyboard. It is only through perseverance and longevity that I have been able to find my voice and express it through a medium.

I have buried my hatchets, I get upset by a lot less, I take it as it comes, and I roll with the punches, but most of all, I write a lot of metaphors. I have a renewed belief in myself. I do believe anything is possible; ask any Red Sox fan about that. I will strive always to be the artist inside me that has always wanted to come out. The genie is out of the bottle and he won't go back.

I don't know where this train ends, but I'm going to ride it to the end with confidence and determination. I'll have my arm sticking out the side, just in case there is a chance to grab a brass ring along the way. I won't accept defeat, but if I don't make it, then that will have to be fine. If I can live my life being who I am, that is the satisfaction. I intend to go on creating because that is what I need to do. If my work is recognized and appreciated by someone else, so much the better. The most important lesson is to be true to myself: "I am what I am," to quote my beloved Popeye once more.

Well, Dear Reader, you have been absolutely fabulous through this whole experience. As the reader you have played your part perfectly throughout this entire narrative. You have made it to the bitter end and I thank you for that. It is always a wonderful thing in life when someone takes the time to hear what I have to say. Of course, my book would mean so much less without you. Like a tango, the author is nowhere without his necessary partner, the reader.

Now it's time to say good-bye to all our company. What's next for Lenny Manzo? What's on the hot stove? What's goin' down? Movie tip #185: Canned answer for what's next: "I have various projects at different stages of development." Having said that, I realize that's not going to cut it between us. After all, we are so much closer now and it wouldn't be right to leave you with such a vague cliffhanger.

When last we saw Lenny Manzo, he was left hanging over the Hollywood Abyss (another great name or title, I just can't stop, Harry, another one for development) hacking out his next project on the new iPhone he bought with his book money. With one hand on some trusted roots, he hangs while writing the dialogue for his next project. Yes, ladies and gentlemen, Leaping Lenny Manzo will be directing his first feature film. Unbeknownst to his book-reading public, he has been secretly developing a movie with a marketing plan. That picture will be green-lit the moment all the funding is in. So, friends and fans of Lenny Manzo, you are now on the ground floor of his next project.

I still have many details to work out about turning this book into a move. As of now, I've settled on Matt Damon in the lead role. I hemmed and hawed between him and DiCaprio. It wasn't an easy call to make, but Matt, I'm offering it to you first. So have your people call my people, I'm anxious to get started.

If this was the end of the movie, I would have to attach an epilogue. Lenny Manzo has gone to direct many major motion pictures. After his first feature film successfully made its debut at Cannes, he hasn't looked back. He has also written several books on various subjects about projects in various stages of development. In between projects, he lives in Tahiti and sips hot coffee in the tropical heat. To this day, he still does not order an iced coffee out.

Now for the real challenge: How do I end this book? Relax, my beloved reader, for it is rhetorical, but this has been a dilemma. The epilogue has the happily-ever-after thing going on. I like that, but that is more of a prediction. Don't worry; when the movie comes out, I'll end up as a major Hollywood player like Harry Zimm or Chili Palmer. Maybe Spielberg can do a cameo for me. We can be seen having lunch at one of those frou-frou sidewalk cafés in L.A.

"So, Stevie, what's next for you?"

"Well, Len, I have a lot of things going on. Why? Are you looking for a project?"

"Well, Stevie, you know I'm always interested in what you have going on."

"I might just have something for you, are you interested?"

"Yes I am; this sounds very interesting."

"I'm glad you're interested, it has a lot of potential."

"I'm certainly interested in potential."

That's OK for the movie, but I'm not there yet. I could go off into the sunset, but that implies I'm checking out and I'm not going nowhere. And I am aware that I used a double negative. You can take the boy out of the city, but you can't take the city out of the boy.

After all my trials and tribulations, ups and downs, glory and failure, I have redefined myself once again. I am not looking back anymore. If I want to, I have this handy-dandy memoir. And when I read back or think back or watch the soon-to-be-made major motion picture *Above the Line*, I'll think I was always made for show biz. I haven't hit the heights of Bugs Bunny and other mega-stars, but I'm not cleaning up after the elephant either.

I've made my living in this madcap world and will continue to do so. Whether it is in my blood, or lack of alternative, I'm here to stay. I won't be holding a boom pole again or laying any more 4/0. I'll leave that for the younger blokes and blokettes. My wake has already been filled and I know films in New England will manage without me.

If I could turn back the clock, would I do it again? This has to be your absolute last question. I believe if a magic genie turned back the clock and I did something completely different with my life, and arrived at the same point in my life again, and the same magical genie came by for the second time and asked if I wanted to do it over again, I could find many reasons to go back again. No matter what I would have done, the road would have been filled with hurdles, pitfalls and the occasional land mine. Throughout my life and career I have learned a lot and have grown because of it. There has been good mixed with the bad, and as I said, that would have happened no matter what path I had chosen.

Like the book cover, I happily sit with a cup of coffee in my hand and a smile on my face. This last year I've made the leap. I am choosing to do what I want to do, instead of what is available to do. The future looks rosy and if it isn't bright I'll rent the Death Star and illuminate my path. That's one thing about show biz: you can always purchase it.

So now that I'm a published author I am officially on *The Road to Oprah*. This was a title that I bandied about for a little while, though I did feel there might be litigation involved. So I decided to play it safe and stick with my industry-upbeat dream title. *Above the Line* or *The Road to Oprah*, it still comes down to the same thing. I'm still moving forward as I live and create. I know all of my dreams may not come to pass, especially since Oprah has reached the end of the line with her show. Beyond everything I hope to achieve in this business, I will always aspire to freedom. I want control over my own life and not have to punch the Hollywood clock anymore.

Writing this book has been my greatest accomplishment to date. I hope you liked it; otherwise it is a rather pathetic-sounding statement. It did take a year of my life, so I hope you will at least award me E for effort.

Now I'm just stalling; we've had such a wonderful time together, I don't want it to end. You need to be moving on as well, I understand. All right, here we go, we're in the final stretch, the horses are well past the clubhouse turn and there's the checkered flag. I went deep into my file cabinet, which resides in the upper portion of my cranium, and I came across *The Magnificent Seven*, the classic remake of Kurosawa's *Seven Samurai*. At the end of that movie, Yul Brynner sits on his horse—he and his band of heroes have cleaned up the town for the villagers—and delivers a line that I think is quite apropos.

"Adios!"

Breinigsville, PA USA
01 April 2011
258941BV00003B/1/P